# THE Filmmaker's Guide
# TO Production Design

## Vincent LoBrutto

ALLWORTH PRESS
NEW YORK

06   05   04   03   02        5   4   3   2   1

Published by Allworth Press
An imprint of Allworth Communications, Inc.
10 East 23rd Street, New York, NY 10010

Cover and interior design by Joan O'Connor, New York, NY
Page composition/typography by Sharp Des!gns, Inc., Lansing, MI

Cover photograph: Photograph of scale model for the production design of the television adaptation *Death of a Salesman* (1986), directed by Volker Schlöndorff, production designer, Tony Walton. Courtesy Tony Walton, The American Museum of the Moving Image, and the CBS Television Network.

ISBN: 1-58115-224-8

LIBRARY OF CONGRESS CATALOGING-IN-PUBLICATION DATA
LoBrutto, Vincent.
The filmmaker's guide to production design / Vincent LoBrutto.
p.  cm.
Includes bibliographical references and index.
ISBN 1-58115-224-8
1. Motion pictures—Art direction. 2. Motion pictures—Setting and scenery. I. Title.
PN1995.9.A74 L63 2002
791.43'025—dc21
2002007998

Printed in Canada

For
Reeves Lehmann and
Salvatore Petrosino

# CONTENTS

# ACKNOWLEDGMENTS

I would first like to thank my chairman, Reeves Lehmann, of the Department of Film, Video, and Animation at the School of Visual Arts in New York City, and Salvatore Petrosino, his director of operations, to whom this book is dedicated. Reeves gave me his full support to teach a production design course back in 1994 and Sal has been my *consigliere* on developing the class over the years. It was Sal's idea to mount a museum show, "The Art of Production Design in Motion Pictures," which we co-curated at the Visual Arts Museum at SVA in Spring 2000. Again Reeves was there with full support and encouragement. My heartfelt thanks to Silas Rhodes, founder and chairman of the board of the School of Visual Arts, for his good graces, for following the path less often taken, and for creating a home for the study of art. SVA President David Rhodes and Vice President Anthony P. Rhodes also provided encouragement and support. I thank Francis Di Tommaso, director of the Visual Arts Museum, Rachel Gugelberger, associate director, and their staff for the meticulous care, good taste, and expertise in mounting such an enterprise.

I learned production design for film at the knee of many great designers and have them to thank for my education in this cinematic art and craft. They include these artists: Ken Adam, Mel Bourne, Patrizia Von Brandenstein, Albert Brenner, Robert Boyle, Norman Garwood, the late Ted Haworth, Andrew Jackness, the late Richard MacDonald, Terence Marsh, Jane Musky, Lawrence G. Paull, Polly Platt, Bruno Rubeo, the late Ferdinando Scarfiotti, Paul Sylbert, the late Richard Sylbert, Wynn Thomas, Tony Walton, Stuart Wurtzel, and Kristi Zea.

I want to thank the late Richard Trupkin who produced productions of *Twelve Angry Men* and *One Flew Over the Cuckoo's Nest*, which I directed as artistic director of the Woodside Kiwanis Players. Production designer Marvin Pastina created environments for our work beyond any expectations of what a little local community theater company could do. I offer respect and remembrance for firefighter Lawrence Virgilio, who performed in both productions and perished on September 11, 2001.

My wife Harriet Morrison is a woman of the theater who over the years inspired me to study the horizons of drama. It was Harriet's idea for me to do an interview book on production designers, and she envisioned its title. She was the first reader of this book and as always lent her "fine Italian hand" to the manuscript. My son Alexander Morrison, who recently studied filmmaking, screened film after film with me during my original research into the subject and warmed my heart with the following story. One night while he was attending American University, he walked into a dorm room where a group of students, kicking back, were watching a video of *Goldfinger*. (I'm sure refreshments were served.) Alex looked at the screen and said, "Oh, that's a Ken Adam film!" as a food fight broke out in his direction.

My appreciation to all the students who have attended my production design course at SVA for teaching me about teaching production design and to all the thesis students who have harnessed the power of design for their films. I cherish all of our discussions and marvel at the results.

My thanks to all the heads of education I have worked with at Film/Video Arts for their support of a production design mini-course I teach there. Thanks to all of FVA's documentarians and guerrilla filmmakers, who at first respectfully listened, then went on blind trust, and then embraced production design as part of their visions.

I want to thank publisher Tad Crawford at Allworth Press for suggesting this project and for his unconditional support. Thanks to my editor Nicole Potter for expertise, patience, and taste, and to Kate Lothman for her understanding and professionalism in coordinating the project. Thanks to copyeditor Diane Moroff for her meticulous attention to detail, and to Joan O'Connor for her elegant book design.

Finally thanks to Andrew Jackness, Wynn Thomas, and Tony Walton for contributing examples of their work that reveal the art behind the art of production design. My respect for and fascination with the work of film production designers is what got me here in the first place.

# INTRODUCTION

The purpose of this book is to make filmmakers aware of the art and craft of production design for motion pictures and to provide practical, technical, and aesthetic guidance. This is a how-to book about production design for film and a why-to book as well.

Volumes have been written and said about the look or vision of a film. Many filmmakers rely on the tools of cinematography and videography to achieve this goal. Burgeoning digital tools enhance the visual properties of a movie but do little on their own to create the total visualization and design of a motion picture.

Production design has long been a mystery to many filmmakers. Often, we are not aware of when production designers are doing their job or the nature of their contribution. Production design is usually associated with Hollywood blockbusters and period films. Historically, independent, low-budget filmmakers have felt they did not have access to production design, and besides, contemporary films are shot on real locations, aren't they?

Although I had made my own independent films, have a B.F.A. in filmmaking from the School of Visual Arts, and worked for the ABC television network in post-production and as a freelance film editor, production design eluded me. As a student of filmmaking for most of my life, I have studied every genre and style of movie from classical Hollywood to the films of international masters, independents, and experimentalists. My understanding of the tasks involved in creating motion pictures embraced directing, screenwriting, acting, cinematography, and post-production, but I remained in the dark as to art direction's' role in the visual and narrative processes.

During the 1990s, I produced a series of interview books on the film crafts. The first craft I investigated was close to home—editing. The second book, on production design, was in less familiar territory. Filmographies produced a list of production designers with experience, craft, and the ability to collaborate with directors on a wide range of film styles and storytelling approaches. I quickly came to the realization that the look of a film couldn't have sprung forth full-blown from the director's imagination, as the *auteurists* would have us believe. Nor did the great artistry of the cinematographer accomplish the visualization of a film—*someone* had to create what was in front of the camera, while the director and director of photography were behind it.

A lot of background research was necessary. For many of the films I had already seen, I had to re-educate my eye to see beyond photography to the purpose and influence of production design in the moviemaking process. When the contribution of production design did appear in front of my eyes, it was an epiphany.

When I was ready, having finished my self-created prerequisite course, I interviewed a number of prominent production designers on the East and West coasts. These in-depth discussions were not only the content of *By Design: Interviews With Film Production Designers,* they also became a series of one-to-one master classes in feature film production design. My professors were legends in the field: Ken Adam, *Goldfinger* (1964), *Dr. Strangelove* (1964), and *Barry Lyndon* (1975); Mel Bourne, *Annie Hall* (1977), *Fatal Attraction* (1987), and *The Fisher King* 1991); Robert Boyle, *Shadow of a Doubt* (1943), *North by Northwest* (1959), and *The Thomas Crown Affair* (1968); Albert Brenner, *Bullitt* (1968), *The Goodbye Girl* (1977), and *Pretty Woman* 1990); Norman Garwood, *Brazil* (1985), *The Princess Bride* (1987), and *Glory* (1989); Ted Haworth, *Strangers on a Train* (1951), *Some Like it Hot* (1959), and *Pat Garrett and Billy the Kid* (1973); Richard MacDonald, *The Servant* (1964), *The Day of the Locust* (1975), and *Altered States* 1980); Terence Marsh, *A Bridge Too Far* (1977), *Absence of Malice* (1981), and *Spaceballs* (1987); Jane Musky, *Blood Simple* (1984), *Ghost* (1990), and *Glengarry Glen Ross* (1992); Lawrence G. Paull, *Blade Runner* (1982), *Romancing the Stone* (1984), and *Back to the Future* (1985); Polly Platt, *The Last Picture Show* (1971), *The Bad News Bears* (1976), and *The Witches of Eastwick* (1987); Bruno Rubeo, *Platoon* (1986), *Driving Miss Daisy* (1989), and *Sommersby* (1992); Ferdinando Scarfiotti, *Death in Venice* (1971), *Last Tango in Paris* (1973), and *Scarface* (1983); Paul Sylbert, *One Flew Over the Cuckoo's Nest* (1975), *Heaven Can Wait* (1978), and *Kramer vs. Kramer* (1979); Richard Sylbert, *Who's Afraid of Virginia Woolf?* (1966), *The Graduate* (1967), and *Chinatown* (1974); Wynn Thomas, *Do the Right Thing* (1989), *A Bronx Tale* (1993), and *Mars Attacks!* (1996); Patrizia Von Brandenstein, *Amadeus* (1984), *The Untouchables* (1987), and *The People vs. Larry Flint* (1996); Tony Walton, *A Funny Thing Happened on the Way to the Forum* (1966), *Murder on the Orient Express* (1974), *All That Jazz* (1979), Stuart Wurtzel, *The Purple Rose of Cairo* (1985), *Brighton Beach Memoirs* (1986), and *The Mambo Kings* (1992); and Kristi Zea, *Married to the Mob* (1988), *GoodFellas* (1990), and *The Silence of the Lambs* (1991).

The concepts and techniques presented in this book have been acquired from the knowledge and experience of these and other production designers. The teaching methods I have developed since 1994 were honed during my course in production design at the School of Visual Arts.

Teaching production design to filmmakers is unlike educating them about cinematography or editing, both absolutely necessary to completing a film. In fact, the early reaction was there was no access, no money, and no way to bring design to their films. This quickly changed; filmmakers learned that production design was a road to achieving their vision of a film and could be accessible to them.

Currently production design is an integral component in independent, student, low-budget as well as mainstream film production. I get many calls and request from filmmakers looking for a production designer. With each passing year the number of film students who have dedicated themselves to becoming production designers increases.

This book has evolved out of this experience and from my work as an advisor to student and independent filmmakers. The results have been affirming and altering. The majority of films now have added a production designer to their creative team; in turn, the work is more visually interpretive and expressive. Filmmakers are visual storytellers, and production design provides possibilities that have been long ignored, misunderstood, and underutilized by moviemakers outside of the old and new studio systems.

Throughout the following eighteen chapters, we will be exploring the answer to one question—What is production design?—with a Zen-like approach. This book is for producers, directors, production designers—in other words, it is for moviemakers.

# GENERAL NOTES

The word "film" is used throughout this book along with "movie" and "motion picture." In the twenty-first century, the media and formats utilized to capture images include film, video, and digital technology. Often "film" is used to indicate a project that in reality may be a video. Eventually the term filmmaker may be replaced with imagemaker, moviemaker, or motion picture creator, but to consider one a filmmaker still has meaning and places that person at the center of the process.

In an Author's Note for his 1976 novel, *Even Cowgirls Get the Blues*, Tom Robbins apologizes for use of pronouns and nouns in the masculine gender, while expressing hope that the English language would in the future find a grammatically correct solution other than use of he, she, his, hers, himself, or herself. Mr. Robbins and fellow writers—including myself—are still waiting. I particularly cringe at the written or spoken use of the phrase "he or she" and generally prefer to use job titles that aren't gender specific, like cinematographer or director of photography or sound recordist, rather than cameraperson or soundperson. My apologies for the English language's insistence on being gender specific when, in the practice of filmmaking, it does not apply. In other words, filmmakers are filmmakers, and this is a book for filmmakers.

Words that appear in **boldface type** indicate their importance in understanding production design for motion pictures and can be found in the appendix B, the glossary, along with other useful terms.

# Chapter 1

## WHAT IS PRODUCTION DESIGN?

Production design is the visual art and craft of cinematic storytelling. The look and style of a motion picture is created by the imagination, artistry, and collaboration of the director, **director of photography,** and **production designer**. A production designer is responsible for interpreting the script and the director's vision for the film and translating it into physical environments in which the actors can develop their characters and present the story.

In its fullest definition, the process and application of production design renders the screenplay in visual metaphors, a **color palette**, architectural and period specifics, **locations**, designs, and **sets**. It also coordinates the costumes, makeup, and hairstyles. It creates a cohesive pictorial scheme that directly informs and supports the story and its point of view.

The production designer researches the world in which the film takes place to establish a sense of authenticity. The production designer must interpret and transform the story, characters, and narrative themes into images that encompass **architecture**, décor, physical space, tonality, and texture. Production designers use sketches, illustrations, photographs, **models,** and detailed production **storyboards** to plan every shot from microscopic to macroscopic detail. Production designers are the heads of the **art department** and manage a creative team that includes **art directors**, **set decorators**, **property masters**, painters, **carpenters,** and specialty crafts people.

### A Brief Historical Perspective on Production Design in Motion Pictures

Production design is an art and craft embedded in the core of the filmmaking process. Production designers utilize imagination, technique, illusion, and reality. They apply discipline and financial restraint, to visually enhance the script and the director's intent, by creating images out of ideas and purpose out of the images.

The earliest films did not employ production design. The Lumière brothers in France recorded the documentary reality in front of their motion picture camera. The first evocation of art direction was fundamental. Filmmakers used painted backdrops and simple props to create a basic setting. Early art direction was not realistic in approach or result but rather a mannered, generic representation that indicated where the story took place. It functioned as an accessory to the screen story, not an interpretive or expressive craft.

The classic Hollywood **studio** system created and developed massive factory art departments, with hierarchies headed by **supervising art directors**, who managed the work of art directors and other unit members who designed and executed each and every studio release. Art direction in movies during the 1920s and 1930s became a sophisticated art form supported by a wealth of organized and systematic resources, but it did not yet encompass the shot-by-shot totality of film visualization that interpreted the story and gave the characters a living and breathing environment.

The advent of the production designer occurred in 1939 when producer David O. Selznick gave the title to William Cameron Menzies for his work on *Gone with the Wind*. Selznick recognized that Menzies did much more than design the sets and décor; he created a blueprint for shooting the picture by storyboarding the entire film. His detailed visualization of *Gone with the Wind* incorporated color and style, structured each scene, and encompassed the framing, composition, and camera movements for each shot in the epic film. Menzies' contribution helped expand the function of the art director beyond the creation of sets and scenery, to include the responsibility for visualizing a motion picture. As a result of his extraordinary vision, William Cameron Menzies is recognized as the father of production design.

Over the decades, leading designers have alternated between the art director credit and the production designer title. Now, most films—both big-budget and low-budget independent productions—bear the job title of production designer, followed by art directors, and a team of art department artisans.

## Production Design Is . . .

- A galaxy far, far away, imagined and built on a sound **stage**
- Scenes that take place in New York or Los Angeles—but are actually shot in Canada
- Gotham City brought to the screen, although the urban environment had previously only existed in the imagination of the comic book creators and was expressed in ink
- An apartment in a Woody Allen film, shot on location in an actual New York City apartment, transformed into the living space of the character through addition, substitution, subtraction, renovation, and alteration
- A visual vehicle that transports the audience back or forward in time
- Visual poetry—a dream, a nightmare, or the mundane reality of the everyday
- The altered psychological state of the audience, created by an emotional mood or atmosphere

- Paint, nails, and tile
- Wood, paper, and stone
- The relationship between the characters, their story, and the environment

Production design functions in the service of the story, in the vision and creation of the illusion of verisimilitude and fantasy.

# Chapter 2

## VISUALIZATION OF A SCREENPLAY

Making a film is a most complex artistic enterprise. Moviemaking is the only creative endeavor that encompasses all of the arts: writing, photography, painting, acting, music, dance, and architecture. The filmmaker must take on the challenge of telling a story via image and sound each time a movie is made.

Filmmakers have myriad reasons for wanting to make a movie. They come to the task with particular strengths. Some are principally writers; others are actors, or come from the artistic disciplines of music, the theater, cinematography, editing, or design. They make films to entertain, to express emotion, tell a story, deliver a message, to dream, to imagine, and because they have a passion that drives them. Filmmaking takes time, patience, dedication, commitment, and an understanding of the process in its totality.

If filmmakers are oriented toward story and performance, they must learn to visualize the narrative. The story must unfold in the mind's eye, as it is conceived and created. The filmmaker has to see the movie while the screenplay is being written and during pre-production before the cameras roll. It must be envisioned not as a movie that has been seen before but as a unique story expressed in a unique combination of image and sound. The filmmaker translates the story into the visual language of the cinema.

If filmmakers come from a visual orientation, they must learn to understand how story and character form the foundation of a film. Image and sound without a compelling and engaging story and actors to bring it to life through performance will not produce a successful or satisfying movie.

Good screenplays are rare gems. Writing a great or even a good screenplay is a difficult endeavor. Even if filmmakers are in possession of a good screenplay, they are only halfway toward achieving their goal. The process of imagining the images that become a motion picture is called visualization. Visualization is a total process. To make a cohesive and expressive film, the director must be in control of the way the project is visualized.

Technically, films can be made without a director. Cinematographers, actors, production designers, and editors can follow a screenplay and record the story on film or video, but without the guidance, leadership, and vision of a central figure, it will never be more than just that—a story recorded on film or video. When a filmmaker visualizes a good story, it becomes a motion picture with intention and purpose.

The great visualists span the history of film, all one hundred years plus. A short but representative list would include these masters: Paul Thomas Anderson, Michaelangelo Antonioni, Darren Aronofsky, Luc Besson, Ingmar Bergman, Bernardo Bertolucci, Luis Buñuel, Tim Burton, Werner Rainer Fassbinder, Federico Fellini, John Ford, Terry Gilliam, Jean Luc Godard, D.W. Griffith, Alfred Hitchcock, Stanley Kubrick, Akira Kurosawa, Spike Lee, David Lynch, F.W. Murnau, Sam Peckinpah, Roman Polanski, Martin Scorsese, Steven Spielberg, Oliver Stone, Andrey Tarkovsky, Francois Truffaut, King Vidor, Wong Kar-Wai, Orson Welles, and Zhang Yimou.

## The Trinity

Many filmmakers embrace the camera as the key element in cinematic visualization, but an all-encompassing visual style or look of a movie comes from the trinity comprised of the director, the director of photography, and the production designer. The aforementioned visualists are filmmakers who understand the total palette at their command. It has little to do with money or cinematic philosophy. It is the nature of the motion picture medium. A screen story is created through cinematography and design.

Critics and theorists often cite *Citizen Kane* (1941), directed by Orson Welles, as the great American movie—the result of its enfant terrible, twenty-something director, crowned *auteur*. Scholarship by Pauline Kael published in *The Citizen Kane Book* and Robert L. Carringer in his book *The Making of Citizen Kane* has revealed that the film is the result of collaboration. The screenplay by Herman J. Mankiewicz and Welles contains a narrative and visual structure that directly served the vision of the film and its thematic content. The visualization of *Citizen Kane* emerged from the artistic partnership of three men: Orson Welles, the director, Greg Toland, the director of photography, and Perry Ferguson, the art director. Welles and Toland have been justly praised, while Ferguson's contribution to *Citizen Kane* has been shrouded by the mysteries surrounding the role of art direction in movies.

*Citizen Kane* was storyboarded in great detail, and Ferguson was instrumental to that process. Welles and Toland discussed and decided on the use of deep focus for the film, but Ferguson had to design deep **perspective** sets with foreground and background details for that visual concept to take shape in the film.

The notion that Charles Foster Kane would be based on William Randolph Hearst evolved during the gestation of the screenplay. Ferguson and the art department were not able to get any firsthand accounts of what Hearst's San Simeon estate looked like. Research turned up a 1931 *Fortune* magazine feature article, "Hearst at Home," which served as the genesis for Ferguson's designs for Kane's Xanadu.

San Simeon's great hall became the inspiration for the great hall at Kane's

Xanadu. Ferguson sketched a massive oak table, a high-backed armchair, and a large fireplace into the room. Xanadu became a combination of Renaissance architecture and Gothic, Venetian, Baroque, Egyptian, and Far Eastern design. Another influence on the design of *Citizen Kane* was the overscaled, overdecorated visual style pioneered in the films of D.W. Griffith and Cecil B. De Mille. The photographic plan to create size, a Gothic atmosphere, and to utilize low and **canted angles** influenced Ferguson's work as art director and the sets themselves made the totality of *Citizen Kane*'s visualization possible. Ferguson was aware of the camera's power to suggest massive space and depth. In turn, this minimized set construction, often allowing Ferguson to design a foreground and background so that lighting, lenses, and composition could do the rest to create the grand illusion and mighty power of Xanadu as a symbol of Kane's wealth and loneliness.

## Writing for the Screen

The earliest advice to screenwriters to write visually may very well have come from Aristotle in the *Poetics*. The Ancient Greek philosopher compelled creators of drama determine the developing narrative by visualizing the action as if the writer were actually present as it unfolded. By visualizing the action as the screenplay is being written, the filmmaker can make measured decisions about what is appropriate for the story and rout out the inconsistencies and distractions that threaten the narrative.

In a screenplay, the prose in between dialogue describes what will be shown on the screen. Here, the writer determines the setting—where the scene will take place, the time, and the geographical location.

The screenwriter invents the action using a sensibility that screenwriter and educator Stephen Geller calls the "dream-screen." Write what you see. Write for the frame. Create for the way in which the camera composes, for space, shape and form, texture and light. The training of a screenwriter goes beyond story and character. Visual storytellers write with an understanding of how lenses, shot size, and camera movement impact on a narrative. They create visual symbols and metaphors that are part of the cinematic language. Visual images associate and correlate ideas, concepts, and meaning to the story. The writer creates the plan for what is known as **mise-en-scène**, which includes the environment of a scene, the décor—the production design.

Writers deal with human reactions to ever-changing circumstances and environment. Changes in the environment instigate change in the characters. The characters are the sum total of their physical being and the influence their environment has on them. Once the screenwriter has imagined the environment, it is created and realized by the production designer and the art department.

## Writing the Screenplay with Design in Mind

A script is a blueprint for a film photographed during the production process and structured during the post-production process. A screenplay is a story written to be told through the cinematic tools of cinematography, editing, sound, and production design.

The idea for your film should have the potential for cinematic storytelling, while your approach can be a traditional, nontraditional, or experimental narrative. The prime concerns of the filmmaker are the presentation of the story and characters in visual and aural terms. A well-crafted screenplay should be revised through many drafts before it is ready to be interpreted cinematically. Don't proceed until you get the script right. If the story is insignificant, unimaginative, incoherent, or poorly constructed, the production design can do little more than decorate, rather than visually interpret the narrative to make a significant contribution to the cinematic storytelling.

The design process actually begins before a single word is put on paper. All films start with an idea, a concept, and a story. The sole purpose of the screenplay is as a text, a blueprint to be used to make a film. You must write visually so the camera and the design can interpret the script.

To find out how past screenwriters have created their mise-en-scènes, read the screenplays of films you are familiar with and have a passion for. Study how the filmmaker visually presents the story. The world around the characters is as important as the story itself. Characters and narrative need an armature to give the story veracity, a sense of time and place, an atmosphere, and psychological insight.

All films, not just period films, have a production design. Here is a short list of movies that contain the rare but essential combination of a good story and an appropriate visualization that contributes to the narrative power the film communicates. They include:

*All That Jazz* (1979)—an autobiographical fantasy of director Bob Fosse's life in the tradition of Fellini's *8½*. Tony Walton's production design provides the show biz glitz, Broadway theatricality, and New York style for the flamboyant Joe Gideon who burns himself out from too much sex, drugs, and rock 'n' roll. Glittering colors, shiny Mylar, drab rehearsal rooms, hip New York Apartments, and a hospital set out of a Broadway musical. Also an excellent reference for designing music videos.

*Amadeus* (1984)—the seventeenth century world of Wolfgang Amadeus Mozart. Period concert hall and palaces, but the attitude is Mozart as rock star. Production designer Patrizia Von Brandenstein used the metaphor of a Madonna tour: outrageous wigs, extravagant décor, powder puff colors, and theatrical excess.

*Apocalypse Now* (1979)—the Vietnam War as an LSD-laced fever-dream. Inspired by Joseph Conrad's *Heart of Darkness* and designed by Dean Tavoularis, the trip down the river to the tribal fortress of a madman includes a phallic symbol-decorated stage for the Playboy Bunnies entertaining the troops, a French plantation, a quiet Vietnamese village devastated by bombs, and a helicopter ballet battle.

*Barton Fink* (1991)—an old claustrophobic hotel and the bungalows where screenwriters lost their souls present the underbelly of the Hollywood dream factory as designed by Dennis Gassner.

*Blade Runner* (1982)—a futuristic, retrofitted, third world Los Angeles with Asian, Mayan, and European influences. Neon nights set the stage for this neo-noir designed by Laurence G. Paull.

*Boogie Nights* (1997)—one of the best references for the 1970s on film. Not an exaggeration or satiric interpretation but a meticulous recreation approach as a period film, designed by Bob Ziembicki.

*The Cabinet of Dr. Caligari* (1919)—German Expressionism on film. The design by Walter Reimann, Walter Röhng, and Hermann Warm features distorted perspective, walls filled with graffiti, and painted shadows are the environment for a sleuth, a somnambulist, and a psychotic doctor who fills this claustrophobic world with murder.

*Chinatown* (1974)—production designer Richard Sylbert's perfect recreation of Los Angeles in the 1930s for a narrative that reflects the cynicism and depravity of the 1970s in which it was produced.

*Citizen Kane* (1941)—the world of Charles Foster Kane ranges from an old boarding house to Xanadu, a castle of legendary proportion, in the design by Perry Ferguson. This larger-than-life character is supported by space and grandeur that represent both his power and his deep loneliness.

*The Cook, The Thief, His Wife and Her Lover* (1989)—utilizes color to symbolize its themes. Designed by Ben Vanos, the restaurant is red to evoke decadence, the exterior is blue to represent the city, the kitchen is green for growth, the toilets are white for purity and innocence, and yellow exemplifies the antique books owned by the lover.

*Dracula* (1931)—a classic horror film made for Universal on their studio lot, featuring the Count's castle, utilized and imitated throughout the decades. The design by Charles D. Hall creates the atmosphere for the ageless undead: a large, cold, dark, stone space that protects the creature who can turn into a bat. The castle is contrasted by the sophisticated home of his victim, old-world elegance, and the sexual overtones of women in white, flowing gowns. A bedroom is defenseless against the elusive Dracula, who can fly through the open window. A room of coffins where the vampires lie in hiding provides the vulnerability that leads to their demise.

*Eraserhead* (1978)—this mysterious and truly weird, no-budget, black-and-white film brought notoriety to David Lynch as a personal filmmaker with a unearthly, psychodramatic vision. The room of a lonely man becomes the environment for his profound alienation and for a part animal, part human baby—one of the strangest characters in all of cinema. Lynch's design of *Eraserhead* is filled with neo-surrealistic images: the man's hair standing on end as a particle-filled sky swirls behind him, a blond-wigged Lady in the Radiator whose cheeks are riddled with mump-like growths, a drawer full of dirt, and that baby that looks like a chicken and human fetus combined (Lynch still keeps the secret of its construction and execution).

*The Exorcist* (1973)—a horror film that takes place in the staid elegance of the Georgetown section of Washington, D.C. The design by Bill Malley contrasts the everyday, normal life of a little girl with the results of her possession by the devil. Her bedroom, where much of the action takes place, is transformed from a sweet little girl's room to a baneful place. The film presents the scariest transformation makeup ever put on film. Religious iconography represents the power of the church in this classic battle between good and evil. An excellent reference for contemporary horror films.

*The Fifth Element* (1997)—New York in the future. Production designer Dan Weil and director Luc Besson set out to avoid the clichés of the science fiction genre. Here cabs and police cars fly but retain their traditional design. Twelve artists and illustrators worked on specific themes, vehicles, apartments, food, and domestic accessories. The traditional grid of Manhattan streets and avenues was retained, but buildings in the design were "futurized" to an appropriate level of technology, without resorting to an exaggerated hypermodernity as seen in the old *Flash Gordon* serials and many early science fiction films.

*The Godfather* (1972)—Paramount expected just another gangster flick, but director Francis Ford Coppola and production designer Dean Tavoularis had in mind an epic film about organized crime as an American industry. The screenplay by Mario Puzo and Coppola stressed the family structure, power, and tradition. The design contrasts the sanctity of a sunny garden wedding with Don Corleone's dark, old-world office, where favors and evil deeds are dispensed. The home is a fortress, a corporate headquarters for the family business with dark wooden blinds, immaculate grounds, and all the trappings of home. Light and dark, and good and evil, are the platforms for a family whose relationships are representative of 1940s middle-class America—except their business is crime, murder, and treachery.

*Interiors* (1978)—Woody Allen's Bergmanesque drama is about an oppressive woman and the psychological damage she has inflicted on her husband and daughters. Production designer Mel Bourne received an Academy Award nomination for creation of an environment that provided the mood to support the drama. Eve, played by Geraldine Page, is a decorator. The premise of the story is that she decorates the family living space. Eve is a woman who is a perfectionist in her work, and the subtle and minimalist space she creates for her family represents her cold emotional state and inability to give love. This space dooms them all to struggle with their feelings toward each other. The walls in the house are a muted clay beige color. The window walls along the part of the house that faces the beach are painted a lighter shade than the other walls, to avoid shadows and create uniformity. The windows are a metaphor for personal reflection and confrontation of the characters. Bourne reglazed every window to have a clear surface for actual perfect reflections. The putty on each window was an exact straight line. Bourne felt it was what Eve would have done.

*Intolerance* (1916)—D. W. Griffith's apologia for the racism of *The Birth of a Nation* presents the intolerance of man throughout the ages and features the biggest set ever built in Hollywood. For the Babylon story, the production design by Griffith and his art department, led by Walter L. Hall, constructed massive steps and gigantic platformed pillars topped with enormous elephant statues. The immense scale of the production design was unprecedented and became the artistic bar for the epic film genre.

*King Kong* (1933)—designed by Carroll Clark, Al Herman, and Van Nest Polglase, this fantasy of a giant ape taken from his African environment to New York City, as an Eighth Wonder of the World spectacle for the entertainment of the cosmopolitan masses is convincing and metaphorical. The themes of beauty and the beast and the dangers of violating the laws of nature are supported by a jungle stronghold, an African landscape, a burgeoning New York City, elevated trains, and a cavernous theater. The New York skyline serves as a jungle for Kong, who displays his power by climbing to the top of the Empire State Building (a phallic symbol) and battles airplanes (the might of modern man). An entertaining film with state-of-the-art effects, it continues to influence any film that takes on the challenge of making a fantastical, altered-reality plausible.

*The Last Emperor* (1987)—not only a fine period film but a good reference for creating environments that express the changing environments of the protagonist. Designed by Ferdinando Scarfiotti, the world of the child emperor is the Forbidden City, which represents Ancient China. It is red and gold with traditional art and architecture. The adult emperor is exiled to a bleak prison in Art Deco Europe. The environments present a history of China transformed by Communism and the psychological impact it has on the life of a man born to rule, who is instead sent on a journey influenced by politics, social, and cultural change.

*The Manchurian Candidate* (1962)—visualized the brainwashing of a group of U.S. military men by the Communists, with a revolving amphitheater that represents both a ladies' garden party and the location where the event is actually occurring. Richard Sylbert created a production design that graphically demonstrates the mental delusional state of the men. A classic reference for the political thriller.

*Magnolia* (1999)—the sheer number of sets, designed by William Arnold and Mark Bridges, that link the large diverse group of characters in their misery makes this over three-hour film a major design accomplishment. The environments include the set of a quiz show, a stage where a macho guru preaches to men, a hospital room, a bar, and a rainy street flooded by frogs that fall out of the sky.

*Metropolis* (1926)—this silent Fritz Lang masterpiece features a sprawling futuristic city powered by throngs of slaves who operate oppressive machines that power the city ruled by the rich. Based on a 1925 vision of a German city in the future, the production design features towering skyscrapers and a Tower of Babel metaphoric structure. The sets by Otto Hunte, Eric Kettlehut, and Karl Vollbrecht contrast the grandeur of the city's power with the evil underground dominated by a medieval industrial complex. This netherworld is filled with steel, platforms of compressed workstations, iron rails, a raked staircase, and blasts of polluted steam pounded out from ubiquitous pipes and orifices.

*Nashville* (1975)—Robert Altman's sprawling film of Tennessee's country music scene as a metaphor for the political, social, and cultural state of America in the 1970s is set in recording studios, clubs, concert venues, an airport, on a highway during a multicar supercrash, and in the living spaces of country music superstars. Set decorator and property master Robert M. Anderson achieves an effective commentary on the extravagance and superficiality of American style.

*Rear Window* (1954)—this Alfred Hitchcock thriller is about a photographer laid up with a broken leg, who uncovers a murder in his apartment complex by looking out the window. The production design, by Joseph Macmillan Johnson and Hal Pereira and built on a soundstage, is a courtyard that becomes the man's universe in his confinement. This metaphor for the filmmaker as voyeur is supported by a set that creates a specific character environment for each of the residents living across from Jimmy Stewart's photographer. In a narrative sense, the set is the story: people living in close proximity, their windows a portal into their lives, ambitions, and their dark obsessions.

*Requiem for a Dream* (2000)—environments created by and perceived by the victims of addiction are the foundation of this harrowing film designed by James Chinlund. The drug dens are detailed and depict the doomed world of the addict, but the Brooklyn apartment of an older woman driven into delusion over her battle with food addiction has the most deadly effective set. The set features a refrigerator as frightening as the goriest digital creature.

*Rosemary's Baby* (1968)—Roman Polanski's brilliant adaptation of Ira Levin's novel of contemporary horror, set in New York's Upper West Side. Richard Sylbert designed quintessential prewar apartments for the mother of Satan's child, a subtly creepy one for their cult neighbors, and a scary basement that sets the scene for evil. This paradigmatic film for the horror that invades the modern everyday world is still going strong over thirty years later, influencing films such as *Scream* (1996) and *I Know What You Did Last Summer* (1997).

*Saturday Night Fever* (1977)—low-budget kitchen-sink realism comprises the world of an Italian-American young man from Brooklyn, New York, who lives at home and works in a local hardware store and explodes into the disco nightlife that he dreams will take him beyond his roots. The design features a multicolored projected dance floor, a white suit, and the real fashion of urban middle-class America at the height of the 1970s disco inferno.

*Se7en* (1995). In this unusual and dark film, designed by Arthur Max, a serial murderer is obsessed with the seven deadly sins. The killer, brilliantly played by Kevin Spacey, keeps detailed notebooks depicting each of the sins—:envy, gluttony, greed, lust, pride, sloth, and wrath—and he executes a killing for each in a fitting setting of his own demented choice and creation.

*The Shining* (1980)—Stephen King's Overlook Hotel was built entirely on a soundstage in Stanley Kubrick's adaptation. The haunted hotel was designed by Roy Walker with large, interconnecting rooms for the psychological atmosphere that overwhelms and influences the maniacal behavior of Jack Torrence. The décor includes Native American artifacts, a gold ballroom, a blood-red and white bathroom, eclectic colors and patterns, long, narrow hallways, a huge labyrinth kitchen, and a topiary maze. The interconnecting design allowed Kubrick to take full and effective advantage of Garrett Brown's then newly invented Steadicam's ability to float and glide without the director's attention to the traditional mechanics of camera movement.

*Star Wars* (1977)—George Lucas and his team created a galaxy far, far away, inspired by his passion for Flash Gordon, myth, and science fantasy. The *Star Wars* saga is about more than movies; the films have become part of popular culture. The design by John Barry, however, was developed with limited resources and a technology created by the filmmakers. The narrative reaches back to themes of good's triumph over evil and forward to New Age beliefs in trusting the force within. The design team had the challenge of creating an alternate reality, consisting of a Death Star military complex, vehicles, Jedi resources for the heroes, a memorable alien bar, two charming robots, and a host of imagined creatures in the Lucasian universe.

*Sunrise* (1927)—F.W. Murnau's first American film is one of the masterworks of silent cinema. The story concerns a farmer who considers murdering his wife when he becomes involved with another woman. The massive exterior city set, designed by Rochus Bliese, was exaggerated in scope to visualize the point of view of the country couple swallowed up the breadth of the cosmopolitan environment. Actual streetcar rails and streetcars were brought onto the set. Buildings, streetlights, and a restaurant are just some of the details that give *Sunrise* artistic realism.

*2001: A Space Odyssey* (1968)—Stanley Kubrick spent four years developing, shooting, and completing the science-fiction film that rewrote the rules on cinematic storytelling and visualization. His objective was to present a projection of the first year of the new millennium from the perspective of futurists and experts he had consulted from a wide range of technology, business, style, and scientific concerns. All of the contributions were factored into the overall production design by Ernest Archer, Harry Lange, and Tony Masters. The imagery utilized to support the cinematic exploration of space and man's relationship to a higher power include a mysterious black monolith, a prehistoric landscape, the inner workings of an onboard computer that displays more emotion than the human astronauts, a moonscape, graceful crafts in space, a red and white space station waiting area, the interior of a spacecraft built inside a centrifuge, and a Victorian room in another universe.

*Vertigo* (1958)—Alfred Hitchcock's psychological thriller about a mysterious woman and a detective with a fear of heights made an uncharacteristic use of location shooting. The director, who enjoyed the control of the sound stage, made dramatic and atmospheric use of San Francisco locales. The film, designed by Harry Bumstead and Hal Pereira, is one of Hitchcock's most emotionally complex and mature and was ahead of its time in using actual locations to bring verisimilitude to the style. It wouldn't be until the 1970s when a new generation of filmmakers took to the streets to express their visions.

*Witness* (1985). This story of police corruption is a study in contrasts, in particular between the serene country setting of the Amish in Pennsylvania and Philadelphia's tough inner city. The old-world is invaded by the new. Director Peter Weir explores the spirituality of the Amish and uses the metaphor of a fish out of water as a tough police detective poses as Amish to solve a crime.

## Production Design as a Narrative Tool

Through architecture, shape, space, color, and texture, the design of a film expresses the story and supports the characters. Before you write your first screenplay or the next one, study and understand the palette and tool box that will empower you to fully execute the production design appropriate to tell the story through your personal vision of the film.

Screenwriters write for the screen. They understand the function and purpose of place and period. The prose is direct and evocative, but it is meant to give instruction to the designer. Write cinematically. Understand the environment that the story takes place in. When does the narrative take place? Where? Be story specific. The locations should reveal information about the character's' economic, social, moral, and political status and views. What is the emotional and psychological makeup of the characters? Where do they live? What is their personal style? How do they relate to their environment? How does physical space impact on their lives? Visualize the story as you write it. How can the inner-life of the story be put into a physical environment? How do you impart the poetic or metaphoric subtext of the story?

## The Vision Thing

We've established that the visual style of a film is largely created through the collaboration of the trinity of director, director of photography, and production designer. The following are descriptions of the nature of each job and the ways in which these three interact and support each other creatively.

### THE DIRECTOR

A movie director is responsible for telling a story visually with a point of view. As the central creative force, a good director must have a firm idea of how to translate the script cinematically. In pre-production and production the director makes countless decisions about matters concerning story, motivation, technical, and aesthetic issues, all to serve the film.

To the director, a screenplay represents the totality of the film—content, story, and character. It's a document that embraces the text to be used to develop a point of view and the manner in which specific tools of cinema craft will be applied. Directors read the script for an overall impression and impact. They must pre-visualize the film and be ready to collaborate with the heads of departments working under their leadership. Directors make all final decisions on design and photographic matters.

### THE DIRECTOR'S POINT OF VIEW

It is the director's imperative to have a point of view toward the narrative and characters. Directors with a strong point of view toward production design, such as Terry Gilliam, Peter Greenaway, Alfred Hitchcock, Stanley Kubrick, and Ridley Scott, communicate design ideas directly. Others directors give the production designer a guiding concept and react and respond to their ideas and drawings; still other filmmakers have little sense of the visualization and rely on the designer for the creation of the production design.

### THE PRODUCTION DESIGNER

The production designer is the head of the art department. Production designers are responsible for the physical environment, the sets, and locations. They oversee the work of the **costume designer**, and hair and makeup design. They are responsible for the selection, creation, and construction of the sets, locations, and environments for a movie. Production designers are fiscally responsible to the producer for the design and construction of the sets. They are artistically responsible to the director and to the creative potential of the screenplay.

Production designers are brought on early in the pre-production phase. They read the screenplay for overall impressions, then begin to formulate a concept for the material. The production designer searches to find the film's visual potential and intent, to be expressed in the physical environment. They begin to make notes concerning period, locations, space, texture, and color. The designer meets with the director and shares impressions of the story and how the film will be visualized. The physical environment of the story is the production designer's primary concern.

## THE DIRECTOR OF PHOTOGRAPHY

The director of photography, or cinematographer, is responsible for rendering the director's vision of the movie on film or video. The director of photography collaborates with the director and production designer to create the look and visual style of a film that will best serve the story. The domain of the director of photography is the camera, composition, light, and movement. Lenses define the frame and perspective. Film stocks, lab processes, and digital enhancements impact on the color and visual texture. Cinematographers don't create production design—they photograph it.

The director of photography generally is brought in later in the pre-production process. The reason is fiscal. Directors of Photography earn a higher salary than the production designer and so, for the sake of budget, are given less preparation time. They get involved in planning the look of a film with the design process already underway. If possible, bring the DP on board early so that he can have input into the design process. Remember that the look of a film is a collaboration between the director, DP, and production designer, and it needs to be solidified by the team from the outset of a production. When the DP comes on later, the design process may suffer, not only because the DP is behind in contributing input, but also because practical aspects like the functionality of the set and approach to color and texture may require changes that could have been resolved during early planning among the three collaborators. If sets have to redesigned, rebuilt, or repainted because of color interpretation issues, it will cost the production time, money, and most important, cohesion. A vision or look of a film must be an interlocking collaboration of design and photographic composition.

Like all production collaborators, the director of photography first reads the script for story and then begins to crystallize photographic concepts concerning light, composition, and movement, color, and texture. The cinematographer's primary tools— the camera, lenses, lighting instruments, film stock, or video format—will all be applied to photographically create the vision and look of the film.

The director, director of photography, and production designer meet to discuss the script in detail. The story, characters, and the director's point of view toward the material must be clear. Everyone must be making the same movie.

### A Production Designer's Credo

- Craft must interpret the script.
- Cinema style should be loyal to the intent of the story.
- Style for style's sake is only style and not content. Eye candy is pretty to look at but is not narrative substance.

- Content = ideas, information, and narrative interpreted through the film crafts.
- A good script properly visualized is paramount in making a good film.
- Skillful casting and high-caliber performances are essential in making a good film.
- Craft gives meaning, interpretation, and emotional and psychological depth to the story and to the actors creating the characters.
- The production design must serve the story and the characters.

## Communication

Everyone working on a film begins with the screenplay. Notes, sketches, storyboards, and discussion are the means of communicating visual ideas. The trilogy of the director, director of photography, and the production designer should screen films and look at paintings and photographs to communicate ideas, likes, dislikes, research, and interpretive insights, and to look for inspiration. For *The English Patient* (1996), production designer Stuart Craig visited the archive of the Royal Geographical Society and studied files of documents and photographs of the real Count Almasy, who was fictionalized in the film. A photograph of a street became a reference for the Cario Bazzar set in the film. Production designer Patrizia Von Brandenstein researched the world of faith healers, psychics, and crystals for *Leap of Faith* (1992). The film starred Steve Martin as traveling tent show evangelist. For her Oscar winning design on *Amadeus* (1984), Von Brandenstein examined Mozart's tax rolls for insight into his extravagant life style. Letters revealed he had tremendous gambling debts and that he spent his money on expensive clothes. She learned that Mozart had moved from house to house ten times. This would have been cumbersome to portray in the film so one apartment was used in the film and it was designed to gradually empty as Mozart lost what he owned to pawnbrokers.

After the production designer reads the screenplay for content and overview, the script is broken down. A detailed list of each location is created, with the following information included for each new location:

- **Interior** (Int.) or **Exterior** (Ext.)
- Identification of the actual location; for example, Ext. Farmhouse, Int. Jazz Nightclub
- Time period
- Destination—in what city, state, town, or country is the location situated?
- Time of day or night
- Season/weather conditions

## Breaking Down the Screenplay

The following script page is from the author's unproduced screenplay, *The Barbière*. This period story begins in the 1940s in a barbershop, where a little boy is learning his father's trade. The last shot of the opening montage is a backtracking shot of the father's shop as the boy, Michael, is now working his own chair as a barber. When a full view of the old barbershop fills the screen, there is a match cut to the following scene:

**1.** INT. PERFECT TOUCH HAIR SALON. BROOKLYN 1976 – DAY

**2.** It is the grand opening of Michael's unisex salon. The CAMERA continues to move now TRACKING FORWARD. **3.** EASY LISTENING MUSIC plays in the background over the P.A. system. All of the chairs are filled with customers. **4.** Assistants bring towels and haircutting capes to their operators. One of the SHAMPOO GIRLS goes from station to station with **5.** a tray of Italian pastries.

A SERIES OF ANGLES
**6.** The MAIN ROOM has five chrome and glass haircutting stations on each side. The hydraulic chairs are covered with white Naugahyde. The spacious floor is white linoleum, cut to look like Italian ceramic tile.

**7.** In the back is MICHAEL'S old station from his father's shop. The antique chair and station is MICHAEL'S way of bringing a bit of the past with him to this venture in a new world. He works on customer while overseeing the activities on the floor.

**8.** MICHAEL TORDELLI has grown up to be a very handsome man. Dressed in a tailored suit, his salt and pepper hair is cut in a sharp European style. His eyes are clear and demanding. His relaxed smile is framed by a dark, full but well-trimmed moustache. MICHAEL has a charisma that has made him popular with women and commands respect from men. He emits an aura of old-world elegance with a touch of New York City street toughness.

**9.** Past a wooden lattice partition is the SHAMPOO AREA. There are five sinks and shelves filled with supplies. Customers are getting their hair washed by SHAMPOO GIRLS. Opposite the sinks is a door with a **10.** sign that reads, MR. MICHAEL TORDELLI – PRIVATE.

To the right of the front door is **11.** A WAITING AREA where **12.** coffee and wine are being served while customers sit on **13.** three designer couches reading the latest newspapers and magazines. **14.** The walls are decorated with silver-framed photographs of new hairstyles.

In front of the door is **15.** A tall, white, marbleized Formica RECEPTION DESK, which is covered with **16.** gift plants and cards congratulating MICHAEL. People wait to make appointments. MARIE, the receptionist, is busy skillfully handling **17.** the telephones, intercom, appointment books and customers with a polite diplomacy. **18.** She is single, very pretty with feathered-back hair like Farrah Fawcett Major. She wears designer disco clothes and is unconditionally loyal to MICHAEL.

Detailed lists of each location, décor, props, and costumes are made by the production designer, art director, set decorator, property master, and costume designer, then approved by the director. The following notes for *The Barbière* indicate what information can be extracted from the script concerning the production design.

**1.** This scene is an interior. The decision will be made whether to build this set or find a suitable location. *The Barbière* is a period film taking place in 1976. Brooklyn, a borough of New York City, can be seen outside the front window, and exteriors are needed for other scenes in the film. If a set is created, the exterior view from inside the shop must be accurate. A location is a possibility here. The designer may elect to find a haircutting salon that has retained its look from the 1970s. If not, the location scout will look for a salon that can be easily transformed into an exact period replica. It is daytime, but the time of the year or season is not indicated. Warm weather would probably be preferable for this story. The characters can wear the disco finery typical for the time period and environment, when unisex haircutting salons took the place of the barbershop for men and the beauty parlor for women—at least for young people and those wanting to be *au courant,* 1970s style. The name of the salon, The Perfect Touch, would be displayed on signs and business cards, and possibly be printed on the front window (which means it would read in reverse from an interior view). An overhead sign might be simpler than removing the name from a location window and painting on the new one. As to the issue of whether to build in the studio or find a location, much of the action in this film takes place inside the shop. Building a set would give complete control to the filmmakers and avoid scheduling problems that would come up with a functioning location. Another possibility would be to find a salon no longer in operation that still has equipment and décor, and refurbish it. The ultimate decision is based on a balance of economic, time, logistic, and aesthetic issues.

**2.** The architectural layout will be described. Knowing the rooms in the shop, their arrangement, and connection to each other will help the designer to create a floor plan for a set if it is to be built.

**3.** To justify the easy listening music that will be added in post-production, speakers for the shop's sound system and a record or tape player can be on set, as well as tapes or record albums that reflect the musical tastes of the characters later defined as Disco and Frank Sinatra.

**4.** Specific props, towels, and haircutting capes are indicated. Research will uncover the kind of scissors, combs, brushes, hair products, and other supplies used to dress the set and for hand use by the actors.

**5.** The pastries are going to be eaten by actors and extras on camera, so they will have to be real and there must be enough on hand for multiple takes and camera setups.

**6.** The description of the main room implies that the shop is modern, state of the art. The materials for the old-world barbershop were porcelain, leather, and Italian ceramic tile. This shop is made out of artificial, faux materials, such as Naugahyde and linoleum. The culture that created the old shop came from Italy; this one is Italian-American, glitzier, and less permanent in nature. The style of The Perfect Touch is the latest and doesn't have a sense of tradition.

**7.** Michael's old barber station is the one from the early scenes that took place in the 1940s. It should be aged and in direct contrast to the brand-new shop it sits in. The old station reflects Michael's character. He still embraces his roots as he strives for success in a rapidly changing America.

**8.** This description provides important information for the costume designer and the hair and makeup department in helping to create the character of Michael. Because the characters in the film are haircutters and the customers are being freshly styled, a haircutting consultant would be helpful. Also the hair and makeup departments need to be expanded to handle the large cast. They will also need to do research on hairstyles of the time to give the film authenticity.

9. Wooden, painted-white lattices are crosshatched fences used in gardens. They became a popular décor element in 1970s hair salons. Lattice was featured in Richard Sylbert's design for *Shampoo*, where it served as a metaphor for the Garden of Eden surrounding the womanizing hairdresser portrayed by Warren Beatty. In *The Barbière*, lattice is not used as a metaphor but as a period décor element. In the 1970s, lattice was used as a room divider and created a friendly, atmospheric mood rather than the isolation of a solid wall. The open design of lattice allows a view through the fence-like structure yet still defines the space. The shampoo sinks would largely have to be operational so customers can be seen getting their hair washed. If working plumbing is a problem, actors could be wet down prior to shooting and the shampoo hose could be rigged so water could spray out on camera.

Props: The shelves should be stocked with uniformly designed bottles of shampoo and hair conditioner labeled with products of the era. There should also be stacks of clean white towels and large combs for combing out the hair after the shampoo.

10. The scenic artists would be responsible for all signs. The sign for Michael's office should be designed to represent Michael's ego and demand for respect.

11. The style of the working door must be determined, as should be the shape and design of the waiting area.

12. Props for the waiting room—such as coffee and wine sets-ups—can be placed either here on view or in a back room. The style of the coffee cups and wineglasses are to be determined. Because it is opening day it may be appropriate to use real ceramic coffee mugs and wineglasses that would speak to Michael's sense of class. Another choice would be to use Styrofoam cups for the coffee and plastic cups for the wine to establish that Michael is a product of his environment and his sense of worldliness is only a façade.

13. The three designer couches should be expensive but made of manmade materials, maybe Naugahyde, to relate to the haircutting chairs. The arrangement of the couches will be determined by the design of the room. A table to hold the magazines and newspapers is not mentioned but necessary. The reading material should be added to this, as well as a book made up by Michael's staff containing photos of models wearing the current hairstyles featured in the shop. This helps to sell customers on a hairstyle before they get to the chair and allows the shop to become associated with a signature hair-styling look.

14. These are professionally posed and photographed pictures to decorate the shop and again to promote the shop's hair fashion sense.

15. The reception desk could be rented or purchased from an industry manufacture or distributor. One may exist in a location. Building this unit allows the designer to create to the character of Marie and contribute to the overall atmosphere of the production design for The Final Touch salon. Marbleized Formica signifies that the surface pretends to be Italian marble but is an imitation. This is another metaphor: while Michael imitates integrity of his father, a hard-working, honest man, he is power-hungry, will-

ing to do anything to succeed but is attached to his family roots. The result is something that is not what it is supposed to be. Formica is not marble—and Michael is not his father.

16. Props are used to indicate that the shop has just opened. Plants with colorful bows sporting small identification tags and congratulatory greeting cards line the desk. Not mentioned but period-accurate would be the shop's first dollar, framed or taped to the wall.

17. The reception desk has telephones and an intercom that do not have to be practical. The sound for this equipment will be added in post-production. The appointment book or chart should be large and made out in pencil detailing every half-hour of the day, the haircutter's names, and the names of their clients. This is Marie's power to control who gets appointments with whom and when. The book should be large and imposing.

18. This description of the character Marie will aid the hair, makeup, and costume team to help the actress create the role.

The filmmakers then share and make comments and notes addressing the atmospheric, architectural, and stylistic specificity of the locations. The script will give some information in the prose description. The nature of the story and characters will also help flesh out indicators from the script. The creative team then adds its own observations about the look of the location and the purpose it serves in the narrative. Authenticity, imagination, and creating the right audience perception are of the highest import. "Real" isn't always best for the film; creating a world with its own inner-logic and truth is. The design must play dramatically and be believable to the audience no matter how surrealistic, fantastical, or imagined it may be. Does the location require or need to be built on a stage or can it be found? If an actual location will be used, does it have to be altered, aged, or restored?

You may be able to find a location, but it may not be suitable for film production. Space is required for the camera, sound, lighting, and crew. If a set is built, the walls can be made **wild**, allowing them to be moved. The set must be designed and built to accommodate the personnel and equipment necessary for production.

It is important for the director of photography and the production designer to meet with the director before the process of location scouting or building studio sets begins. A production deal to shoot in Canada or another county may have been made by the producer or director for budgetary reasons. The decision to shoot the film entirely in the studio may have been made. Martin Scorsese decided to shoot *Gangs of New York* (2002) on sound stages in Italy. Oliver Stone informed production designer Bruno Rubeo that sequences set in Massapequa, Long Island, during the 1960s, for the film *Born on the Fourth of July* (1989), would be shot on location in Texas due to a two-picture deal made with the Texas Film Commission. That decision required a massive effort on the part of the production designer and the art department. Shooting on location in Texas meant a restoration effort to recreate Massapequa in the 1960s. It demanded a total transformation that included **façades** covering existing houses, the uprooting of trees and landscaping, the importation of trees, plants, and bushes indigenous to Long Island, and the refacing of several blocks of a Texas town's shopping district.

## Set Decoration

On a major or independent production, the set decorator, a member of the art department headed by the production designer, executes the set decoration. The set decoration begins after the set has been built or after a real location has been selected. The set consists of the walls, floor, ceiling, **windows**, doorways, and doors. Decoration includes rugs, furniture, wall hangings, and window treatments. The script will give some indication of the décor, but the set decorator will be influenced by the aesthetic decisions made by the director, director of photography, and the production designer and the way in which the actual set and characters have been realized.

The set decorator makes a list of what décor elements are necessary for each location in the script. They include paint, wallpaper, floor coverings, furniture, paintings, photographs, books, magazines, newspapers, appliances, and audio-visual equipment.

## Props

Items handled by the actors are designated as props, including pens, weapons, cigarette lighters, eyeglasses, and wineglasses.

They are gathered, designed, or purchased by the **property master** who is responsible for their placement and care during the shooting phase of a film. The property master is, of course, also acting under the supervision of the **set designer**. The script will indicate specific props necessary for the story and representation of the characters. Often it is the unique and specific prop that will enhance the visual texture of the design and bring verisimilitude and imagination to the story. The red paper lanterns used in *Raise the Red Lantern* (1991), a film designed by Cao Jiuping and directed by Zhang Yimou, identified which of his many wives he wanted to bed on a particular night. The designer considered the lanterns as witnesses of the tragedy that unfolds throughout the film in the courtyard of the estate. The most significant prop in American film history is the children's sled in *Citizen Kane* (1941). Initially it is a gift given to Kane by Thatcher, as he is about to take the boy away from his parents to an affluent world they couldn't afford but can now give to their son, as young Kane's mother has come into a stock fortune. Kane's dying word "Rosebud" becomes a mystery that may be a key to his complex personality. In the final seconds of the film, when many of Kane's personal artifacts are thrown into a furnace, we see that the name of the sled was Rosebud and that for Kane it represented a childhood he was never allowed.

Every visual element should complement, support, and develop the cinematic narrative and fit into the overall design plan. The property master lists the props needed for each scene, and includes necessary items that will give the film, via the design, distinction.

These "shopping" or "laundry" lists are an instrumental part of designing your film. They organize your approach to the design and stimulate ideas and creativity. The lists will be used to find, create, build, rent, and execute the design.

## Special Effects

All special effects need to be added to their own laundry list, and the consequences of special effects sequences need to be taken into account as well. Practical effects like the walls in Brian DePalma's *Scarface* (1983), designed by Ferdinando Scarfiotti, had to be replaced after each take when they were riddled with bullet holes. Many replacement walls were prepared in advance.

Digital technology has made a tremendous impact on production design. For the Oscar-winning *Gladiator* (2000), the decision was made to create the stadium and backgrounds of Rome with CGI, or computer-generated imaging. The production designer can and should be involved in this process. When the industry used hand-painted mattes for **matte shots**, the production designer conferred with the matte artist. CGI, like matte shots, are a tool that should serve the design. Computer graphic artists and special effect creators have to understand the needs of the production designer. Currently CGI is employed for budgetary and logistical reasons, to create impossible shots and to augment, change, and enhance. Roman Polanski's *The Ninth Gate* (1999) features a very traditional-looking design that recalls the Hitchcockian sense of artificiality. The design looks old fashioned and very low-tech. Polanski's DVD commentary for *The Ninth Gate* reveals that almost every shot in the film has a CGI element—though most of the alterations were admittedly motivated by the filmmakers' desire to experiment with the miracle toy, not because CGI was necessary for substantive contributions. Richard Sylbert and other major designers have expressed concern over when and where CGI should be utilized in creating film design and when traditional methods are most effective.

## Finding the Look of a Film

The look of a film comes out of the content and the director's conception of the story. Pre-visualize the film. Translate the script into visual images. Details come out of concepts. Don't proceed until you have a working metaphor, a specific psychological, atmospheric, and emotional image of what you want to visually project.

The key to the look of the film is not in an imposed or personal attitude toward visual style—the story will lead you there. Some questions to answer:

- What emotional impact does the story have? *Carnal Knowledge* (1971), directed by Mike Nichols and designed by Richard Sylbert, follows the sexual obsessions and failed relationships of two males from college to middle age. Sylbert saw the film as a chamber piece. The sets were designed to drive the characters into the corners of the rooms by putting every door in every room in a corner. All of the windows look out to another window. The walls were bare and only decorated with light fixtures. The physical environment emphasized the emptiness of their lives.
- How does the environment of the narrative reflect the characters? The vivid characters in the screenplay for Ingmar Bergman's *Fanny and Alexander* (1984) suggested settings that evoked their personalities. The grandmother had been a diva of the theater. She behaved as the queen of the family. Production designer Anna

Asp designed an environment that conjured up power and a sense of theatricality. This was accomplished with heavy drapes that suggested a theater curtain, lush carpets, sophisticated paintings, a crystal chandelier, oversized potted plants, a bookcase full of fine volumes, and hand-crafted furniture. The home of the Bishop reflected austerity with white stone walls, a single tall candlestick holder and white, lit candle, and a music stand with instrument and sheet music. The ascetic nature of the bishop created an environment the designer saw as a metaphor for a prison for the children. The home of Jacobi, the puppet-maker, was warm and magical, filled with red and a large puppet stage that allowed the children to escape from their puritan environment into an enchanting world of fantasy.

- What is the psychological nature of the story? In Andrey Tarkovsky's last film, *The Sacrifice* (1986), a catastrophic event takes place during the birthday celebration of the main character that impels him to search for an act of faith. The great director's theme was the lack of spirituality in modern life and the importance of the exploration of belief. The design of the man's house developed out of a collaboration between Tarkovsky and designer Anna Asp. The result was a timeless atmosphere that could have been set after nuclear devastation. The scale of the exterior of the house was four times the size of the interior to emphasize that it sat surrounded by total ruin of rock, polluted water, and dirt with no sign of life around it. The trees were nearly bare, tall, and thin as crooked pencils. The design interpreted the psychological state of mind of its main character.

- How can the atmosphere of the architecture and physicality of the settings contribute to telling the story visually? *The Name of the Rose* (1986), directed by Jean-Jacques Annaud, was based on the novel by Umberto Eco that took place during the inquisition in the thirteenth century, where a monk is entwined in the strange happenings in a mysterious Italian abbey. Production designer Dante Ferretti was taken with the way Eco had evoked the atmosphere of the Dark Ages. Ferretti started with the concept of a "subterranean, mysterious quality" and came up with the idea of vertical labyrinth. The design was inspired by M. C. Escher, a Dutch graphic artist who used optical illusion and the ambiguity between flat and three-dimensional shapes to create surrealist effects, like staircases that seemed to run both up and down in the same direction. Ferretti made graphic use of high medieval arches and interconnecting staircases and passageways to visualize Eco's vision of this dark period of history.

- What is your attitude toward the story? Federico Fellini created a fantasy world in his films. To him, films were like dreams, not reality. Dante Ferretti designed many films for the maestro. During an early collaboration, Ferretti designed a set with a sink. He presented Fellini with his drawing, which encompassed all of the details of the basin, the water taps, and the pipework. Fellini ordered the pipes out of the picture. He wanted to maintain a dream state and felt that particular detail of realism would shatter it. For *And the Ship Sails On* (1983), the two men spent hours studying the seaside just outside of Rome for inspiration on how to recreate it on the sound stage. As they drove back, Fellini noticed a tomato field covered with plastic that moved in the wind and picked up the light of sun. In

Fellini's imagination it looked like the sea and that is what they used to create the sea set of the film.

- What is your point of view? *Working Girl* (1988), directed by Mike Nichols, was a message comedy about a working-class secretary who tries to move up the societal ladder. Production designer Patrizia Von Brandenstein had a specific point of view toward the story. The young woman took the Staten Island Ferry to work in Manhattan every day. To Von Brandenstein, the boat trip was like immigrants coming to the new land, or Dorothy coming to Oz. This point of view influenced Von Brandenstein's approach to the way the character saw Manhattan and the office building that became her yellow brick road route to success. The office set was built in a Lower Broadway building with a square corner and curved front facing the harbor. Von Brandenstein had to create the geography of how to get the protagonist from the elevator, through the pool of secretaries, to the power office she craved.

## Exercises to Develop Visualization Skills

- Read a screenplay of a film that you have not seen. **Breakdown** the script into lists of sets and décor. Make notes about the color and texture. Develop a working visual concept based on the story and its intent. When you are confident you are ready to begin the design process, screen the film. How close did you come to the film director's concept? Do you understand the approach? If your visual concept differs, would it succeed in maintaining the integrity of the story and characters? Does it have a directorial point of view?
- Study your personal environments. What do the architecture, furnishings, and décor communicate about time, space, place, and the people who live there?
- Read a short story or novel. Visualize the literary work as a film. Put it down on paper in words and sketches.
- Read a novel or play that has been adapted to a film. Then, see the film. How has the cinematic process transformed the story visually?
- Select a painting that depicts a scene before the invention of photography. How has the artist visually rendered the scene in color, form, and environmental detail? What story does it tell? What does it reveal about the figures depicted?
- Keep a visualization diary. Make notes on every film you see. How is the physical world of the film visualized? How does the production design define and inform the story and characters? What is the role of cinematography in the overall result?

# Chapter 3

## DESIGN METAPHORS

A production design **metaphor** takes an idea and translates it visually to communicate or comment upon the themes of the story. An object or an image is transformed from its common meaning and stands in for or symbolizes an aspect of the narrative, and thus adds poetic complexity to the story. The metaphors evoked by images may be complex and be comprehensible to varying degrees, but often the viewer easily reads a latent meaning. Unlike the intangible words in poetry that conjure up multiple meanings and symbolic imagery in the reader's mind, images in movies are concrete. Using an object or image to transcend the purpose of its physical reality is a challenge, because the metaphorical intent may appear vague. It may be difficult to get the audience to understand the narrative objective of the metaphor.

A visual metaphor in a production design may communicate to only part of an audience or only be accessible to a critic or theorist. A visual metaphor may act on the subconscious level, while the viewer consciously follows plot, character development, and the physicality of the design. These subconscious visual metaphors work on another level, presenting subtle layers of poetic imagery that can impart ideas, concepts, and significance in the narrative.

By nature, production designers visually interpret screen stories both into a physical design that is easily comprehended and through poetic metaphors that communicate on an intellectual, subconscious, psychological, and emotional level. For the designer, the metaphor may be a conduit for various design decisions concerning the myriad details that have to be addressed in architecture, color, space, texture, and spatial relationships.

*The Graduate* (1967) takes place in suburbia and concerns two families. For production designer Richard Sylbert, the classic 1960s youth-culture film—directed by Mike Nichols and starring Dustin Hoffman, Katherine Ross, and Anne Bancroft as the legendary Mrs. Robinson—was a modern version of Shakespeare's *Romeo and Juliet*. Sylbert's metaphor was a variation on the notion that the families were like the Montagues and the Capulets. The Montagues and Capulets were antagonists, the

Braddocks and the Robinsons are not—they are much alike. Sylbert designed both family houses in an identical architectural style, but inverted. One faces left, the other, right. Sylbert's intent was to visually imply the suburban rat race metaphor of keeping up with the Joneses. The houses were designed and then built on a sound stage. Benjamin Braddock's family's house is white with black detailing, the staircases are straight, and all the openings are square or rectangular. Elaine Robinson's house is black and white, too, but with a round staircase, arches, and openings. The Braddock house has a pool and the Robinsons' has a solarium. Mrs. Robinson wears leopard skin, a symbol for her sexual prowess and attitude toward young men like Benjamin, while Mrs. Braddock is attired in the traditional manner of a wife and mother of the time.

Richard Sylbert and producer and star Warren Beatty intended *Shampoo* (1975), directed by Hal Ashby, to be a modern retelling of Jean Renoir's *Rules of the Game* (1939). Sylbert researched Hollywood beauty salons and came up with the metaphor of the salon setting as the Garden of Earthly Delights. The main character, a womanizing hairdresser, perceives his workplace as a Garden of Eden where he is surrounded by beautiful women he can have his way with. Earlier I mentioned that white lattice was a popular décor element in the 1970s, found in most hair salons of the era; it is also emblematic of a fence surrounding a garden. Sylbert carried the lattice motif over to the design of the outside deck at the Goldie Hawn character's home and into the wallpaper of a dining room and The Bistro. (The fashionable restaurant was selected because the lattice motif was already a part of its design.) Sylbert also visually indicated the social status of characters by their placement in the landscape. Jack Warden's office was high up, Hawn's home was halfway up a hill and Julie Christie's house was further up on Hutton Drive. Beatty was always on the bottom.

In *Silkwood* (1983), designed by Patrizia Von Brandenstein and directed by Mike Nichols, the management of the plutonium plant scrubs down exposed employees with wire brushes, flaying the employee's skin. Karen Silkwood is put through the brutal assault. When the officials of the plant send workers to her home to check radiation levels, they scrape down the walls, turning the paint and walls into a metaphor for Karen Silkwood's skin and body. They flay the walls of her home in the way they had scraped down her flesh.

*Rush* (1991), directed by Lili Zanuck and produced by Richard Zanuck, was designed by Richard Sylbert's identical twin brother Paul and is the story of two police officers, one a junkie. Paul Sylbert judged the story as about two naturally repellent elements, police and drugs, likening this to oil and water. The Zanucks wanted to shoot the film in Austin, Texas, but Paul Sylbert suggested Houston, Texas, which is on the coast, because it was near oil and water. Another metaphor Paul Sylbert discovered in the story was the male drug addict as a sacrificial figure. Paul Sylbert saw *Rush* as a descent into hell. For hell imagery he used oil installations because oil comes from the bowels of the earth—the oil shoots out in bursts of flames from the mouths of the wells. He also wanted to use railroad tracks as a means of transportation. The imagery of the shiny train tracks and lines evoked mainlines associated with cocaine use. Paul Sylbert shot photographs of oil on the ground of a gas station after a rain. When light hits the ground at twenty-eight degrees it causes a rainbow to appear. The set decorator and costume designer employed the rainbow oil colors in their work. *Rush* was a period film that took place in 1975, and the metallic properties of the oil and watercolors both fit the metaphor of natural repellents and was period accurate.

The method of finding a design concept and a poetic connection between content and visual style defines the job of the production designer. Taking the script literally will give you an accurate but soulless result. Illustrating the screenplay with images will not establish a thematic relationship between the story, the characters, and their environment. The production designer can accomplish this by obeying the rules of style that pertain to the period the story takes place in, by finding the metaphors and resonance of the story, and realizing them through the art and craft of art direction.

A design metaphor is a visual image employed by the production designer to make a poetic analogy that informs the story and characters; specifically, it is an associative allusion to the character. In *The Untouchables* (1987), directed by Brian DePalma, production designer Patrizia Von Brandenstein perceived Al Capone as a Sun King, an extraordinarily powerful man who controlled Chicago. Von Brandenstein conceived the idea that the city revolved around Capone and created a floor mural visualizing the mythic image of a powerful sun figure. She placed the mural on a barbershop floor where Capone gets his haircut.

Design metaphors can be seen and interpreted by the audience or can be a hidden avenue for the production designer to subconsciously impart ideas. *Chinatown* (1974), directed by Roman Polanski, takes place during a drought. Production designer Richard Sylbert removed the color green from the design, except at the home of the murder victim—where the grass is green because the murder victim has secret access to water. The door to investigator J. J. Gittes' office has a wooden frame surrounding thick pebbled glass. The materials here are period correct, and in addition, Sylbert perceived that the textured glass was evocative of frozen water. Spike Lee's *Do the Right Thing* (1989) takes place on the hottest day of the year, the setting for a violent confrontation of the different races that cohabit in a Brooklyn neighborhood. Production designer Wynn Thomas created a hot color palette. The color scheme expressed the heated emotions of the characters and was supported by director of photography Ernest Dickerson's use of oppressive, broiling summer light. Thomas used a street location devoid of trees so the characters had no relief from shade. Even sound designer Skip Lievsey contributed to the metaphor by creating sound effects and backgrounds that were dry in nature.

## The Psychological Nature of Production Design

Design is not only a physical representation. Environments can have a metaphysical impact on how the audience perceives the story and the characters. Do you want the viewer to feel claustrophobic? Do you want the viewer to experience a sense of massive space? Do you want the viewer to feel frightened? Comfortable? Uneasy or enveloped in dread or doom? The story can be visually interpreted to convey a myriad of psychological states generated by the narrative and point of view of the director.

For Joel and Ethan Coen's film *Barton Fink* (1991), production designer Dennis Gassner received an Oscar nomination for his visualization of Hollywood in 1941. This tinsel town recreation concentrates on the squalor behind the glamour, as the title character, a Broadway playwright based loosely on Clifford Odets, deals with the personal horror of encountering writer's block and selling out in the netherworld that filmmaker Kenneth Anger identified as "Hollywood Babylon." This city of broken dreams, booze, murder, and moral deprivation enters the heart, mind, and soul of Barton Fink as he struggles to write a wrestling picture on studio demand. Fink lives in a decrepit hotel that becomes the prison for his mind. His room is confined, stifling, and squalid, and the hall outside the door is cavernous and spooky. The environment envelops Fink as he pounds his typewriter in vain and suffers torture by mosquitoes. He also encounters a mysterious neighbor whose back story results in a fiery hell that drives the writer into the fantasy of a beachside painting on his wall, signifying his escape from the confines of Hollywood's formulaic prison of commercial product into a world of art and beauty.

In *The Servant* (1964), directed by Joseph Losey and designed by Richard MacDonald, a servant and his master slowly change social roles. The tense black-and-white film is dialogue- and behavior-driven. Losey's metaphor for the environment where this psychological shift of power takes place is to feature the masters' house as the shell of a snail. MacDonald visually interpreted this concept as a three-story structure with a spiral staircase that went through the entire space, encapsulating and swirling the characters in a vortex of confrontation and transformation. MacDonald's design creates an atmosphere that seals the destiny of the two men.

## Atmospheric Qualities of Production Design

The design of a film can create a sense of place. The atmospheric qualities of the sets, locations, and environments are essential in establishing a mood and projecting an emotional feeling about the world surrounding the film. Atmosphere contributes aesthetic properties and visceral fabric to the film. The director of photography can bring atmosphere to a set by applying color gels, through choice of lenses, lighting, and with smoke and diffusion, but the production design must provide the physical elements. The architecture, use of space, color, and texture are the physicality of the design. The contributions of the production designer and the director of photography can work together to impart an emotionally evocative sense of atmosphere.

*Dead Presidents* (1995), directed by the Albert and Allen Hughes, is the story of a young middle-class African-American man who goes to Vietnam instead of going on to higher education. When he returns and experiences societal rejection, a life of crime seems the only way out. Director of photography Lisa Rinzler approached the story as a "three-act experience." The first act before Vietnam was bright, saturated, hopeful, and sunny. Act two, Vietnam, was "hot, frenetic, urgent, and confusing." The conclusion that takes place back in America is "colder, drabber, more dangerous and mysterious, with more darkness." Studio work on *Dead Presidents* was accomplished at Empire Stages in Queens, New York, where production designer David Brisbin created a poolroom set as part of the environment responsible for the young man's descent. The space looked old, a place where a lot of the life had been lived. Brisbin did the room in a russet orange palette and a checkered linoleum floor. The ceiling was patterned tin, representing a culture gone by. At another site a character dies of a drug overdose. When Rinzler first read the scene she decided to express the emotion of the moment with green and asked Brisbin for a green lamp. The designer provided a lamp with an oval light green shade that motivated the use of green light later **gelled** a darker shade of green to visually interpret the dread of death by overdose.

*Seconds* (1966), directed by John Frankenheimer, is a contemporary, socially critical horror film about a middle-aged, upper-class suburban man dissatisfied with his life who is offered a second chance at youth in exchange for his wealth. The director's central theme was that society had distorted this man's values, and the nameless company performing the transformation further corrupted his morals and sense of reality. A visual metaphor for distorted values was achieved by extensive and creative use of wide angle lenses by the veteran cinematographer James Wong Howe, who shot the black-and-white film in canted angles with controlled but disturbing optical distortion. This motif was supported and enhanced by production designer Ted Haworth, who designed some sets in distorted perspective to be photographed with normal focal length lenses and others in normal proportions that were shot with extreme wide-angle lenses. The result was a warped visual presentation that created a paranoid, hallucinogenic atmosphere expressing the man's nightmarish experience.

Haworth's set for the company's mazelike offices consisted of a long corridor with interconnecting offices, a waiting area, and an operating room. Shooting with 9.7mm and 18mm lenses, Howe was able to bend the walls of Haworth's labyrinth. For a scene where the man experiences a drug-induced hallucination in which he imagines he is molesting a young woman, Haworth designed a bedroom with heavily textured walls raked at extreme angles, creating a false sense of perspective. The floor undulated beneath black-and-white checkerboard tiles, bringing the specter of Franz Kafka to the mise-en-scène.

## Translating the Narrative into Visual Ideas

In addition to creating metaphors the production design of a movie can also serve the purpose of identifying the places inhabited by the characters. In the early days of Hollywood filmmaking this was a principal function of art direction. The content and intent created by the screenwriter on paper awaits visual translation. The contemporary moviemaker must be aware of the many tools and palettes available through production design to accomplish this task. One must be specific and precise in a number of areas:

- Authenticity
- Emotional truth of the story and the characters, through their environment
- Interpreting the director's intent
- Defining space
- Details and details within details

## Interpreting the Characters Visually

The production designer must create a breakdown of the characters, in the spirit of the screenwriter who created them, and focus on how the following aspects are translated visually:

- How old are they?
- What is their ethnic and social background?
- What social class do they belong to?
- What is their role in the story?
- What is their personal style?
- What is their physicality?

The screenplay holds the answers to be deciphered by the production designer. Where we work and live is a reflection of who we are. Therefore, production designers must apply their understanding of the characters to create their environments. A production designer is not an interior designer or decorator, however. The latter primarily creates a sense of style based on fashion and practicality to create a visual harmony and consistency, while a production designer is a storyteller. Most environments represent spaces assembled by the inhabitants over a period of years; what they own has been purchased over time. Many characters have a complex sense of style. Not every character lives in a contemporary time frame—some remain in, or are attracted to, the styles of an earlier era. All characters within the same age group will not have the same social status, and not all characters in the same social group have the same sense of style.

The actor playing the part has an influence on your choices. Costumes, hair, makeup, and accessories are all design decisions that, when combined with all of the visual elements of a design, create an environment that fills the frame and signifies the life around it.

The last thing a production designer wants to do is create a generic design. Every space has its own nature and character. Think of all the homes and apartments you have visited. What personality do they project? How are they related to the people who live there?

## Establishing an Environment for Cinematic Storytelling

If the filmmaker considers each location where the story takes place as a set—a literal representation of what is indicated in the script—that is all it ever will become. Rather, consider each location as an environment to reveal the lives of the characters and for the story to unfold. An environment surrounds and embraces the characters. There is a direct relationship between the environment and the characters. Are the environments hostile? Confining? Comforting? Chaotic? Claustrophobic? Vast? Warm or cold?

## Visualization Exercises

- Keep a diary of places you visit. Detail their characteristics. What makes them special? In your design diary, capture, in prose, diverse environments—an urban city scene, a desolate beach, a library filled with students studying, a studio apartment, or a restaurant kitchen on Saturday night.
- Observe environments.
- Read poetry and literature to understand how words can translate form into metaphoric, symbolic, and poetic ideas, which impart meaning beyond story and plot. Keep notes on phrases that become metaphors the author uses to create layers of rich meaning. What are the metaphors? What do they represent?
- Look for visual metaphors in the production design of the films you see. List them. Analyze their purpose and impact on the narrative and the characters.

# Chapter 4

## RESEARCH

Research your film—to avoid generic design. Research and development of the production design will enrich the material in the same manner that the specific emotions and behavior an actor discovers when working on a script enriches a character. The screenplay will inform you about where and when the story takes place, but that's only the beginning. Researching a project is a multifaceted, in-depth process. Research reveals specific design information and presents the scope of history so the production designer can select what elements are needed to express the content of the film's design. The production designer has to read and interpret the research in reference to the story. But don't be a slave to research—always keep the objective of the design concept in mind.

Production designer Christopher Hobbs told Peter Ettedgui for his *Screencraft* volume (Focal Press, 1999) on production design and art direction that, "One should never seek to recreate a period—one should attempt to reinvent it. The primary function of design in film is to comment on and boost what's in the story. It's a theatrical medium. One telling detail in how a set or location can suffice to evoke a whole period." For *Velvet Goldmine* (1998), the Todd Haynes film about glam-rock in the 1970s, Hobbs created a painted wall mural for the front of a boutique of an American Indian face with red and white angled bars emanating from the head. This helped to recall the style of Kings Road area of England in the 1970s, the home of British Glam, where such a mural once existed. Once rooted in the period reality, Hobbs, who designed most of visionary Derek Jarman's film, used his design imagination to illustrate and narratively enrich the story.

As the design concepts and metaphors are created, research to nurture and elaborate your plans. Research is one of the most exciting aspects of the production designer's job. It is a time of possibility, and of attaining knowledge and fulfilling the potential of the project.

Experienced production designers and studio art departments have a working library built up through years of acquired research from earlier projects. Each film explores new areas and expands the designer's knowledge in subjects and places visited in the past. Over the years of his long and successful career production designer Mel Bourne has developed a library of research for the films he has designed. He has notebooks filled with details concerning the lifestyle of families that live in Newport for *Reversal of Fortune* (1990). For background on baseball for *The Natural* (1984), he had a researcher compile data and make arrangements with baseball equipment manufacturers for additional research and props. The baseball museum at Cooperstown also provided information. To build a carnival from scratch in a field for a scene where Hobbs pitches against The Whammer in 1919, massive research was done on carnivals from the period. Bourne found a Toronto company that outfits carnivals all over the world and went through their entire stock. He amassed a major collection of photographs of baseball stadiums. He found a book on psychiatry at the turn of the century and collected research on hospitals for Woody Allen's *Zelig* (1983). Bourne has files on lofts from his research on *FX* (1986), and 250 photographs of lofts for *Fatal Attraction* (1987). He maintains files on bars, saloons, supper clubs, and period bars, and he has scores of photos of firehouses, from the contemporary to houses with old oak trim to those with tile walls.

The research period is the most fertile aspect of the production design process. It is a time for discovery. Be expansive in your search—decisions will be made later after much thought and consideration.

### Design Files

Create an alphabetical series of file folders labeled by subject: Chinese Restaurants, Independent Bookstores, Laundromats, New York Apartments, Outdoor Swimming Pools. The files of an experienced production designer will have photographs from magazines, illustrations from books, and original location photographs of a wide range of sites. Specificity is key. Don't think in generic terms but for atmosphere and detail. What sort of Chinese restaurant is necessary for your story? Is it a Chinatown restaurant with simple tables, minimal décor, and an emphasis on authentic food? Is it a suburban up-market Chinese restaurant with oriental vases and Ancient art? Is it a down-market restaurant, small, frugal, with faux décor? Is it a take-out with a few tables or a vast modern space with several eating areas and a full bar? Do you need a lounge area or the kitchen for the story? Do you need an exterior view? Is the name of the restaurant important? Can you locate it, or will signs and menus have to be created? Are windows necessary? How about the table settings and the style of service? Is it a family style restaurant or one that specializes in intimate couples seating? What neighborhood is the restaurant in? Economic class is always a consideration, as it speaks to the sophistication of the taste and style of the characters, as well as the reality of their lifestyle.

Pictures in a design file do more than just capture an image of the location for research. A well-developed design file will document historical eras, which is necessary for designing period films. Each picture contains vital information for the designer concerning materials and texture. Color or the gray scale is represented. The color will give the designer information as to the shade, value of each color and its relationship to others, as well as the psychological impact. The pictures will reveal the overall mood and atmosphere of the settings so the designer can determine if it is right for the story or if there are elements that can contribute to the look intended for the film. The pictures will document props, furnishings, vehicles, and **set dressing** elements, all critical to understanding the world the designer is creating.

If this is your first movie or you don't have a research library—start now. Scout and photograph the locations you need. Cover the location in full shots from various angles, and then methodically in details, for future study.

Cut out photos from magazines, collect books, photocopy library materials, go on the Internet. Don't be selective. Put in your folders any image that clearly depicts a location, setting, prop, articles of furniture, architecture, color, texture, or time period. These will come in handy on future productions and can be helpful to fellow filmmakers. Your design library could become a source of income. Subscribe to *Architectural Digest, Home and Garden,* to any magazine that features design and environmental ideas. Comb through your personal and family snapshots for reference.

On *Dead Presidents* the Hughes Brothers utilized snapshots of their father and his friends taken during the 1970s to communicate their impressions of how they wanted the film to look. The pictures captured the period, style, mood, and atmosphere the brothers were looking for. They became a visual bible for the twin directors, director of photography Lisa Rinzler, and production designer David Brisbin. The photos, along with other specific research from the art department and Rinzler's choice of film stock, exposure, color, and compositional approaches, determined the style and look of the film.

## Paintings

If the project takes place in a time frame before the development of photography, paintings are a prime research source. Every large city has museums filled with valuable inspiration and historical information. Familiarize yourself with their permanent collections. Get on mailing lists and Web sites so you can track upcoming exhibitions. Paintings can be an excellent resource. Unlike photographs, which may seem to offer a true reflection of reality, paintings offer unique ways of seeing and interpretation. Representational works contain information about architecture, clothing, status, attitude, social mores, and history. Nonrepresentational paintings can provide psychological and atmospheric inspiration, in addition to ideas about the use of frame, spatial relationships, color, texture, and composition. Libraries are a great resource for books on art. Many bookstores carry a good selection of volumes containing excellent reproductions of paintings. They are a good investment for the filmmaker's art department. Rembrandt and Edward Hopper are especially important artists to study for their affinity to filmmaking. There is a direct connection between Rembrandt and the design and photographic style of *The Godfather. Pennies From Heaven* is just one of many films inspired by the art of Edward Hopper. Hopper's use of natural light as a sole, realistic source, and his photographic sense of composition in framing street scenes and landscape in his work as a painter make him a major influence on cinematographers. Hopper's inspiration to cinematic creators has been so great that in the 1990s a traveling exhibit highlighted the connections between his work and the medium. Bernardo Bertolucci, his production designer Ferdinando Scarfiotti, and director of photography Vittorio Storaro were so inspired by the work of painter Francis Bacon, images from his paintings appear in the title sequence of *Last Tango in Paris* (1973), in addition to illuminating the actual design. The tortured deformed human figures surrounded by massive space became a metaphor for Bertolucci's directorial attitude toward the story and characters.

Throughout art history there are painters whose work can be valuable to reference when developing the production design of a film. Here are examples:

Winslow Homer (1836–1910)—American landscape and marine painter. Homer's work is naturalistic but personally expressive. His bold and powerful watercolors are an excellent reference for depicting the pioneering spirit of America. He painted the sea on the rugged coast of northeast England and on the Maine Coast. Winslow Homer is best known for works that demonstrate the power of the sea and man's battle with the forces of nature.

Giorgio de Chirico (1888–1978)—this metaphysical painter contrasted the common with the fantastic. His work set architecture into new and mysterious relationships. A surrealist whose work greatly influenced the films of Federico Fellini, de Chirico is a principal reference for altered reality.

Pierre-Auguste Renoir (1841–1919)—French impressionist best known for beautiful flowers, children, idyllic settings, and especially paintings of beautiful women.

Hieronymus Bosch (1450–1516)—this Netherlands artist painted half-human, half-animal creatures and demons in imaginary environments. Bosch is an excellent reference for the themes of the grotesque, evil, temptation, greed, the consequences of sin, and religious allegories.

Michangelo Marisi da Caravaggio (1571–1610)—this highly influential artist is known for his homoerotic imagery, deep color style, and striking use of chiaroscuro. His large-scale religious work offended the clergy by its lack of decorum and what, today, might be called political correctness. Caravaggio rejected the notion of ideal beauty that dominated his era and was accused of being obsessed with the smut of sin.

Edward Hopper (1882–1967)—American scene painter whose theme was the loneliness of city life. Hopper painted motel rooms, filling stations, cafeterias, and deserted offices at night. His work had a psychological impact in evoking modern city life. Many of his paintings capture settings rather than groups of characters or action, which makes him especially influential as a cinematic reference for production design.

George Groz (1893–1959)—German-born painter known as a caricaturist who expressed his disgust for the military regime. A social satirist, Groz depicted a decaying society obsessed with gluttony and depravity, contrasted by poverty, disease, prostitutes, and hustlers.

Jean-Antonine Watteau (1684–1721)—French Rococo artist who painted perfectly dressed young people in romantic and pastoral settings. Watteau was associated with the theme of young lovers in a Garden of Eden, or parkland settings. He created an atmosphere of melancholy in his paintings, a poetic depth that expressed the feeling that youthful pleasures of the flesh are fleeting.

## Photographs

Photographic research is an effective source for planning production design. The art department utilizes two categories of still photographs, archival and original. Still photographs are a medium that directly relates to how the film or video camera will render the design.

Archival photographs: Historical shots of interior or exterior locations are a valuable and accurate reference to study, understand, and determine physical space, architecture, details, dimension, texture, and color. Archival photographs are available in libraries and museum collections, magazines, photo houses (for a fee), on the Internet, and in book form. It is helpful for filmmakers and designers to have a working knowledge of the history of photography and what subject areas specific photographers have concentrated on. Matthew Brady's superb photographs of the Civil War have been invaluable to projects from *Gone with the Wind* (1939) to *Glory* (1989).

Original photographs: The art department can take their own photographs to record scouting trips, document locations, and other reference materials.

## Magazines

Magazines are an excellent and accessible research source. A range of magazines covering every conceivable contemporary subject is currently on the market. Most topics have a multitude of titles to select from, especially the areas of home design and decorating. Libraries are a good source for back issues, and older magazines such as *Life, Look*, and the *Saturday Evening Post* are excellent repositories of history, culture, and style across many decades. These three magazines in particular are key. *Life* and *Look* magazines were photo story oriented so they provided pictorial coverage of their subjects. Both focused on cultural, social, and lifestyle development of America from the 1940s on and are a standard reference for U.S. films as a source for fashion, architecture, trends, food, travel, and a scope of regional America. Stanley Kubrick began his career as a staff photographer for *Look*. His short films *Day of the Fight* and *Flying Padre* (both 1951) were developed out of photo stories he shot for *Look*. His second feature film, *Killer's Kiss* (1955), was inspired by the photos of the middleweight boxer Walter Cartier who was the subject of *Day of the Fight*. *Killer's Kiss* is filled with images of New York that have the tabloid sense of street grit taken from *Look*, which give the film a realistic design environment. Steven Spielberg is an avid collector of Norman Rockwell's paintings. The artist's painted covers for the *Saturday Evening Post* created iconic images of the innocence of America. They have influenced the design of many Spielberg films, especially *E.T: The Extraterrestrial* (1982) and *Always* (1989). In designing Volker

Schlöndorff's expressionist adaptation of Arthur Miller's play *Death of a Salesman* (1986), production designer Tony Walton fragmented the world of Willy Loman as his mind underwent the same process. "It's sort of like an exploded Norman Rockwell—the ungluing of America," Walton explains.

Just some of the information to be found in magazines includes images of appliances, architecture, fashion, food, furniture, geographical locations, hair, makeup, props, and vehicles.

Magazines are also good reference sources for color, texture, and materials. Go through your own magazine collection and clip out and file. Haunt used bookstores, antique shops, and the attics and cellars of relatives and friends for back issues—the treasure hunt is fun and rewarding. Images and samples from magazines can be mounted on a display board to present the color palette, architectural ideas, and other design concepts to the director.

## Literature

Design ideas can come from all the visual arts, but fictional literature and nonfiction literary works are important sources, too, because words stimulate visual ideas and deliver prose descriptions that contain details about a time and place. Period novels and contemporary works of literature will provide background that can bring insight to the visualization. Reading will bring literary intelligence and a poetic sensibility to your ideas for the movie.

Writers who evoke a strong sense of place include these below:

Jane Austen (1775–1817) wrote about domestic life in middle and upper class Britain of the nineteenth century. Her novels include *Sense and Sensibility* (1811), *Pride and Prejudice* (1813), and *Mansfield Park* (1814).

Charles Dickens (1812–1870) wrote about the evils of Victorian industrialized society. His prose displays an encyclopedic knowledge of London. His novels include *David Copperfield* (1850), *Great Expectations* (1861), and *A Tale of Two Cities* (1859).

William Faulkner (1897–1962) is the Southern master who created the mythical Yoknapatawpha County, peopled with families representative of the South. Faulkner covered the region from the days of the Indians through the pre–Civil War era to modern times. He wrote about the psychological depths of poor white families, the effects of flood on the lives of hillbillies, moral awareness, and race relationships. His works include *The Sound and the Fury* (1929), *Light in August* (1932), and *Absalom, Absalom!* (1936).

Marcel Proust (1871–1922), a French novelist, wrote *A Remembrance of Things Past*, a seven-part social panorama of France just before and during World War II. His principal themes were love and jealousy, and the relationship of art to reality. Marcel Proust's exquisite prose evoked images of memory in detail that translates to vivid imagery in the reader's mind.

Leo Tolstoy (1828–1910), in *War and Peace* (1865–69), set against the Napoleonic Wars, explored complex characters in a turbulent historical context.

*Anna Karenina* (1875–77) is a study of an aristocratic woman who leaves her husband and searches for meaning to her life.

Anne Tyler (1941– ) is American novelist whose fiction is often set in small Southern towns. Her recurring themes are how families deal with separation from isolation and death. Her work includes *Dinner at the Homesick Restaurant* (1982), *The Accidental Tourist* (1985), and *Breathing Lessons* (1988).

Tom Wolfe (1931– ) is an American journalist and novelist who documents in exacting detail contemporary American culture. Wolfe has written about the counterculture of the 1960s, U.S. astronauts, architecture, and the pretensions of the art world. His novels *The Bonfire of the Vanities* (1987) and *A Man in Full* (1998) use his florid journalistic style to satirize the greed and personal obsessions of the rich and powerful and those who aspire to that life. His nonfiction books include *The Electric Kool-Aid Acid Test* (1968) and *The Right Stuff* (1979).

## Video

If you have a camcorder, regard it as an invaluable research tool. It will enable you to capture images on location-scouting expeditions and to create a library of architectural styles, terrain, backgrounds, cities, towns, and countries you investigate in search of the film's design. Video also gives you the opportunity to see design elements on camera, in motion, and within a movie frame. There is a wealth of archival material available on tape and film to study. Documentaries are also a valuable asset in investigating a wide range of subjects.

Since the 1980s, production designers have made extensive use of portable video to create a motion picture diary of locations scouted for films. The digital revolution of the 1990s has produced compact, inexpensive, and easy to use digital video cameras that have made the use of video during the scouting process even more common. Often the director, producer, production designer, and director of photography are unavailable for preliminary scouting. By reviewing the tapes, these key members of the production team can begin to pre-select the locations that they will later visit on site. The late director of photography Ralf Bode (*Saturday Night Fever*, 1977; *Coal Miner's Daughter*, 1980), made widespread use of digital video in his work on projects like a television adaptation of the classic American musical *Gypsy,* which starred Bette Midler. Bode personally shot rehearsals on video to work out camera blocking and for visual ideas on how to shoot the set.

For *Saving Private Ryan* (1998), Steven Spielberg and his production team screened archival material of World War II, much of it available on video, to create the combat photography, cinematographic style, and realistic production design used so effectively in the dramatic opening recreation of the D-Day invasion.

Most film archives have their collections on video so production designers and their researchers can easily go through material relating to their films. For independent, low-budget, and student filmmakers, video documentaries on a myriad of periods, topics, and subjects are available for free in public libraries and on television. Cable television is especially valuable. Outlets like the Discovery Channel, the History Channel, and A&E, as well as public broadcasting stations, are a fine resource for documentary research. Most book and video stores have a documentary and nonfiction section of video and DVD selections that can be inexpensively purchased and become part of a design research library. The Internet has many outlets for a wider and more eclectic catalogue of this material.

## Oral History

When production designer Patrizia Von Brandenstein set out to research *Silkwood* (1983), based on the true story of whistleblower Karen Silkwood who exposed the dangers of working in a plutonium plant, she was confronted with the dilemma of plutonium plants being off-limits to outsiders. There were no visual records, and access was impossible. Von Brandenstein sought out a retired plutonium plant worker, and as he described the facility in detail, she sketched each separate element of the factory. The details were rendered into full-scale sketches that recreated the plutonium plant. Working drawings and architectural plans were developed and the set was built on a sound stage. The result, when photographed by Miroslav Ondricek, was a realistic environment that looked like an actual plutonium plant.

The testimony of real people can often be of valuable assistance in visualizing a film. Interview subjects can relate details of time and place with accurate specificity. There are oral history archives across the country, which compile human histories of neighborhoods, events, and places. Start by reading the collected works of Studs Turkel, the dean of oral historians who has interviewed hundreds of people, documenting a wide range of experience, memories, and information with a personal, humane point of view.

## The Internet

The Net is like having a research library at your fingertips. In addition to surfing Web sites that feature the subject you are interested in, you can connect with libraries and archives that provide a wealth of resource for production designers. Print out images from Web sites, file them, and use them for reference and presentations.

## Clearance and Permissions

During the research process, be careful to check if any design element is trademarked or copyrighted. In such cases, you must get clearance or permission. These are often negotiable. If your film is a student project or a short for the festival circuit you can make a deal in which you pay the full fee only if the movie is sold for commercial distribution. Unauthorized use of a design element can result in a lawsuit against the film company by the owner of the trademark or copyright. If such an item is used as an inspiration and is not an exact copy or the actual original piece, no clearance or permission is necessary. Many if not all objects and décor have a copyright or trademark. It is always helpful—if not imperative—to have legal counsel in entertainment law available for the production of a film. They are experienced in knowing what items need clearance and permission. Common sense is also helpful.

All contemporary photographs are automatically protected by a copyright held by the photographer, professional or otherwise. Check all paintings and sculpture for ownership. It is unlikely that you will have any problems using general purchased items such as furniture, appliances, or vehicles, but tapestries and rugs can require permission. To acquire permission, determine the owner of the copyright or trademark by the name on the product or the company that manufactures or distributes it. Artists and photographers are generally represented by galleries, agents and lawyers. If the project is independent and low-budget, appeal to the owner for permission without fee in return for an on-screen credit or deferred payment should the film make a profit in the future. Always get clearance and permission in writing, stating the production company, object, use, fee, or waiver of fee. It is a good idea to have a lawyer draw up or check your documents. Mark Litwak's book *Dealmaking in the Film and Television Industry: From Negotiations to Final Contracts* is particularly helpful and useful.

## Product Placement

During the research and design process the filmmaker may choose to bring income into the project though product placement deals, which occur when a company pays the filmmaker a fee to clearly feature its product in a film. This may seem like a good resource for income, but it has its artistic downside. The product must be part of the design style of the film and part of the lives of the characters and their environment. Cereal boxes, snack food, or beverage bottles with their labels directly facing the camera often stick out as planned advertisement and pull the viewer out of the narrative. If you involve such companies, try to negotiate a reasonable use so that the artistic integrity of the film is not compromised.

## Guidelines for Conducting Research

- Use all resources, photos, paintings, books, video, film, the Internet, personal accounts, museums, libraries, and location scouting. Each will bring a specific facet to your knowledge.
- Explore all possibilities you discover and their tributaries.
- Think out of the box. Don't dismiss anything without consideration. Keep organized access to all the information you come across during the research period; you never know when something that seems irrelevant will become central in the design of a film.
- Screen every film that relates to your project. Study how other designers have handled the subject of your film to understand the concepts and ideas. Don't imitate—be inspired to discover and innovate.

# Chapter 5

## THE ART DEPARTMENT

All sketches, illustrations, models, and **drafting** are produced in the art department, and most studios have set up functional and fully equipped art departments that productions can use. For the independent filmmaker, the art department can be set up almost anywhere: in the studio, in a storefront, a rented space, a loft, or in an apartment. Some basics you will need are a drawing board or table, pencils, markers, supplies to build models, drafting materials, ink, pens, and watercolors, or other paint mediums. Become acquainted with a reliable art supply store. Budget the items you will need.

### The Design Team

The production designer supervises a team of artisans and craftspeople who execute and produce the work generated by the production designer's plan. The nucleus of the art department staff consists of the art director, set designer, set decorator, and property master followed by a support staff that includes a **buyer, construction coordinator, construction crew, production illustrator, scenic artist**, set dresser, **greensman**, draftsman, **location manager**, painters, carpenter, and location scout. The costume designer and hair and makeup crews are separate departments all under the supervision of the production designer. Because the production designer is responsible for the look of the film, hair, makeup and costume design must be coordinated in order to achieve a singular design result. Just as a director needs to understand all the crafts to be able to communicate his vision, the production designer must be aware of how hair, makeup, and costume design integrate with the overall design of the film. The amount and intensity of supervision varies. If the makeup, hair, and costume designers are highly experienced, basic meetings may be all that's necessary. If they are not, the production designer must get involved in careful supervision of research, style, and execution of these crafts.

## Art Director

The art director runs the show during production. He supervises the art department crew on set and reports directly to the production designer. Depending on the relationship between the production designer and the art director, the production designer may remain off-set and continue designing and coordinating, meeting with other department heads while the art director works with the shooting crew on a day-to-day basis. The art director, an executive assistant to the production designer on the film, fields phone calls and is responsible for dealing with vendors and the logistics of getting materials to and from the set. If there is no production designer on the film, the art director is responsible for the design of the movie. The title of production designer is honorary.

Prior to William Cameron Menzies' groundbreaking accomplishments on *Gone with The Wind* in 1939, art directors were responsible for the visual look of the film. It is now recommended that the person in charge of what used to be known as "art direction" be assigned the title "production designer." This status encourages the designer to be a partner in the visualization team and acknowledges the role of art direction in films as a craft with storytelling capabilities. If you are producing or directing a small, low-budget production, make sure the person who has the title of "production designer" has a clear sense of the importance of that position's input. The scope of the job will motivate the designer to be an active part of the trinity that creates the look of the film.

## Set Designer

The set designer is responsible for designing and supervising the construction of sets based on the ideas and input of the production designer. A set designer can be brought in for one or all sets to be designed, or on a small production, this job can be done by the art director or production designer.

The set designer, brought in by the production designer to plan and create the elevation drawings used to construct a set, drafts blueprints based on concepts, descriptions, or conceptual drawings and then oversees construction of the set and any modifications ordered by the production designer or the director. The set designer collaborates with the director and director of photography to plan how the set will be employed and photographed.

Established set designers collaborate with many production designers and directors. Set designer David Klassen has worked on many projects including *The Blues Brothers* (1980), director John Landis, production designer John J. Lloyd; *Beverly Hills Cop II* (1987), Tony Scott, Ken Davis; *The Toy* (1982), Richard Donner, Charles Rosen; and *Blade Runner* (1982), Ridley Scott, Lawrence G. Paull.

On *Blade Runner* Klassen worked directly under Lawrence G. Paull and with Ridley Scott, drawing plans of back lot streets, vehicles, and other design elements for this massive production. Klassen moved up to art director on many films including *A Few Good Men* (1992), *Radio Flyer* (1992), *Dave* (1994), *Waterworld* (1995), *Six Days, Seven Nights* (1998) and *Lethal Weapon 4*. David Klassen became a production designer on *House on Haunted Hill* (1999). Often the position of set design-er leads to a career in production design.

## Set Decorator

As noted earlier, the set decorator is responsible for the décor of a set or location. Décor includes rugs, practical lighting fixtures, furniture, window treatments, wall hangings, and all details of the interior decoration of the space. The décor must reflect the period, characters, and intent of the story.

## Lead Man

The **lead man**, or assistant set decorator, locates objects, furniture, and other décor elements used to dress the set.

## Swing Gang

The **set dressing** crew, also known as the **swing gang**, works under the supervi-sion of the lead man to find, gather, and collect décor elements.

## Hair and Makeup

Hair and makeup design and application can be performed by one or two crafts-people, or by a team. The hair crew researches, creates, and administers the proper hairstyles for the characters, story, place, and time period to serve the director's point of view toward the story.

Robert Altman's *M\*A\*S\*H* (1970), is based on a novel that takes place during the Korean War in the 1950s. When the film was conceived and produced it was 1969. The Vietnam War was raging, American soldiers were dying in the bloody conflict, and at home the country was experiencing massive antiwar protests. Altman's point of view was that the film, which took place in a mobile military medical unit, was an antiwar message pertaining to Vietnam. Altman and his design team took out all references to the Korean War. The text had a 1960s counterculture attitude. Period hairstyles for Korea's 1950s would have been short tapered haircuts for the men, with no facial hair. To visually communicate the 1960s era, many of the characters had long, layered, shaggy hair cuts, and Elliot Gould sported a busy Fu Manchu– style mustache, done up in a style popular in the Age of Aquarius. The women of the Korean War wore their hair either up or in a short teased look set on rollers. In *M\*A\*S\*H*, the female charac-ters had short, natural or blown-dry hairstyles, or long, straight hair worn down. *M\*A\*S\*H* has a large ensemble cast and their hairstyles, and the hairstyles at the time of the film's release, clearly connected the audience to Vietnam and the tribal culture popular with hippies of the time. Ironically, the studio, Twentieth Century Fox, was angry at Altman's political message and forced a crawl at the beginning of the film that identifies the scene as taking place in Korea. The corporate message had little impact on audiences of the time, who totally "got" Altman's political statement.

An on-set hairdresser is invaluable to cut, style, color, set, and maintain the hairstyles. If your film needs special styles, and hiring a specialist is not viable, make an arrangement with a salon to create the hairstyles at the shop. Have the salon's hairdressers instruct the actors as to care and maintenance of the characters' hairstyles. Wigs, hairpieces, and hair extensions can transform an actor into the character. The visual image that is projected by an actor wearing the right hair will help the audience "buy" the character, and it will also help the actor in the process of "becoming" the character. Hair is a critical design element. The reality of many a period film has been shattered by inaccurate or insufficient hair design.

The haircuts on the men in *Spartacus* (1960) look more like late 1950s crew cuts and the slicked back hipster look of the time than the Roman Empire period in which the film takes place. Iconic actors such as Steve McQueen, Clark Gable, Robert Redford, and Julia Roberts rarely allow their signature hairstyle to be cut and styled to the exact standards of a period film. War films and Westerns often fall prey to anachronistic locks. This is due to a number of factors: a desire to attract a contemporary audience; a lack of attention to detail; or to a reluctance on the part of the actors to cut their hair, fearing it will prevent them from getting another role before their hair grows out and can be restyled for another part.

Talk to your actors in advance. Costume, hair, and makeup are essential tools for the actors. If they are unwilling to change their hairstyle for a role, or can't agree on the way the character should physically appear, they may not be right for your movie.

Makeup for film can also be transformative. The makeup artist on a movie must understand how the tools of foundation, rouge, lipstick, and eyeliner will read on film. Makeup is corrective and additive. A makeup artist should be on set to apply the makeup before shooting each day and for touch-ups during the filming. If you can't find a trained film makeup artist for your production, search for a salon makeup artist or a person familiar with and talented at applying street makeup. For prosthetic makeup to age, create a creature, or for special makeup effects, a qualified person familiar with the proper materials, tools, and techniques is necessary.

The use of prosthetic character makeup was an integral part of the production design of *Dick Tracy* (1990). One of the challenges of this film based on the famed comic book crime fighter was how to depict the villains seen in newspapers by millions of people for decades. The makeup design and execution by John Caglione, Jr., Hallie D'Amore, Richard Dean, Doug Prexler, Lynda Gurasich, Virginia Hadfield, Kevin Haney, Ceri Minns, Ve Neill, Craigh Reardon, and Roland Blandcaflor brought Flattop, Pruneface, the Brow, and Lips Manlis from ink to three-dimensional life by transforming the actors into these bizarre, freak-faced characters. The comic book look the makeup achieved worked perfectly with Richard Sylbert's Oscar winning primary color, generic architecture production design, and the expressionistic matte paintings that helped create Tracy's city environment.

Science fiction films such as *Star Wars* and *Star Trek* also depend on transforming character makeup to render the characters and universe of the narrative believable.

Aging makeup is necessary for films where a young actor is playing an old character, like Stacey Keach in Robert Altman's *Brewster McCloud*, or when a character ages throughout a film, like Robert DeNiro in *Raging Bull*, F. Murray Abraham in *Amadeus*, and Dustin Hoffman in *Little Big Man*. Recent films *Hannibal* and *Vanilla Sky* use transformational makeup to create the illusion a character has been horribly deformed by an attack or accident.

Makeup and hair are visual elements that impact on the look and personality of the character and help establish period, mood, and atmosphere. They must be designed and created within the overall design of the film. The final word on hair and makeup comes from the director and production designer. Often a designer will have long associations with hair and makeup artists they have worked with in the past and will be instrumental in hiring them.

As with hair, makeup directly concerns the actors. Talk to them in advance about makeup and be clear about what is expected of them. Have sketches of the makeup design prepared, do makeup and camera tests, and schedule accordingly. Makeup applications and hair styling take time to apply and require patience and careful scheduling for the actors to be prepared for each shooting day. Most actors will need an hour or two depending on the character work to be done on them. Extensive prosthetic makeup for aging, transformation, and creature makeup takes much longer to apply. A complex application can take up to four to six hours each day. The daily call sheets for cast and crew are coordinated by the production manager and line producer. They will schedule time for the actors, makeup, and hair teams to begin the appropriate time prior to the day's first shot so that the cast will be character-ready when shooting begins. Many actors, especially those trained for the stage, are knowledgeable and have experience with applying their own makeup.

The production designer should have an initial consultation with the makeup and hair department during pre-production to discuss issues concerning the visual interpretation of the movie. The discussion will vary depending on the film, as some will have more emphasis on special makeup and hair design (especially horror, science fiction, and fantasy films), but there are basic issues to cover.

- **Period.** When does the story take place? What's the point of view toward the period? Is it realistic or stylized?
- **Region.** Where does the story take place? Discuss the locations, mood, and atmosphere of the environments, and the personal styles of the people who reside there.
- **Characters.** Who are the people in the film? What are their social/economic circumstances? How do they wear their hair and makeup? Are there hair and makeup transitions throughout the story? Where do the characters have their hair done: barbershop, beauty parlor, at home, in an exclusive salon, or a neighborhood Unisex shop? How does the hair and makeup of the characters reflect on their personality? Are they neat or casual? How do the characters maintain upkeep of their hair and makeup? Do they do it themselves? What methods do they use? Natural, blown-dry, set with rollers? Do they use hair spray, gels or mousse?
- **Time frame of the story.** Do the hair and makeup styles progress or maintain the same look during the narrative? Is aging involved or some other transformation, like hair color or facial hair?

- **Costumes.** Hair and makeup directly interact with the dress of the characters. Production designers should share their views, but it is essential that hair and makeup talk to the costume designer about style and coordinating a total look for each character.
- **Logistics, materials, and budget**. The production design goes through the shooting schedule with the hair and makeup departments. Who is being photographed on what day? When do the actors need to be in full makeup? Where will makeup and hair be done? In a studio facility, a private shop, or a makeshift area? Will there be hair and makeup people on set for touch-ups? Do any of the actors have their own personal hairstylist and makeup artist? The production designer controls the total art department budget and, along with the producer, supervises spending and purchasing. This is a critical issue: The hair and makeup department must know what is available and expected from them and whether they can deliver the result intended based on the existing budget.

Makeup and hair will have read the screenplay and have begun preliminary drawings of hair and makeup design, color, and texture so those issues can be discussed with the production designer, who then gives his notes and suggestions.

### Construction Coordinator

The construction coordinator, responsible for the building of sets, follows the working drawings and drafting of the art department and supervises the construction crew. The set is built to the exact specifications of the plan. There are professionals who specialize in construction coordination for film production design. Set construction differs from conventional construction in several distinct ways. A set is not a permanent structure; it often is a two or three wall construction. Many sets are built with **flats**, wooden frames covered with stretched canvas or board. Not everything in a set is practical (meaning operational). Materials for sets differ in quality and authenticity. Sets can be a section of a structure that is the only element needed to create the illusion of a larger building or a detail that implies a larger space around it.

In Hitchcock's *North by Northwest* (1959), designed by Robert Boyle, there is a sequence that takes place in the United Nations building. The exterior was established with a shot of the actual building. A matte shot shows an expanse of the interior with several open floors heading upward, creating a feeling of size and grandeur. The Cary Grant character walks across the floor in this wide shot, which then cuts to a medium shot of Grant walking, and finally to a shot of a woman at a reception desk. The shot is tight. The blue walls match the wide shot. There is the indication of a desk, a microphone to make announcements over the public address system, and a wall divider to create the illusion of depth and angled walls. This is a separate set. Small and simple to build when intercut into the other footage, it gives the impression of a large reception area, although we just see hints of it. The scene did not require that the whole reception area be built, so the small set was an inexpensive and effective solution for this part of the plot.

Sets are built directly on a stage floor, not on a foundation. The low-budget independent filmmaker can utilize friends who are familiar with building techniques or local construction workers. Reference books on theater stagecraft are useful if you are not using a professional crew. Safety of the cast and crew is essential. The set should not be built for permanence but must be stable enough to work in; it must withstand the opening and shutting of doors and windows and other aspects of physical endurance. Since sets are built to be photographed, many have **wild** walls that can be removed for a camera position and special effects.

Wild walls that can be moved are common and essential aspects of designing and building a film set. Logically, the camera requires more room for maneuvering than that part of the set that actually ends up in the picture, especially for wide and full compositions. The camera and crew take up room, and some lenses need distance to achieve their effect. The director of photography may be using a dolly or a crane that needs the additional space to operate in.

Production designer Kristi Zea had to incorporate wild walls for the scene in Martin Scorsese's *GoodFellas* (1990), when characters walk through the Copa. Filmed in a single uninterrupted Steadicam shot, the scene follows them from the street, through the basement and kitchen, then into the club's showroom itself. Scorsese wanted the impression that Ray Liotta and Lorraine Bracco were moving through a long passageway. The famed Copa had been renovated, so Zea and the art department had to transform the location to suit Scorsese's wish to execute a long, continuous Steadicam shot that followed the characters getting out of their car and walking into, then through, the backstage maze of the Copa, until they were seated by waiters to hear Henny Youngman say "Take my wife" from the stage. "It was constructed so that as the camera was following them through the hallway, there were carpenters off on the right getting rid of two or three of the walls that were going to be in the way when they came into the Copa," Zea explains. The long hallway seen in *GoodFellas* didn't exist at the location. Zea and the construction team built the long corridor, so that when they got down the stairs there would be a long corridor that led through the kitchen. In reality, after going down the back staircase seen in the film, you arrive right into the Copa showroom.

## Construction Crew

The construction crew is made up of many artisans:

- Carpenters: The majority of sets are constructed out of wood. Skilled carpenters are necessary to build sets and also to be on call during shooting to provide solutions for problems that may come up concerning the set.
- Painters: Sets must be painted; existing locations are often repainted to create the proper design objectives. Specialists in movie work understand how the camera reads color and texture and how lighting affects the surface. Again, permanence is not essential here, and the choice of paints and texture materials should be based on the intended result, budget, and the aesthetic properties sought.

Remember, it is the design process and its results that are important. Big-budget films have a person or team for each of these jobs. If those resources are not available to you, combine these jobs and aspects of the production design process. Get your crew to multitask. It is the purpose, intent, and result that will enrich the design of your film, not an art department army. Wear many hats or delegate, but understand the nature of the craft of production design and the visual storytelling tools in your power.

## Property Master

The property master is responsible for objects and props handled and used by the actors. He works with the set decorator and production designer to identify all necessary props and is responsible for obtaining them. The property master consults and collaborates with the production designer to identify and then go out and get all the props needed for the story. Veteran production designer Albert Brenner explains, "The little things like the eyeglasses somebody wears, or a wristwatch, or the plate of food—that's the prop master's job. He will take care of that, but what he hands the actors for the most part is decided by the art department."

Sources for props include industry prop houses for film and theater, specialty stores, antique shops, pawnshops, and private collections. Studio art departments may have a prop department that can be utilized. Experienced property masters have a working collection of basic props. Often multiple copies of one prop will be needed as a backup in case of wear or damage from repeated use. During production, the property master is in charge of all props and sees that they are in place for each shooting day.

Filmmakers should always have a backup plan and backup equipment if possible. It's a good idea to have a selection for each prop in case minds are changed on set. It's a good work ethic to have an identical backup for any prop, but there are categories of property items that need reserves because they get used up or damaged. Bottles, glasses, or dishes that are broken on camera, and food and beverages that are consumed during the story, need a backup supply. Calculating the exact amount needed is based on how complicated the action or shot is, the take ratio the director is required to shoot at, and the available budget. Fresh flowers seen in a location shot over a long period of time, candles, practical pens and pencils need reserve. There is also the issue of continuity. Props must match from shot to shot. If they are used up or worn down during shooting, replacements need to be at hand.

Firearms and weapons are handled separately by an armourer who supervises safety at all times and instructs the actors on how to employ the weapons. To avoid confusion and misunderstanding, always notify police officials when using weapons on a set, whether the location is interior or exterior. Never use a real loaded weapon on a film, and practice the utmost care when working with any weaponry on set.

## Location Scout

After discussions with the director and production designer, the location scout searches for the places indicated in the script. He takes still photos and shoots video to aid in the search process and reports back what he has found to the production designer. After locating and documenting a selection of choices and disseminating the material, the location scout takes the production designer and the director to the sites he has found. Once a location is selected, a deal is struck with the owner or managers of the property. Kristi Zea has designed many films, such as *Married to the Mob* and *GoodFellas*, that require location work. "First, I have a conversation with the director, and the general look of the picture is discussed," she explains. "Once that's determined, then I go out with a location scout and usually the location manager. We drive around for days, going to a variety of locations that have been found previously, or we start from scratch. I'll say, 'Stop here; let's look at this for a second,' whether it's a street or a building, a rooftop, a palatial mansion or a store. Once I like something, then we take pictures and show it to the director. Then we take the director to see it. If he likes it, we go back a third time with the technical crew. They talk about what they need in terms of lighting, electrical equipment, where we're going to house all the necessary back-up personnel, where to put everybody between shots, and if there are enough parking facilities. A deal is struck between the production company and the people who own the property."

There are many arrangements between filmmakers and proprietors. Of course, the best case scenario for the production is when permission can be obtained for no fee. However, home and shop owners have become less willing to allow filmmakers to use their space for a variety of reasons. Understanding these issues can help supply solutions. Moviemaking can be a long and disruptive process. Be prepared and don't overstay your welcome. When you are using someone's living space, offer other quarters to the inhabitants, if necessary. If they are going on vacation, that would be a good time to schedule shooting. Work around their schedule. If they are staying in part of the space, do not violate their privacy; keep to your work area. The producer, unit production manager, and the location manager should be the liaisons between the film company and the landlord of the space you are using. Often the production designer is the person who makes the initial contact and arrangements. He must see to it that what has been promised to the owners is carried through by supervising the art department and working closely with the production manager and the director of photography on the set during shooting to make sure that the crew works carefully, respecting the location. Good diplomacy is important for the reputation of the production designer and the company. The location manager is the person on duty during the shoot. It is his job to make sure everything goes smoothly; he is responsible for maintaining the safety of the location. When trust is violated with the public it damages the reputation of all filmmakers—student, independent, and commercial—and makes it more difficult to secure future locations.

The filmmakers must be covered by an insurance policy to repair or compensate for any damage done to the property. Make sure the production crew is respectful and careful, especially when taping lights to the walls. Let the owners know about all production design plans in advance. Advise them about any structural changes or repainting and make sure the location is left just as you found it when shooting is completed.

Check to see that the neighbors know about the production. Late night shoots, chaotic, violent, or loud scenes, or scenes involving nudity, can disturb and offend neighbors. Also inform the local police if the film contains action depicting drug use or any illegal activity that may be misconstrued by observers. If a block or area needs to be cordoned-off, have enough staff to assist. Make sure they are polite and helpful. Let the community know in advance—put up notices. Personally inform all parties concerned.

If a location can't be found or there is no budget for the original conception of the production design, alternate plans must be developed and realized. The glitzy, showbiz conclusion of Bob Fosse's *All That Jazz* production designed by Tony Walton is a Broadway-like production number, and is actually a fantasy in the mind of the dying director/choreographer, Joe Gideon, an autobiographical character based on Fosse. The original ending was the opening night of Gideon's production *N.Y. To L.A.* "We had planned to film at the Opera House at SUNY, Purchase," Walton remembers. "They owned a gargantuan organ given to Carnegie Hall by Holland, but it turned out to be too big." The opera house had constructed a building next door to house the giant organ, then created a track so the organ could ride onto the stage at the Opera House. Walton had designed a New York skyline for the production number that matched the profile of the massive organ pipes. The skyline would be painted on a scrim so that they could cross fade from the images of the skyline through the organ pipes. On cue, the organ would track off stage to expose a palm tree representing Los Angeles. "I had worked on computer adjusted imagery of the recurring images, the eyedrops cuts and 'It's showtime, folks,'" Walton explains. "They were supposed to segue from the hospital monitor via hallucinatory medical imagery to the big opening night showbiz, ending the way Fillmore East and West had used organic liquid projection in the sixties, but we couldn't even afford the projectionist to project the footage." None of this material was ever shot by the production. When the original plans were put to a halt by the studio, Fosse and Walton relied on design elements from earlier sequences where Gideon and the angel talk about his life, in a surrealistic set that represents an attic of his memories. Walton was able to use many of those design elements and tests for the planned ending, including translucent paintings of the heart and abstract heart operations, to film the final concert sequence staged in the Black Box theater at Purchase. At the time, Walton was designing a ballet that utilized a half-mirrored material, Mirrex Mirror Scrim. When Walton showed Fosse that the material could present the illusion that Lange was with Gideon in the reflective surface, though at times seemed to be in front of the mirror and at others, behind it, Fosse found it the perfect visual representation of an angel. When Columbia Pictures shut off the budget, the Mirrex saved the day.

Often the public and business community, under the erroneous impression that all filmmakers are well financed and will make money from the project, will overcharge. If their fee is too high, offer a film credit, publicity, or points or percentages if the film turns a profit.

## Location Manager

The person responsible for the location in pre-production and during shooting until the crew is finished is the location manager, who is accountable for the security of the property and equipment.

## Greensman

The greensman is responsible for the care, maintenance, and style of grass, shrubbery, flowers, trees and plants. Locations can be transformed with creative landscaping that deals with continuity and regional specifics. Sixty North African palm trees Kubrick selected for *Full Metal Jacket* (1987) were shipped from Spain to England to recreate Vietnam during the war. The trees were purchased through a nursery and cost the production £1000 per palm tree and an export permit for them to make the trip. On many films, lawns and topiary are maintained in a manner similar to that provided by a commercial gardener or landscaper. Other projects, like Tim Burton's *Edward Scissorhands* (1990), involve artistry from experienced film landscaping experts.

## Buyer

This member of the art department purchases furniture, décor, clothes, props, and other design elements. Buyers must know vendors and sources well and have good negotiation skills. Items can also be rented and loaned. The low-budget filmmaker must rely on networking skills and the gift of getting others to participate and contribute to the project.

## Scenic Artist

An art department specialist who creates all painted backgrounds, prop paintings, signage, any illustrative material, magazine covers, book jackets, and murals indicated by the story, a good **scenic artist** can paint out hot spots, shadows, or other factors that may interfere or concern the cinematographer during production. Scenic work is also necessary to touch up and maintain the set on a daily basis. Bertolucci's *The Last Emperor* (1987) required skilled calligraphers who recreated the work of China's Forbidden City. The scenic artists on *Pollack* (2000), directed by and starring Ed Harris, meticulously recreated hundreds of paintings including the seemingly impossible task of copying the landmark drip paintings of Jackson Pollack. In this film the scenic artists played a major role in the plausibility of the story and the principal character.

## Costume Designer

The costume designer creates or selects the clothing to be worn by the actors. The costume designer must have an in-depth background in period dress and an in-depth understanding of character and story. The costumes may have to be conceived, drawn, and then manufactured from scratch due to the nature of the narrative, the characters, and the actors playing the parts.

Historically the costume designer comes onto a film after the production designer, who begins early on in the process. The color and texture concept has been established and agreed upon by the director and production designer. When the costume designer comes on the project, the production designer tells him the parameters of the colors the film will be set in. The costume designer takes samples of the color scheme and begins to draw designs for the characters' costumes.

Most production designers let costume designers work from their own inspiration, based on their interpretation of the story and characters. If the designer is established and highly experienced—such as Ann Roth (*Midnight Cowboy*, 1969, *The Unbearable Lightness of Being*, 1988, and *The English Patient*, 1996); Patricia Norris (*Days of Heaven*, 1978, *Victor/Victoria*, 1982, and *Blue Velvet*, 1986); or Albert Wolsky (*Grease*, 1978, *Sophie's Choice*, 1982, and *Bugsy*, 1992)—there is little back and forth necessary after talking to the director and production designer. With an inexperienced costume designer, supervision may be more intense, especially if the production designer comes from a British tradition of theater and has designed both the costumes and sets, like Tony Walton, or has worked in film as a costume designer first, such as Kristi Zea and Patrizia Von Brandenstein. Directors may also have long relationships with costume designers, and in this case they, are the ones to hire them—not the production designer. Milena Canonero was the costume designer for many films directed by Stanley Kubrick and Jeffrey Kurland has worked with Woody Allen for almost twenty years.

The costume designer designs directly to the body type of the actor playing the part. The project is cast by the time the costume designer is hired, so the costume designer takes measurements and begins to design for each actor and character. An example of how the actor can influence the costume design can be seen in Paul Schrader's *American Gigolo* (1980). The main character, Julian Kay, is an L.A. male hustler who makes his living performing sexual favors for women. Julian is in his mid-twenties, handsome, and lives in a sparsely decorated but very chic apartment. He is highly fashion-conscious and well groomed. The original actor cast as Julian was John Travolta. Giorgio Armani was brought in and personally designed everything from suits, shirts, jeans, and overalls tailored to the actor. However, when Travolta had to leave the film before shooting began for personal reasons, Richard Gere was cast in the role. It was decided that since Gere was a "real person," as opposed to the iconic movie star Travolta had become, he should not be dressed by one designer. "I told Schrader, 'Let's keep Armani, but let's mix it up with other designers. Let's go real American,'" production designer Scarfiotti explains. "If he wears jeans, they should be Levi's; they can't be designer jeans." Scarfiotti also had to make changes in the apartment set already built for Travolta. The wall color was changed to suit Gere's personal style.

To create the costumes, costume designers use many of the same criteria as the production designer. They are also storytellers. The period, region, social class, profession, and personality characteristics of the characters are the costume designer's guide. Fantasy or otherworldly characters demand imagination and an understanding of the world the characters live in.

The costume and character design for the title character in Tim Burton's *Edward Scissorhands* (1990) came from a drawing the director made years before. He thought of a character who wanted to be able to touch but couldn't, one who was simultaneously creative and destructive. The result, as designed by Coleen Atwood, is a young man with a formfitting, dark skin-suit with belt buckles, protruding points, and straps all over his body. Edward has a high neck collar and long, multiple length working scissors for hands and fingers. This extreme fantastical visualization projects the personality and inner-life of a lonely, confused man unable to make human contact.

The famous white suit designed by Patrizia Von Brandenstein and worn by John Travolta in *Saturday Night Fever* (1977) transformed middle-class working kid Tony Manero from his everyday life in Brooklyn to a disco dance king at night. The tailored suit was made for the dance and gave Tony the supreme confidence and sharp silhouette that defined his angular ever-changing movements on the brightly colored disco floor.

The red Eisenhower zip-up jacket designed by Moss Mobry and worn by James Dean as a tormented teenager in *Rebel Without a Cause* (1956), expressed the rage, sexual repression, and emotional upheaval of the character of Jim Stark.

In a low-budget situation, the actors may own clothes appropriate for their character. The costume designer should work closely with the performers to participate in the selection process, whether it's in their home closet or the mall. Up-and-coming fashion designers welcome exposure in a film. A deal can be negotiated for a fashion designer to dress one or more of the characters for an individual credit, in addition to designing the other clothes needed for a film. If you are coordinating a low-budget or student film, visit schools with a fashion or costume design course to find burgeoning costume designers for your project.

## Production Illustrators

Production illustrators are artists who paint or draw a conception of the production designer's ideas for a set or a design moment for the film. They are helpful in fantasy or sci-fi films such as *Star Wars* (1977), for which Ralph McQuarrie created illustrations. Production illustrators are not often used in low-budget filmmaking. The added cost is not a necessity, but production illustrations can be a valuable tool when trying to raise money for a specific set that needs to be built.

Ralph McQuarrie's concept paintings for *Star Wars* (1977), which included color illustrations of the droids C-3PO and R2-D2 and Darth Vader, helped to get much-needed seed money from Twentieth Century Fox when the script was put into limbo at the studio.

The cliché that a picture is worth a thousand words is applicable here. A full-color illustration of the set will sell it faster than any pitch or rough sketch.

## Draftsman

The draftsman makes technical drawings that detail a plan to build a set. They are precise, uniform technical drawings created to exact scale. Drafting for a film is the same as any architectural plan, so any competent draftsman can assist your project.

## Set Dresser

The set dresser works under the supervision of the set decorator and is responsible for putting the décor on set. An experienced set dresser has a background in furnishing and decorating, a sense of style, and understanding of the role of design in storytelling is necessary.

## The Production Designer's Responsibility to the Art Department

The production designer supervises the entire design team. All of these details flow from the production designer's vision, skills, and leadership. The production designer answers to the director for creative issues and to the producer for fiscal matters. Art and commerce go hand in hand in moviemaking; production design must be carefully planned and budgeted so the film gets the look it deserves and doesn't fall victim to the red pencils of the front office.

## Understanding the Role of the Art Department During the Early Stages of Pre-production

- The final draft of the screenplay during the pre-production period is a shooting script. This blueprint for the production process includes detailed information concerning use of the camera, the physical action, and dialog. Each scene and shot in the screenplay is numbered consecutively.
- The production manager breaks the script down into individual components, determining what days in the shooting schedule each scene and each shot is to be photographed. The art department must plan accordingly to have the locations ready for these specific dates.
- Pay careful attention to the credits of all the films you screen. The team assembled for each film will give you insight into what resources were necessary to create and produce the production design. Seek out productions that resemble the circumstances and conditions concerning your project and use them as a guide and model.

# Chapter 6

## PRE-PRODUCTION

The pre-production process is a time of discovery and invention. This is when the production designer and the art department develop ideas and create the blueprints for the design of the film. The production designer enters a systematic process of planning stages to create the design of a film.

### Concept Drawings

Production designers think by drawing. The first stage of the design process, after absorbing the screenplay and understanding the director's point of view toward the visual style of the film, is the process of physically designing the production. Concept drawings are impressions of the sets drawn with pencil, charcoal, or marker. Concept drawings put the visual ideas on paper. They then are shown to the director for approval. Beginning with shapes in a sketchy, broad-stroked fashion, the designer is thinking out loud on paper.

Visually oriented directors often draw their own simple concept drawings. Alfred Hitchcock, Martin Scorsese, and Brian DePalma have been known to pass their ideas on to production designers, who then develop them into full, detailed drawings or paintings of the proposed set, which they present back to the director for approval.

For *Vertigo* (1958), Hitchcock gave production designer Henry Bumstead a sketch comprised of just a few pencil lines of what he wanted to see outside the window of the Jimmy Stewart character's apartment in San Francisco. The sketch showed a tower on a hill. Hitchcock wanted a view of Coit Tower, which for him represented a phallic symbol. A monochrome wash sketch of the apartment was worked up by the art department and outside the large window was a view of San Francisco and the historic Coit Tower in the background. When the director okayed the proposed set, construction plans were drawn, and the set was built on the studio stage. A translight was also created with the image of the Coit Tower and lit from the back to appear like the outside view.

For the Francisco club attended by the villain, Hitchcock's conceptual sketch had large ribbed columns, a door, and men seated in chairs and at a table. The art department sketch developed the set but retained the design principles of Hitchcock's thumbnail. The approved sketch depicts an old-world, wood-paneled room with antique chairs, overstuffed chairs, a chandelier, fireplace, and the columns suggested by the original concept.

Many drawings can be made for each design element. For the shack outside the city in *Dick Tracy* (1990), production designer Richard Sylbert made over fifteen conceptual drawings. This one location was key to helping him understand the world of the film (for which he won an Academy Award). Concept drawings can be small with many possibilities on a page or can be full-size charcoal sketches, as created by Ken Adam when he designed the early James Bond films. Adam's work established the visual atmosphere for the franchise that has lasted over forty years.

The rumpus room, used by the master criminal who is the title character of *Goldfinger* (1964) to entertain and plan nefarious capers with international mobsters, was developed by Ken Adam in sketches that define the massive space. The ceiling is supported by angular beams that are set in dynamic angles that create an atmosphere of power and the expansive reach of the criminal mastermind.

### Approval

After a presentation of the concept sketches, the director and the designer enter a discussion about the ideas. A single drawing may communicate and capture the director's intent, or elements from several drawings may be combined to achieve the design's objectives. An idea from a concept drawing may be altered or the designer may be sent back to the drawing board to come up with additional approaches. Director Stanley Kubrick immediately approved Ken Adam's triangular shaped, bilevel presentation of the war room set for *Dr. Strangelove or: How I Learned to Stop Worrying and Love the Bomb* (1964). As Adam prepared to move on to the next stages of design development that would eventually lead to construction, Kubrick had second thoughts and about what to do with staging in the upper level. Kubrick ordered Adam to come up with a completely different concept. Designers must be prepared to move away from their original ideas and may or may not be given specific guidance from the director. Some directors are very design-oriented and remain part of the process, like Ridley Scott, a former production designer on commercials. Scott worked as part of the design team on *Blade Runner* (1982) with production designer Lawrence G. Paull. Throughout his career, Stanley Kubrick spoke repeatedly about not always knowing what he wanted until he found it by exploring seemingly endless possibilities. Before arriving at the shape of a monolith in *2001: A Space Odyssey* (1968), described in Arthur C. Clarke's short story *The Sentinel* as a slab, designers Tony Masters, Harry Lange, and Ernest Archer conceptualized the marker from an alien power as a transparent cube, a pyramid, and a tetrahedron. Each object was discussed, logically analyzed, and ultimately dismissed until the monolith appeared in a sketch presented to Kubrick.

closer —

as we move through glass
snow thickens — when we
find the house again

move around to side
window

Center window

Move in to Window

3.

Three pages from the storyboard to *Reckless* (1995), directed by Norman Rene, drawn and designed by production designer Andrew Jackness. Courtesy Andrew Jackness and the Samuel Goldwyn Company.

Sc. 15 Rachel talks to
Lloyd

Sc. 16 Rachel opens door
and sees party in closet
We move on with
Rachel

They talk

Rachel sits on bed

Lloyd gets atlas

18.

Roy Leaves.

This is probably the wrong
Relationship for the following
bits.

Rachel finds her sash

21.

What are directors looking for? How do design ideas evolve? When Ken Adam came up with a new concept for *Dr. Strangelove*'s war room he sketched the large oval table with circular light fixtures. Kubrick asked about the texture of the table. "Could it be covered in green baize?" Adam said "yes," knowing the film was to be photographed in black-and-white. Kubrick was sold. The U.S. president, Russian ambassador, and pentagon officials were "playing poker for the fate of the world." The metaphor fit Kubrick's directorial concept of the scene—it was a visual metaphor and presented dramatic possibilities for camera positions and overhead lighting effects.

## Storyboards

Storyboards visualize a film shot by shot. The storyboard can be drawn by a storyboard artist who specializes in the craft or by someone who can visually interpret a story and understands cinematic grammar. The storyboard can be comprised of expressive drawings or little more than stick figures. The ideas should generate from the director, director of photography, and the production designer. On a low-budget film the production designer may storyboard the entire film. The storyboard clearly shows the relationship between the characters and their environment; it is a guide that reflects the director's visualization of the project and how the director of photography will photograph it. For the production designer, the storyboard will indicate how the design will appear in the frame and what has to be created by the design team.

Production illustrations can visually communicate a particular set or location. If a fantastic, experimental, or highly inventive design needs to be created, a detailed illustration will help visualize the idea and is a great tool to generate capital in a fundraising campaign.

After the concept drawings and specific design direction is agreed upon, more drawings, in pencil, pen, or marker are done; then a plan is made. A draftsman executes this architectural drawing. The construction crew will follow the drafting plan to build the set.

Scale models of a set, which present the physicality of a set in three dimensions, can be built out of cardboard or other materials. The construction crew can examine the architectural structure by studying a model. The model can be used to sell the design to producers to obtain financial resources. The director and director of photography can plan shots, camera positions, and the blocking of action by working with the model. A member of the art department, a specialist, or the production designer can build models. The model visually displays the architecture and sense of space intended by the design in three dimensions. Production designer Anna Asp, who has worked with Ingmar Bergman and Andrey Tarkovsky, makes extensive use of models in her work. A scale model is built for each set; then the models are painted exactly the way they will look as completed sets. Experiments with lighting can then be made on the model, and camera movements and compositions can be planned. Asp finds this process satisfying and effective. "When the set is constructed on the stage, it's like walking into my model," Asp explains.

## Drafting

Drafting is an exacting art with specific equipment and standards, though you may have to assign this job to someone who is not an experienced, trained draftsman. The most effective and thorough way to learn drafting is to take a course as part of a design or architecture curriculum or in a continuing education program. Drafting can be self-taught with the aide of an instructional book, supplies purchased at a local art store, and the time to learn and practice this exacting craft.

Drafting does not involve freehand drawing; it is a mechanical skill executed with pencils guided by a ruler, T-square, compass, and other tools that help produce precise and uniform lines for creating design plans. The purpose of drafting is to draw objects to be constructed. Drafting is practical drawing not intended to be displayed and enjoyed as art. There are many methods employed in the drafting process; the most commonly used is called Orthographic Projection, which allows the drawing of objects that have depth, although the paper used has only length and width. Length, width, and height are words used to describe the dimensions of an object. In drafting terms, basic dimensions are shown by width, height, and depth.

Drawing paper used in drafting can be bought in pads or rolls. Vellum is a common drawing surface, and white paper is most often used in drafting. Finely grained cream or light green paper is also used, as are transparent materials, such as linen and glass cloth.

To arrive at the proper scale of a drawing, the size of an object and the space available on the paper are the primary considerations. A draftsman starts with the overall dimensions, then measures the drawing space. A single object ten feet wide and four feet deep using one-half-inch scale will take five horizontal inches on the paper. The side view is two horizontal inches. If the object is six feet high, the front view will be three vertical inches, the top view two vertical inches. The three required views—front, top, and side of the object—will take a total space of five vertical inches and seven inches horizontally. There must be room in between to organize the drawing and make it pleasing and clear to the eye. To create more space between the three views, a smaller scale may be desirable.

## Sample Exercises

Before any real drafting can be done in creating a plan or view of a set, getting comfortable and skilled with the tools is necessary. Begin by making clean lines, consistent in weight, one below another or next to each other. Drafting or technical drawing is not like freehand drawing; it must be precise and clean, free of smudges and inconsistencies.

As you get familiar with the various grades of pencil leads and rulers, experiment with the pressure applied from pencil to paper and the angle of lead to paper. In creating line after the line, the order in which lines are created and where the ruler and your hand are positioned is critical in not smudging the work you have already drawn.

Once good results have been achieved, move on to connecting lines at right and left angles until you can make a perfect join. Practice curves with a French curve and circular lines with a compass.

Next, readable, consistent lettering is necessary to identify aspects of a technical drawing. Practice basic block lettering using a soft, sharp pencil. Use clean-cut, dark strokes, and accent the ends of each line. Lightly drawn top and bottom guidelines are necessary to create uniform letters and word.

To set up a drafting space, the necessary tools include:

- A stable drafting table with adjustable height and tilt of angle. A 30" × 46" table can accommodate 24" × 36" paper, with room to work with a T-square.
- Another table or space to hold the drafting tools. A tabouret functions as a table and also has drawers to store drafting tools.
- The drafting table covered with a rubberized material that will give the pencil a flexible surface to draw on.
- A drafting machine, also called a parallel, that allows the draftsperson to draw in any angle.
- A parallel straight edge attached to the drawing table by a cable system allowing it to glide up and down so the designer can draw straight parallel lines.
- A T-square, which can be moved up and down the drawing to facilitate drawing straight lines.
- A French curve, which allows a range of complex curves to be drawn.
- An adjustable triangle, which takes the place of having a series of fixed triangles. It can be set at any angle.
- A bow compass that has a sharp point to secure it to the table and an arm with a piece of lead to draw circles.
- A lead holder to hold drafting lead that comes in seventeen different degrees of hardness.
- A lead pointer, used for sharpening the lead, but not on a standard pencil. A wooden drafting pencil can be sharpened in a pencil sharpener.
- An eraser shield, which is a thin, aluminum sheet with cutout shapes of various sizes. It allows for precise erasing.
- A white plastic eraser, manufactured for erasing drafting vellum.
- Drafting dots and drafting tape to secure the drawing to the table without causing damage to the corners when removed.
- A triangular architect's scale rule that has twelve measuring scales on six sides.
- A stomp, which is a stick of compressed fiber that is used to add shade and texture to the drawing.
- A lettering guide to aid in drawing letters.
- A furniture template to allow the quick and accurate drawing of furniture in plan views for one-quarter-inch or one-half-inch scale.
- A circle template, which is the only effective way to draw precise ellipses.
- A square template, used for drawing multiple of squares repeatedly with consistent accuracy.

Additional drafting supplies include drafting powder, an electric eraser, and a drafting brush.

Every line in a technical drawing represents meaning and information to the reader who will eventually build from this blueprint. The American National Standards Institute has endorsed these standards. A line gauge showing all the established weights from .005 inches (.13 mm) to .079 inches (2.00 mm) should be purchased. In a technical drawing, all lines must be dark, cleanly drawn, and uniform. To reproduce the drawing lines should be spaced at least .06 inches (1.5 mm). The width of a line is established by the smallest size the drawing will eventually be reduced to.

Three weights of lines can give the drawing a clean look. Thin lines can be drawn with one weight, then another, to represent parts of the set that will not be visible to the viewer of the completed set but which must be shown in the drawing in order to explain the mechanics of the design. A still thinner lead weight is used for lines other than the main ones. These include centerlines, extensions, and lines indicating dimensions. Thick lines should be drawn in a softer lead than thin lines. H or F grade pencils are recommended for this work.

## Drafting Requirements and Standards

- Lettering should be one-sixteenth or one-eighth inch high.
- Guidelines should be created first. Letters should be consistent in style throughout all the project drawings in a low wide form that is easy to read.
- The title describing the view and subject and title of the project should be one-quarter inch high.
- A stamp can be made with the title block that can be used for each drawing. The block should include these details: the title of the project, the company logo, space for union stamp to indicate if the film is a union production, set title, date, sheet number, name of producer, director, production designer, draftsman, date of production, date drawn, and the scale of the drawing. Detailed information for each drawing can be added in pencil to the prepared stamp block.
- The thickness of a drafted line communicates specific instructions and is called the line weight. Line weight is controlled by the degree of pressure, lead weight, and overlapping lines to create a thicker line.
- Soft leads will produce very thick black lines. Leads to achieve this are 8B, 7B, 6B, 5B, 4B, or 3B. The higher the number in the B series used for sketching and drawing, the softer the lead. 2B, B, and HB produce a thick black line used for thick lines and for indicating scenery. F and H leads give a dark gray line and are used for lettering. 2H, 3H, 4H, 5H, 9H, and 10H are hard leads that make light, thin lines. A dimension system utilizes arrows to specify all dimensions throughout a drawing.

## Plans

A staging plan, used to visualize how the set is laid out on a sound stage, should include the following:

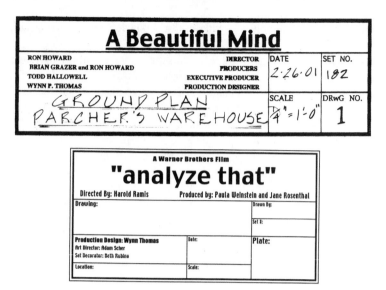

Two examples of title blocks. *A Beautiful Mind* (2001), directed by Ron Howard. Courtesy production designer Wynn Thomas, Imagine Entertainment, Universal Pictures, and DreamWorks Distribution LLC. *Analyze That* (2002), directed by Harold Ramis. Courtesy production designer Wynn Thomas, Warner Bros., Baltimore Spring Creek Productions, Face Productions, and Tribeca Productions.

- The stage dimensions and space
- Where the set walls, platforms, and stairways are laid out
- Drawn and labeled furniture, rugs, and décor
- Indications of drops, backings, and cycloramas
- Labels for any scenery intended to fly
- The title block in the lower-right-hand corner

A floor plan is a view of all scenery. A platform plan, drawn in one-half-inch scale for the construction of platforms and stair units, should include the following:

- The breakdown of a larger platform built in smaller sections.
- Construction and material details.
- Any openings in the stage floor and platform.
- All dimensions.
- Radius of curved platforms.
- Moving platforms—type of casters, swivel or rigid—wheel diameter and caster height.
- Tracks, turntables, and control devices to move elements on the stage. Each element must be fully dimensioned.

All drawings must have title blocks.

**Elevation** Drawings show a particular angle of a portion of the floor plan elevated to a direct flat view of the front, side, or rear of the set. The elevation is a no-perspective view of the set.

A series of elevation drawings of a living room set may be created as follows: a straight-on full view of the window wall with hanging mirror, radiator cover, and plant table. The opposite long wall would be presented in a separate elevation with a fireplace in a dimensional protruding three-sided section coming out from the main wall, doorways on the right and left, and built-in L-shaped shelving units on both sides of the right doorway. Side or short wall elevations have connecting, matching architectural elements. The side wall elevation view of the wall next to the built-in shelves would present the shelves on the left, an upright piano, and a doorway on the right leading to a short entrance hall and front door.

An elevation drawing lists all construction information, all details concerning paint, moldings, and windows. The drawing should be made with a medium pencil line. The title block should reflect all the necessary information. There should be a three-quarter-inch border around the drawing. If needed, create elevation drawings for the side, rear construction section and details of a set.

Elevation drawings give the construction crew a detailed plan of the architecture of each wall of a set with all its dimensions and seen in isolation from a straight-on view—not at an angle that would distort or obscure this view.

A section view drawing is a sliced-through view of a portion of a set that may be complex in its design and construction aspects. A revolved section is a sliced-through view of the set or a detail of the set revolved 90 degrees. Textures and materials are indicated with pencil shading techniques put in with a stomp—for instance, pressed paper formed into a pencil shape is used to blend lines and create shaded areas.

A section view of a plywood box would reveal the inner-structure of the box. A removed section view would make an imaginary slice through the box, turned 90 degrees. This would show that the box is hollow and has 45-degree angle corner supports at each joint. An extra thick line is drawn to indicate the parts of the drawing where the imaginary cut was made. These lines are called section lines.

Textures should be drawn using a photograph as a guide, not from memory. Pencil drawing technique can indicate rough stone, brick, concrete block, wood paneling, lumber, wallpaper, clapboard, concrete, cut stone, and glass. The camera view method of drawing is camera specific and shows the set from a particular aspect ratio. A camera lens MM/field-of-view chart is necessary to create these drawings. The chart is a transparent sheet with a selection of superimposed rectangles that represent a field of view related to a specific millimeter lens and camera distances. This allows the drawing to be made in the proper scale to represent the chosen lens for the shot.

A scale plan is drawn to determine the dimensions of the designed set and how it will fit in the studio space. This plan is drawn with a drafting ruler on tracing paper in scale that can range from a one-quarter inch up to twelve inches, depending on the size of the set.

A series of overlays show the studio plan, an overhead view that includes the dimensions of the sound stage, the set, furniture, and décor. Each element is on a separate sheet of tracing paper. When combined, they present the composite of the design allowing control over each individual drawing element.

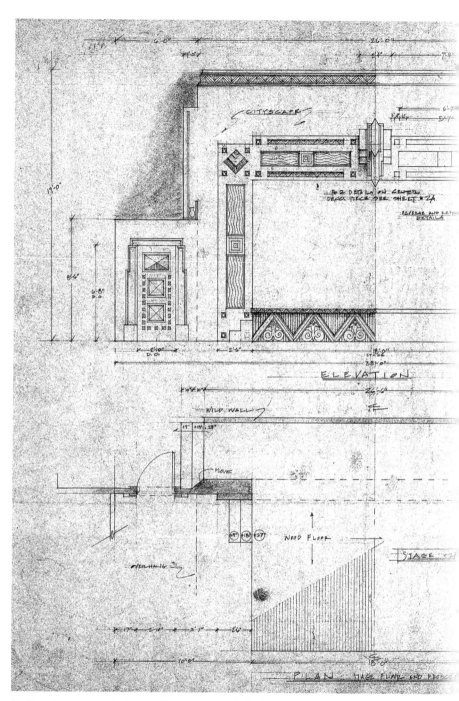

Drafting plans from *Malcolm X*, (1992), directed by Spike Lee, created by production designer Wynn Thomas. Courtesy Wynn Thomas, Spike Lee, 40 Acres and a Mule Filmworks, Warner Bros., JVC Entertainment, and Largo International N.V.

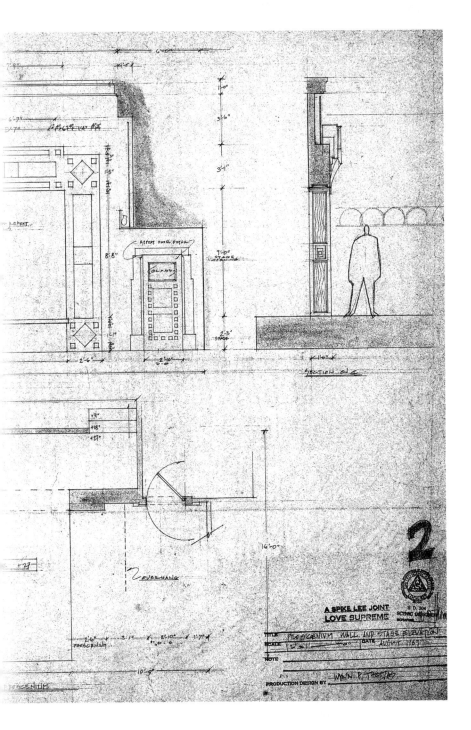

A SPIKE LEE JOINT
LOVE SUPREME

PRODUCTION DESIGN BY  WYNN P. THOMAS

The approved staging plan indicates each flat, all doors and windows, furniture, props, window treatments, platforms, and sets of stairs. This plan will be used by the director of photography to design the lighting plot and establish camera positions and movement, as well as sound equipment positions.

If the project is being produced at a professional studio with sound stages, a basic studio plan can be obtained upon which you can overlay your set plans. The studio plan available from the studio where you are working will include:

- Location of studio entrances and exits
- Location of storage areas, dressing rooms, shop space, and restrooms
- Layout of power sources, electrical outlets, and water
- Rigging and hoists to raise lighting equipment and scenic pieces, as well as the track used to hang a cyclorama
- Blue screen/green screen for matte effects

The studio plan is numbered. The numbers relate to marks on the studio walls. These are used to precisely locate the position of all scenery, décor, and sets.

The furniture plot, which details where all the furniture pieces will be positioned, and the prop plot, which details the location of each prop, are used by the set decorator, the assistant set decorator, and the set dressing crew and property master to plan, prepare, and organize their work.

## Location Scouting

When embarking on a location scout, preparation is necessary. The scout should have available some specific items, as detailed below, on all trips to record and retrieve information, to properly represent the production, and to negotiate with the proprietors of a location. A basic location scout's kit should always be readied with a number of items necessary to evaluate and document the locations visited during the scouting process in pre-production.

Location scouts should carry a Polaroid camera with a flash to make a photographic record of the location. Pictures should be taken from all angles necessary to cover the space in detail. Take full shots and close shots of specifics, moldings, fixtures, doorways, and windows. When the scout returns, the Polaroids will be shown to the producer, director, production designer, and the director of photography for their inspection, input, and decision on the feasibility of using the location for filming. Each of the team members will assess the pictures for their specific responsibility, among other issues. The producer will look at the economic aspects and production values inherent in the location. The director is concerned with storytelling and visual potential. The production designer will examine the photos for the period, architecture, and stylistic elements that are part of the design plan. A location may be usable for a particular room or section that can be combined with other locations. So the designer is not only looking at the long view but for the components and details as well. The director of photography is interested in the photographic opportunities, light sources, size of space where the camera, equipment, and lighting instruments can fit, and intriguing camera angles. A video camera is also helpful to capture the scope of a location, present how rooms or areas connect, and to see the location in a motion picture medium.

The scout should have Xerox copies of the storyboard and production design sketches. These are essential to determine if the location will satisfy the requirements of the film and meet the artistic and technical standards of the director, director of photography, and production designer.

Location releases must be available during scouting. These official forms contain the production letterhead and contact information that, when signed by the owner or representative of the location, gives the film company permission to use and photograph the location for the movie.

Business cards should be given to the landlords, owners, and contact people of locations visited by the scout. A professionally printed business card will aid in building business relationships with vendors, suppliers, and independent contractors, and bring legitimacy to the production company. Keep it simple; fancy logos and typefaces are often the sign of an amateur.

The production must carry insurance to cover any damage or loss occurring while working on location. A document known as a certificate of insurance should be shown to owners and representatives to acknowledge insurance coverage is in place.

Location scouts must navigate in any area they are exploring. A compass will assist in plotting travel routes and keep the scout aware of their location. A cell phone, pager, lap top computer, and palm pilot are all important communication devices helpful in maintaining contact with the production office and the location site.

The scout must accurately measure the location in detail for the production designer to determine if the space is adequate and to plan the design. A reliable professional retractable tape measure, which can be purchased in a hardware store, is necessary for this task. A series of metal rulers, from one foot to a foot and a half in length, with the smallest fractions that can be found, are needed for measuring fine point dimensions and to get into small or inconvenient spaces.

The scout must have maps of the area to be scouted. A general collection of maps is helpful to plan scouting trips, to determine travel routes, and to get an overall understanding of an area's logistics and resources. Digital maps are available on the Internet and in software. A vehicle with OnStar or other navigation services would be helpful but is an added production expense and not necessary. The scout should be an experienced driver and have a backup plan or alternate routes if necessary. The Automobile Club of America (AAA) has detailed maps for the entire United States available to their membership. It is also a good idea to be a member in the event of breakdowns, as they provide repair and towing services. If the trip involves going out of state or out of country, the scout needs the proper transportation information and schedule and ticket arrangements to be made.

Stationery Supplies are essential. The scouting kit should contain notepads, pens, pencils, erasers, Scotch tape, scissors, Post-It notes, paper clips, and a stapler.

The scout should always carry petty cash for gas, tolls, meals, and lodging expenses. A production credit card comes in handy. If the production vehicle has E-Z Pass, it is economical and efficient in this time-is-money business.

The scout needs to have an accurate timepiece to record travel time and to coordinate schedules. Mileage to and from the production office and the location must be recorded in writing. The time it takes to get to and from locations can be an important decision factor in selecting a location.

Location fact sheets should be prepared in advance and put into folders labeled for each location needed in the film. The forms are available from production service companies but can easily be created on a word processor and copied in bulk. This would allow the production company and production designer to tailor the information to their prerogative.

The following information is absolutely necessary to document during a location scout:

- *Name, address, phone number, and e-mail address* of the owner, property manager, electricians, janitors, doorman, elevator operators, and other relevant contacts. While working at a location, these people are essential in the smooth running of a shoot.
- *Parking availability.* Does the location have its own parking? Can parking permits be obtained? Is there a municipal lot or private parking garage nearby?
- *Back entrance for delivery and pick-up access.* Most locations have strict rules for this. Locate and note them for all concerned. Make contact with anyone involved in supervising these areas.
- *Freight doorways.* Measure the dimensions of the doorway and note all accessibility information.
- *Stairways.* Document the location, width, and height of all stairways to be used during production.
- *Elevators.* Examine the passenger and freight elevators. Take dimensions and note weight and number of passenger restrictions. Find out the hours of operation. If the shoot is an overnight, arrangements for a night operator may be necessary.
- *Doorways.* Carefully measure the height, width, and depth of all doorways.
- *Location of restrooms, dressing areas.* Note which restrooms can be used by the film company. Does a portable unit have to be brought in? Is there a room that can be designated for dressing the actors? Also consider space for hair and makeup. If not, a trailer may be necessary.
- *Diagram of location floor plan.* This will be used by the production designer in planning decoration or restoration work. The camera and sound crew will use it to plan their work. The unit production manager and the location manager need to have location floor plans of all locations to organize and supervise all work done on location shoots.
- *Floor and ceilings.* Examine surfaces for floor problems that may affect camera placement and movement. Check and test ceiling for lighting and sound conditions.
- *List all equipment that can be supplied by the location owner.* Are there telephones, fax machines, and computers on the premises? Can they can be used by the production company? Is there refrigeration, heating, air conditioning, tools, a working kitchen?

- *Note any construction projects taking place in the area.* Check the area surrounding the location for anything that may disrupt production.
- *Note what days and time surrounding lawns are mowed.* This activity would disturb sync-sound recording.

New York, Los Angeles, and other cities with active film production have many support services available for production designers and art departments. Although the production often has to pay for these services, they may be necessary for the design of the film. The plethora of services and set dressings available to the filmmaker in these production-oriented cities runs the gamut, from airline and aviation mock-up to candelabras, from firearms to taxidermy.

## Organizing the Property Department

The prop master makes a list of props needed based on the script, discussions with the production designer, and their collaborative decisions, and then designates them into distinct categories:

- Personal props are worn or directly used by the actors—eyeglasses, rings, and wallets, for example
- Props such as appliances that are not used on camera are listed as nonpractical. They do not have to be in working condition, just look like they can operate.
- Hand props are used by the actors—for instance, wineglass, cigarette lighter, and telephones.
- Practical props are fully operational and in working order.
- Any prop that is not directly used or operated by the actors does not have to be practical.
- Key props that are often used or visible should be backed up with replacements in case they're needed during production. The back up props must be an exact match not to disturb continuity.

Before shooting begins the production designer and the art department go through a final checklist.

## Final Steps of Pre-production

Each shot in the storyboard and on the shot list is checked to make sure the camera will not be shooting off set. The production designer goes through the compositions, lenses to be used, and planned camera movements, making sure that the set supports all angles to be employed. The set is scrutinized for its ability to project its objectives; when lit and photographed by the cinematographer, final corrections are made.

- Are there any hot spots? The simple solution is for the camera crew to adjust the lighting or to spray down the area with dulling spray. Often a scenic artist can spray the appropriate color paint and finish on the area to resolve hot spots. In an extreme case, the production designer may have to replace or substitute materials on the set that are causing problematic glare on camera.

- Any reflections? Glass, shiny, and mirrored surfaces can be sprayed down with dulling spray by the camera crew. The materials can also be replaced by the set dressing crew with nonreflective ones.

- Are the colors too dark, too light? This should be resolved before shooting begins by consultation between the director, director of photography, and the production designer. Colors should be camera tested in pre-production. If the problem arises on the set, the painters and production designer must resolve the problem by making the necessary changes.

- Will the camera cables or equipment obstruct a shot? Often the camera crew can resolve this, but more serious problems should be handled during pre-production. The design might have to be altered to accommodate the production crew or the director of photography may have to use other equipment or method of routing cables.

- Are the details on all surfaces the right pictorial balance? A model built to scale, painted, and decorated to match the set, will give the designer the best chance to check if the pictorial balance is correct. The final test is examining the completed, constructed set. The production designer should schedule time before the set is to be shot so that it can be checked and adjustments can be made before shooting, without causing costly production delays.

- The placement of every piece of furnishing should be checked. Is the environment too busy or too sparse? Is it effective from every camera position? The set decorator examines all furnishings and décor. The production designer, director of photography, and director inspect the set dressing from every camera position and lens application.

- What is the overall impact of the set? Is it too dark, producing an oppressive impression, or too light, causing the surroundings to look vacant? The director is the final judge of the look of a set. It is the director's vision, and he is the principal storyteller. The production designer should have the director sign-off on each set as it is finished, still allowing time for changes. Steven Spielberg made major changes to aspects of the sets for *Hook* after the sets were built but before production. Production designer Norman Garwood, who received an Oscar nomination for his work on the film, redesigned Spielberg's requests in time for the shooting.

- Is the set completely stable and safe for the cast and crew? It is the responsibility of the construction coordinator and the construction crew to guarantee the set is safe to work on. Everything must be braced and supported.

- Doors and windows should be checked for sticking and mobility problems by the construction crew. Any sticking problems can be resolved with silicon spray or three-in-one oil.

- The props are checked for arrangement, placement, color, texture, and authenticity by the prop master.

- The aging is adjusted so the set doesn't look too old or new for the story. The painters and scenic artists enhance or reduce aging effects with paint, asphaltan, dust, dirt, India ink, and water solution, powder, and other materials.

- The height and brightness of all practical lighting fixtures should be adjusted. Lighting is the domain of the camera crew. Practical lamps are chosen and placed on the set by the set decorator. They are wired and bulbs are augmented by the electrician. The height and brightness of all practical lamps is adjusted by the gaffer under the supervision of the director of photography.
- Is the furniture stable? Are the actors able to work with it comfortably? The set decorator is responsible for making sure the furniture is safe and user-friendly for the actors.
- Does the set work for the characters, performers, and story? After all the collaboration and consultation, the director will determine whether the set is right for the film.

## Deadlines

The art department must plan a detailed schedule, coordinated with the shooting schedule and with appropriate arrangements for rental and access of the studio space.

The art department should estimate the time every step will take, so a starting date can be determined by backdating everything involved.

- How much time will it take to acquire all materials necessary to build the sets?
- How long will it take to get all of the props, furniture, and décor?
- How long will it take the construction crew to build the set?
- How long will it take to transport the set to a studio, assemble it, and secure everything for the first day of shooting?

Other aspects that affect the art department schedule include:

- Riggings for the cinematography team
- Special effects that concern the set, such as fire, water, explosions, gunshots, snow, and digital effects
- Tests for camera: lighting, color, and texture
- Tests for special effects
- Tests and accommodations for sound

## Keeping Ahead of the Company

When the schedule is tight, the crew will shoot as soon as the first sets are ready, so the production designer and the art department try to stay at least one step ahead to maintain the shooting schedule. That schedule must be maintained throughout the shoot. If problems arise with the preparation of set and location, let the production manager know immediately so the schedule board can be rearranged. The production designer never wants to be the cause of delays once shooting has begun.

The extensive and impressive sets designed by Norman Garwood for Steven Spielberg's *Hook* (1991) required a long pre-production period and many changes were demanded of the art department. Spielberg made major changes in studio sets that he had originally approved as he came up with new ideas. This involved redesign and new construction. These changes could have delayed production and extended pre-production, but when shooting started, the film remained on schedule due to the diligence of the art department.

A check and balance system should be in place between the art department and the production team so details or major plans don't fall through the cracks. Filmmaking is a creative endeavor, but it is also a business and demands military precision regarding logistics. Don't even think about beginning production without at least plans A, B, and C in place. Always have a contingency plan and be ready to solve problems.

## Cover Sets

Lost time is lost money. In the event of inclement weather, a cover set—an interior space where the company can shoot if prevented from shooting on location—is crucial. During pre-production designate cover sets and have them available before shooting begins on exterior work. Have crew on call to support the cover sets during outdoor production so when rain and snow hit you will be prepared to make the shift indoors without losing valuable time and money.

## Pre-production Advice

The following suggestions are critical for all filmmakers and projects but especially on a first film where the production team is not experienced. The producer, unit production manager, and production staff are responsible for planning and scheduling. The director must be fully prepared by the end of pre-production. The production designer is directly affected by the plans and schedule made during pre-production. Read the screenplay again. Certainly the director needs to do this, but the production designer also needs to maintain objectivity and re-think his work before shooting begins.

- Schedule plenty of time for the pre-production phase of the project
- Don't shoot until you are totally prepared
- Have as much backup and as many alternate plans as possible
- Plan for cover sets where the company can shoot in the event of inclement weather
- Check and recheck everything
- Read the screenplay again with an objective eye for perspective, details, and clarity toward the production design of the project

Most of the work of the production designer is completed before shooting begins. During production the art director runs the day-to-day operation of maintaining the sets and dealing with issues that come up.

If the entire production is not designed by the first day of shooting, the production designer will continue with the process of creating concept drawings, working drawings, and plans, and overseeing construction.

# Chapter 7

## COLOR

Color performs many functions in production design. Color is not only used to achieve verisimilitude in the images; color can communicate time and place, define characters, and establish emotion, mood, atmosphere, and a psychological sensibility. In visual storytelling, color is one of the moviemaker's greatest assets. As in all areas of filmmaking, the color design must be given serious thought and must be carefully planned. You are not just presenting pretty or eye-catching colors; you are telling a story and defining the characters. A set, location, or environment is interpreted by its use of color. Color is a powerful design tool that often works subliminally. Many colors come with an intrinsic symbolic meaning. In *Silkwood*, production designer Patrizia Von Brandenstein made notable use of the color yellow in the plutonium plant. When it appears on road signs and in urgent public messages, yellow signifies a warning of danger. The yellow in *Silkwood* had a metaphoric power. The plutonium plant Karen Silkwood and her friends worked in was a great threat to their health and safety. The yellow was both a warning and a dramatic foreshadowing of what was to come in the story.

The production designer creates a color palette for a film. The chosen range of color is a way of expressing and defining the world of the film. Color allows the designer to create a tonal context that can complement or contrast with the narrative. The goal is not to color-coordinate as an interior designer might when decorating a living space but to consciously select each color for its dramatic impact.

On *Dick Tracy* (1990), production designer Richard Sylbert used the primary colors red, yellow, and blue to signify the comic book world of the story.

*The Last Emperor* (1987), designed by Ferdinando Scarfiotti, featured golden tones and rich saturated reds for the Forbidden City sequences that presented the magical, insular, old world of the young emperor. For scenes where the adult emperor is placed in a prison camp, director Bernardo Bertolucci, director of photography Vittorio Storaro, and Scarfiotti dramatically shifted the color palette to somber blues and grays to indicate the change in China's political climate.

In *Married to the Mob* (1988), directed by Jonathan Demme, production designer Kristi Zea employed an eclectic juxtaposition of bright colors to illustrate the downtown New York scene. For the ornate and tacky Florida hotel room scene, which concludes the film, Zea used the color turquoise to demonstrate the mob's lavish and cheesy taste in décor. Tony the Tiger's office is all wood, old-world, with overt masculine hues and materials to represent the power of the mob boss.

## The Color Palette

To create the color palette, start with markers, paint, color swatches, or any color media, and make samples. Color illustrations can help plan the color scheme. Richard Sylbert painted small square wooden boards to plan out the color scheme for *Dick Tracy*. The boards were labeled *Dick Tracy* Red, *Dick Tracy* Blue, and *Dick Tracy* Yellow, and were used as references for the design team.

The color palette should be defined before you proceed. Controlling the mood with color has a great impact on the audience. Be certain that the director, the director of photography, and production designer are all in agreement on the color approach. Will the cinematographer be using color gel, a film stock, or developing process to alter or affect the color negative? Is the movie going to be shot on video? What format—digital video, Beta, PAL? How does the format render the color and texture?

The critical difference in how color is recorded is between film and video. Film has a high contrast range and the ability to present highly saturated color. Video as a medium has improved enormously over the last ten years but inherently doesn't render contrast as well as film. Areas of image on the high and low end can lack contrast and detail. Very saturated colors tend to blossom and lose definition. In film, stocks vary in their ability to render contrast and grain pattern, which ranges from fine to grainy. Fine grain produces sharp, clean colors that are desirable for many photographic styles. Some films require a grainy look. Heavy grain creates a dark mood, soft-edged color that is great for edgy, raw subject matter. Low-end video is used for low- or no-budget productions. The color, sharpness, and contrast is quite good, considering how inexpensive the cameras are, but any commercial production striving for good production values should consider at least a three chip camera or high-end professional video camera, not what is now considered prosummer equipment. New high-definition digital cameras come close to achieving a film look. Panavision and Sony have developed a state-of-the-art digital camera that runs at the film standard of twenty-four frames per second. One of these cameras was used to film *Star Wars: Attack of the Clones* (2002), which comes even closer to capturing color the way a 35mm camera can. Most feature films are still shot on film. Kodak still dominates as the film stock of choice, but some filmmakers prefer Fuji film stock that produces what cinematographer Ed Lachman (*Desperately Seeking Susan*, 1985; *The Virgin Suicides*, 1999; and *Erin Brockovich*, 2000) calls "juke box colors," which have a candy color quality appropriate for projects with a bright, post-modern photographic approach. The production designer should talk to the director of photography, screen examples of these results, and know what shooting medium is to be used, before beginning to design the color scheme.

Color gels have a significant effect on the color scheme of the production design. Gels come in all colors and have a wide tonal range within each color. A subtle use of a gel on a light or on the camera lens can heighten or slightly augment the color, but extreme use of a saturated red or blue gel will override any color palette inherent in the production design. It is critical that the production designer and the director of photography discuss this so the design will stay within the original concept once filmed. Gels can help accent a location in lieu of painting a wall and could be an inexpensive and quick solution. Gels can benefit both the production design and the cinematography when both members of the team understand each other's tools and the best result for the story.

If the director of photography has a problem with the color of a set, the time to resolve it is in the planning stages, not at the onset of production.

Because the production designer historically is brought on before the director of photography, this collaboration starts late—after color decisions have been made between the designer and the director. "I was hired to do a TV movie that later became a series called *The Flash*," director of photography Sandi Sissel remembers. "It was a $6 million TV movie, which was almost unheard of, but when I came onto it, we had two weeks before production started so all of the locations had been chosen and they were great, really wonderful lofts. The production designer described it to me as 'the thirties meets the nineties.' We had a relatively short shooting schedule, but the gaffer, key grip, and I were going around looking at locations, and we said, 'This is really weird, why do we have all these white lofts? What does this have to do with a cartoon character?' So we went on to the director and said, 'You're going to think we're crazy, but what if we put colored gels on all the lights and washed all these sets so that they were no longer white but were absolutely bright colors?' This idea came to me because I had been reading about *Dick Tracy* at the time, and how Vittorio Storaro and Richard Sylbert were doing all these sets with primary colors. So it just seemed logical that this cartoon character would be something like this. It didn't make sense that it would be white because that was so unreal, such a fantasy. So we literally turned the offices into yellow, green, red, purple, and these bright colors. Later on the production designer was nominated for an Emmy for his colorful work on this film, none of which was in the production design—all of it was the gels on the lights. Now, had he not given us white sets, we wouldn't have been able to do that at the last minute, and perhaps had he given us weird colors, it would have been even more difficult to do. It worked out collaboratively; he was very nice about it. He loved what we did and the way that we did it."

Colors should be used to visually transcribe the layers of feeling and meaning that are in the script. Color should not be imposed on the design to convey the story, or the audience will be aware of the manipulated mechanics of the color and only see it, rather than feel it. An effective color design operates on a subconscious level and allows the colors to impart ideas and feelings separate from the conscious story and physical setting.

On Bernardo Bertolucci's *Little Buddha* (1993), scene after scene is bathed in blue. At first it establishes the spirituality of the story and the isolation felt by this young American boy believed to be the next Dalai Lama. However, the overpowering presence of this single color application eventually tires the viewer, becomes self-conscious and obvious. The color is a distraction rather than a complement or an integral element in visually illustrating and narrating the theme and story.

Ridley Scott's *Black Hawk Down* (2001) utilizes a limited color scheme executed in the production design, cinematography, and costumes. The film is based on a true story concerning a U.S. mission in Somalia. The predominant colors are green and a sand tone. The military is associated with green, so the uniforms and artillery are this color. The buildings and terrain in Somalia are sand-colored. So the color scheme is consistent with the environment and characters. But Scott and his creative team go too far. The color approach extends to the final color correction when the color of a print can be adjusted and altered. *Black Hawk Down* is so heavily green-toned that the color extends to the sky and skin tones. Part of the motivation is that when the massive attack against the Americans begins, and the blood begins to flow, red has a visceral power it might not have achieved if warm or hot colors had been introduced into the overall design. In the example of *Black Hawk Down*, the green palette is so overwhelming it distracts from the characters and action. The viewer wonders why this color dominates, consciously looking for a metaphor or meaning that is never delivered. The film quickly begins to look more like a music video than a dramatic motion picture story. Subtle use of a wider palette, at least in some locations and scenes, would have tempered this obvious exercise in style as style and not as storytelling.

Production designer Richard MacDonald utilized color to create vibrancy in his designs. His technique was to first paint a wall gray or a cold brown color, such as a raw umber. After the cool color dried, MacDonald splattered the surface with a warm color. Although the camera primarily records the warm color, the splattering technique allows the cold color underneath to show through. In MacDonald's design for *The Addams Family* (1991), directed by Barry Sonnenfeld, he designated the house as a character in the film. In a variation of the splattering technique to achieve optical vibration, one wall in the spooky fun house was painted a light ochre-yellow on encrusted paper with a textured pattern. MacDonald then rubbed a very light lavender blue over the ochre that transformed it into a gray but also projected a vibrating aura that burst forth with vitality when photographed.

During the pre-production stage of *The Morning After* (1986), director Sidney Lumet told production designer Albert Brenner that he interpreted the color of Los Angeles as a tube of Necco Wafers—a candy that combines a palette of light, dusty-colored pastels, encompassing a range of colors from warm to cool. Brenner ran with Lumet's color metaphor. He went back to the script and made a list of the exterior locations where the Jane Fonda character walked. Brenner assigned pastel colors to specific shots and scenes and then searched for each color scheme on location. Although this concept and process involved a little more traveling for the company during the shooting of the film, Lumet was convinced it was worth the effort for the contribution the color choices made in emotionally interpreting the environment, as he perceived it. The production design supported the director's vision of the film.

Tony Walton had designed the original Broadway production of the play *A Funny Thing Happened on the Way to the Forum* (1966). Richard Lester, who directed the film adaptation, wanted a different impression of Ancient Rome than the scrubbed-

and-polished look often presented in movies. Walton's design solution for the 1966 film version was to employ reds, oranges, and yellow-golds that were linked to the terra cotta hues popular in Ancient Rome. The designer also accentuated the vaude-villian roots of the play. During their research, Lester and Walton found that in the Ancient Roman era, statues were painted. Moreover, architectural landmarks such as the temples in the Roman Forum, were polychromatic; they were colorfully painted. Slaves from the same household, played by Zero Mostel and Jack Gilford, were ref-erenced by colors that conflicted with the interior coloring of the house, to empha-size they were in a different social class than the residents. The background charac-ters were presented in muddied, sludge colors, but the principal characters were dis-played in radiant, jewel colors.

For the design of *Last Tango in Paris* (1973), the theme of isolation and desola-tion boldly captured in explicit human horror by the painter Francis Bacon influenced director Bernardo Bertolucci. The principal apartment utilized in the film had been selected when Bertolucci and production designer Ferdinando Scarfiotti visited a retrospective exhibit of Francis Bacon paintings. They left the museum deciding that the flesh color that often dominated Bacon's paintings would be effec-tive in the apartment to express the psychological state of mind of Marlon Brando's character. Scarfiotti painted a series of color tests on large sheets of cardboard. The designer always envisioned creating a color gradation on the walls. The Francis Bacon paintings inspired Scarfiotti to paint a burnt sienna color on the top of the walls that gradually blended into a flesh tone and then a cream tone at the bottom. The environment evoked the color of flesh and became a metaphor for the torment-ed sexuality of the Marlon Brando character.

In Woody Allen's *The Purple Rose of Cairo* (1985), production designer Stuart Wurtzel used color to contrast with the glamorous world of the black-and-white Hollywood movies that enchanted the Mia Farrow character, who lived in the down-trodden world of the Great Depression in the 1930s. The movie palace provided her comfort, and the world outside was dark, cool, and green. Colors in the apartment she shared with her belligerent husband were dreary, heavy, and somber. Wurtzel and his art department painted the exterior of every building in the actual town used as a location for the film, to cast the pall of economic and social strife. The exterior loca-tions achieve this with a palette of dull, dreary blues, dark colored wood, beige, shades of subdued gray, brown, black, and the color of dark, worn brick. The main character's home is done in dark greens and muted browns. The movie theater that is a haven to the woman has cherry-colored wood; the interior of the spacious, majestic theater is lush red, orange, and glowing amber. The original black-and-white movie within *The Purple Rose of Cairo* was carefully shot as a separate pho-tographic element by Gordon Willis so it would glitter like a 1930s Hollywood enter-tainment film. It was projected onto the screen in the movie theater, which had been restored to its glory years by the art department team. It created the illusion that the picture palace captured the character's heart and soul and gave her hope and the strength to escape her dead-end life.

Color can be very subjective, but particular hues and palettes do represent, indi-cate, and communicate narrative messages to the audience. Warm colors tend to represent tenderness and humanity. Cool colors represent cold, lack of emotion, and distant feelings. They can also express power and force. Hot colors represent sexuality, anger, and passion, as well as physical and visceral heat. A monochromatic palette is a limited range of colors that can establish a colorless world, sameness, masked emotion, or a sense of simplicity and unity. Earth colors communicate a sense of home and environmental stability. Red is a color with many symbolic meanings attached to it—fire, Hell, Satan, sexuality, and rage. Blue shades can represent water, sky, ice, or a remote emotional state. Green is associated with trees and rolling fields of grass. White can suggest cleanliness, sterility, or spirituality. Black can characterize mystery, evil, darkness, or luxury. Yellow signifies the sun or danger. Gray can reflect a state of calm, lifelessness, or neutrality. Bright colors represent happiness, frivolity, and joy, or they can be loud and garish.

## A Concise Lesson in the Nature of Color

Combination of colors, hues, and tints are unlimited in what they can express and communicate in the production design of a motion picture. Color can be sublime, indifferent, or overwhelming. For the low-budget production, color is an inexpensive and effective medium to create a visual style and to embellish and emphasize the narrative.

The six basic colors of the spectrum are red, orange, yellow, green, blue, and violet. The principal hues are red-orange, yellow-orange, yellow-green, blue-green, blue-violet, and red-violet.

A value is the light-to-dark variant of a color. A hue on the spectrum is either lighter or darker than other hues. The natural value alignment of a hue can be raised in value by adding white and darkened by adding black. The eye can see about seven separate steps between black and white.

## Color Theory

The science, art, aesthetics, and application of color theory is divided into two distinct areas: light and pigment. Light is the science of how the spectrum creates color. Pigment is the study of how colors are physically created with paint. The production designer deals in pigment. The director of photography works in light. Both must understand the application to achieve the desired results.

Personal perception of color is subjective. Everyone has a unique emotional reaction to a particular color; even descriptive language can vary as it codifies what is seen and felt about a color. Several theorists have devised systems of notating color. Many of the defining terms used by color theorists are similar, and the language of color notation is employed by the designer to communicate the use and purpose of color in the design process.

The principle concepts of color can be seen in most theories on the subject. What follows are the basic principles of the Munsell Color Notation System. When the light of three primary colors are together in the correct proportions they can produce any color in the spectrum.

The primary colors of light are blue, red, and green. Complimentary colors, also known as secondary colors, are produced by overlapping two primary colors. The light of a primary and secondary color mixed together produces white. When two complimentary color paint pigments are mixed together, they produce black.

Luminance is the light reflected from any color. Luminance designates the brightness or darkness of a particular color.

A hue is the predominant sensation of a color—the viewer's perception of it as having, for example, the qualities of red, blue, or green. The spectrum is created by the refraction of light through a prism, with the sun's white light creating several distinct hues. Each theory has a different number of hues. The Munsell theory is based on ten principal colors, the Ostwald Color Theory has twenty-four hues, and the Pope theory starts with twelve principal colors. A six- to twelve-color system is recommended for mixing pigments for scenic painting. The basic colors of the spectrum are red, orange, yellow, green, blue, and violet. The intermediate hues create the twelve principal colors. The intermediate hues are yellow-orange, red-orange, red-violet, blue-violet, blue-green, and yellow-green. A shade is a hue mixed with black. A tone is a color grayed by the addition of white.

A value is the brightness of a color, the light to dark variants. The seven value steps of each color in the spectrum are:

- White
- Medium
- Black
- High light
- High dark
- Light
- Dark
- Low light
- Low dark

Primary colors are three spectral colors that when mixed together in the correct proportions, produce any other color in the color spectrum. A tint is a hue that has been diluted with white. For example, pink derives from red and white, beige from brown and white.

In paint, saturation describes the intensity of a color—so, 100 percent saturation is the color in its pure form. Desaturation is the process of graying-off a color by adding white, which produces pastel colors. In cinematography, saturation is achieved by exposure rate, choice of film stock, developing of the negative, and development and printing of the release print.

The chroma of a color refers to its hue combined with its saturation. The intensity of a hue or the intensity of a color is referred to as chroma. A color that is free of white or gray properties has chroma. The following are some principles of color psychology and the cause and effect of color application:

- Warm hues such as orange, yellow, and red appear to be closer to the camera than cool colors like blue, green, and purple. Cool colors make objects look larger and farther away.
- A smooth surface will give the impression that colors are more saturated than they would be if the same color were applied to a dull, matte texture that makes them appear desaturated.
- The lighting has a critical impact on how color appears on film. All colors can be

checked and tested on film or videotape. Reflections caused by the lighting can dim the luminance and hue of a color or crush the density of the color. Diffusion desaturates color and gives the area a consistent level of brightness.

- A background and foreground color can modify each other. In contrast and relationship, an individual color can be modified by other colors appearing within the same frame.
- Colors appear lighter against a black background.
- Colors appear darker against white. The intensity (chroma) of a color is the degree of pureness.
- Limiting the palette to cool or warm, or even monotone color, is effective in communicating sameness, calm, and a lack of identity or unification.
- In designing the color scheme for a space where a group of characters live or work, the designer must decide the point of view. Does one of the characters dominate the stylistic tastes of the environment? Are they responsible for the color scheme? The color palette can represent the individual's emotional state or it can express a sense of doom, happiness, or sexual tension that will become a platform for the characters and story.
- To plan the color scheme, production designers use a painter's elevation that shows the colors in their true form without the influence of lighting. A scale drawing of the set is created in a line drawing, and a boxed grid numbered on the top and lettered on the side is put over it to identify each box. A notion of the actual color and the painting technique is indicated.

## Black-and-White Filmmaking

Designing black-and-white productions is an art and craft in itself. During the classical Hollywood studio era, production designers and art departments were well trained in working in the black-and-white medium. The principal difference in designing in black-and-white as opposed to color is that the designer's palette does not consist of the color spectrum. The black and white designer is working within the gray scale and must understand how each color translates to a value from black to white.

If your film is being photographed in black-and-white, watching other films in the medium will motivate and inspire, but it will not help you to learn how colors are interpreted in the gray scale. Practicing and experimenting with black-and-white still photography will give you an understanding and feeling for how black-and-white film records a color scene. Since a bright green and a bright blue of the same hue may read as the same tone on the gray scale, colors in a black-and-white film are not chosen for their color value but for their tonality on the gray scale. To the untrained eye, the colors of a well-designed set prepared for black-and-white photography will look unbalanced and may appear to be garish and to clash in relationship to each other. The production designer works to achieve balance, contrast, and a sense of space and dimension, using the range of the gray scale. The architectural silhouette is the same, but the detail and modeling must be projected through gray scale values.

After each value is tested, the set is built, then carefully checked and tested with the black-and-white film stock to be used. Camera tests are made to discover the tonal range. During shooting, a black-and-white video assist system will help the designer to see how the set will look in black-and-white. The art department must be prepared to make corrections and changes to enhance, augment, or correct the design so it can best serve the characters and story.

## Color Correction

Color correction is a process where the color of the original negative or master video tape can be corrected for hue, tone, intensity, and value to achieve the original intent of the director of photography, or altered to achieve special, specific color effects that create, mood, and atmosphere.

Historically, color correction was done at a film laboratory where a color timer would time each individual shot and correct flesh tones and the overall color feel, be it warm or cool. A new film print was then struck from the negative using the corrections.

A film negative can be transferred to video and the color correction can be done on a video console that provides more latitude to the specificity of altering areas of color.

Now, digital tools are revolutionizing color correction. Many non-linear editing platforms, such as Final Cut Pro and Avid, provide the ability to correct and alter the color of images digitally. Sophisticated digital color correction consoles allow the moviemaker to make major changes to the color palette of projects shot originally on film or video. This role of color correction has gone from a generalized application, to the ability to literally paint the image at will.

Color correction occurs during post-production and is supervised by the director of photography and the director. The production designer has not officially been a part of this process but color correction and augmentation can have a major impact on how color is used and perceived in the production design.

It is recommended that the production designer be consulted during the creation of the final version of the project. More and more moviemakers are buying their own non-linear editing systems, making it easier to utilize color suggestions from the production designer during the color correction process. Moviemakers are no longer confined to expensive supervised sessions at labs and editing suites where the color correction is done in marathon sessions paid for by the hour. The access of home digital technology now empowers filmmakers with greater control over the color in their work.

## Developing a Color Sense

Study art history. Painters were the first artists to use color to express both reality and creative impressions. By familiarizing yourself with classical and contemporary art, you will develop an eye for the application, use, and purpose of color in creating images.

Pablo Picasso (1881–1973) was an artist of great range. In 1890 he arrived in Paris from his native Spain and began to paint beggars and outcasts. Picasso expressed his own sense of isolation in a series of paintings later identified as his Blue Period. Picasso applied a palette of cool, blue colors to express melancholy and despair. *The Old Guitarist,* painted in 1903, is a fine example of this approach. The old man is seated on the street bent over his instrument; his white hair, face, arms, and exposed legs are tinged with blue; and his expression communicates that he accepts his face as an outcast of society. The Blue Period paintings are an excellent reference for how color can create an overall somber, depressed mood.

Expressionism is a vital source of influence for filmmakers wanting to use color in a nonrealistic manner to express deep emotions. In 1905, a group of young European artists created a radical style. They were called Fauves (wild beasts). The style combined violent colors, such as those seen in the work of Vincent van Gogh, and the use of distortion such as executed by Paul Gauguin. This radical movement was lead by Henri Matisse (1869–1954), whose work presented flat planes of color, heavy pulsating outlines, and primate forms. The painters of Fauvism used pink, orange, green, and dramatic, clashing contrasts of color that created an expressive emotional atmosphere that stimulated a physical upheaval in the viewer. The German Expressionists include Ernst Ludwig Kirchner (1880–1938), Erich Heckel (1883–1970), Emil Nolde (1867–1956), Oskar Kokoschea (1886–1980), and Wassily Kandinsky (1883–1970). Their work with color and texture vividly evokes emotional states through a nonnaturalist application of color to figures and nature. German filmmakers introduced this style in film during the 1920s, and its impact influenced film noir and contemporary films that evoke the deep emotional state of their characters and story.

Piet Mondrian (1987–1944) is an excellent reference for post-modern design. This abstractionist painted flat hard-edged squares and rectangles using primary colors, creating exciting spatial and optical relationships. His work is a lesson in how colors and shapes create movement and rhythm strictly through their contrast and relationship to each other.

The area of color field painting contains significant lessons concerning color, mood, and atmosphere. The large block-like color fields of Mark Rothko (1903–1970), demonstrate the power of large color fields, which can be applied to landscapes and to the overall color feel created in the film frame by deep-hued, soft-textured color relationships. Helen Frankenthaler (1928– ) poured thin consistencies of oil paints to get a watercolor wash effect. The color work of Willem de Kooning (1904–1997) addresses the interior life of a character and altered states of emotional reality.

### Discovering Color

Purchase an inexpensive watercolor set and explore how colors are created through mixing and blending. Practice hues and tints. Create color schemes that project specific moods and emotional states. When you feel more adventurous, move on to oil or acrylic painting, for a more complex investigation into color creation. Fill a brush with one of the primary colors—red, yellow, or blue. Make your application of paint to paper as opaque as possible to get the deepest hue. The better quality watercolor sets will give a better result in achieving a vibrant opaque color. Create a two-inch square of the opaque color. Then create a series of tints by painting additional squares and adding a little more water each time to lighten the color until the final square is clear water. Study each square. How do the various tints of the original colors impart mood? Write a line or two of prose to capture your emotional and psychological reaction to each tint. To develop skills in creating mood, select a specific mood, whether it's somber, joyful, sad, or happy. Then, using one color, paint a background that captures the mood. Experiment with different colors; try gray, green, or blue for sadness. Try red, yellow, or blue for happiness.

Research, study, and learn how to photograph, develop, and print color still photographs. Sit in on a film or video lab timing session to understand how color can be rendered and manipulated on film and video. Create a color diary filled with color samples you come across your travels. Identify each color and note its derivation, properties, and capacity of expression.

# Chapter 8

## TEXTURE

Texture is critical in creating authenticity; evoking age, wear, use, and passage of time; and reflecting the results of environmental conditions on a surface. The Europeans call it patina. The surface of an object must reflect that it has been lived-in or has existed in time. Dust is a common aging agent, easily accessible to the filmmaker.

On the West coast, dust has an earthen, clay color due to the geological properties of the landscape and the quality of reflected light in the region. The nature of East coast dust is often black and sooty. The properties of the soil, car, industrial pollution, and chimney soot in a crowded, architecturally cramped metropolis contribute to the color and texture of the dirt and dust.

The purpose of texture in building materials, fabrics, and furnishings is to provide contrast and complement and to add realism and a tactile sense to the design. The materials chosen for the production design serve many purposes. The textures of building materials communicate the properties of the structure: wood, metal, glass, brick, and tile. If the texture is believable, whether real or created by the art department, it will contribute to veracity of the story.

One of the missions of the production designer is to create the appearance of real materials through art direction. A set built of wood can be transformed by covering the surface with other materials to create the illusion that it is made of stone, any variety of high quality wood, or sheet rock.

Materials and texture are storytelling devices. They inform the audience about the economic status, time and place, and social and political conditions of the story's environment. Materials can become metaphors. In *Terminator 2: Judgement Day* (1991) the Terminator and T1000 are made of metal. The production design by Joseph Nemec III is filled with metal surfaces of all varieties, even molten metal. All the metal structures in the film are related to the power of the cyborgs.

Part of the art of production design is using materials that are available, easy to work with, and sensible for a film production. All the metal materials in the design of *Terminator 2: Judgement Day* are not exactly what they look like. Surfaces are treated, painted, and textured. To use real metal in every case would be difficult to manage in building and working on a film set during construction and production.

The following examples demonstrate how the texture of set construction materials can convey a specific look, mood, and atmosphere to a scene by aging new material so that they appear to be old and worn.

## Aging Wood

The wood is painted with a coat of asphaltum, a tar-like substance that dries slowly. The surface is then painted the color of driftwood. As the paint and asphaltum mix and dry together, the texture of the treated area begins to look like unpainted or raw wood. In a matter of hours, this technique can create the illusion that a structure built with new wood appears to be seventy or eighty years old. Acrylic paint is a quicker drying medium, and is another method of aging wood. The technique involves applying a base coat color and then creating the highlights of the wood with a second coat painted on by brush. The result is not as naturalistic as the asphaltum technique because the acrylic paint leaves visible brush strokes.

## Aging Stone

To age or weather a lightweight stone prop created by the production designer out of dried or baked clay, concrete, or compressed paper, first apply a base color of gray or brown depending on the variety of stone intended. This color will indicate areas where the stone is dark from picking up dirt from the outdoor elements. Then apply a coat of a light color of the first coat all over the stone. The stone is then carefully wiped down with a cloth until the dark sentiment of the base color settles into the dimples of the stone, and the light color forms highlights and contrast. The result looks like aged stone where dirt has built up over the years and settled into dimples and crevices, while other parts of the stone are lighter in tone.

A set comprised of surfaces painted with acrylic paint can be quickly aged with a mixture of 2 percent black India ink and 98 percent water. When sprayed onto the set, the black tone sinks into the texture of the surface. Do not wipe the surface down, because the natural runs of the ink will replicate natural dirt lines.

## The Role and Purpose of Aging in Production Design

Aging must appear authentic on camera. A badly aged set looks like a new structure smudged with dirt, not a real location naturally and organically aged by environmental elements.

Director Sam Peckinpah was meticulous about the aging of the sets in his movies. Peckinpah's Westerns demystified the romantic, poetic westerns of John Ford and Howard Hawks. Peckinpah made movies that depicted the Old West as it really was—dirty and dusty towns put together for functionality, not architectural beauty. The materials are raw—a Western bar is made of untreated wide wooden planks, not the shiny polished surface of a high quality wood. By adding layers of aging to production design, Peckinpah was able to recreate the period, as he perceived it. Peckinpah's *The Wild Bunch* (1969) and *Pat Garrett and Billy the Kid* (1973) are textbook examples of authenticity in aging production design elements of the real West to reveal those elements without romance and myth.

To age the exterior of a home or building, production designers employ painters in the art department to apply several coats of paint, each in a different, distinct color. When the surface is carefully chipped and scrapped, the layers of color show through the final coat, giving the impression the façade is old and has been painted many times over the years.

Production designers use Fuller's Earth, a clay with absorptive properties, to age surfaces. It has been used for litter and bedding for poultry and pets, and is a soil conditioner for greenhouses and golf courses. Fuller's Earth is widely used on film sets. Sold packaged, and more sanitary than going out and getting real dirt, Fuller's Earth is rubbed into wood to create a dusty, age-worn look. It can also be spread out on a floor to create a dusty dirt floor. Fuller's Earth comes in especially handy when designing a Western or in aging down an old or haunted house.

The look of dirty, grimy windows can be achieved by applying several layers of dulling fluid or a wax spray. If the windows are in a deserted location subject to years of neglect or are in the residence of a character that has not kept his home clean, they should be grimed up in this fashion. Fuller's Earth or dirt can be applied while the spray or fluid is still wet. This will create the illusion that dirt has been kicked up from the outside and has adhered to the smeary, grimy glass.

Cobwebs can be created with fine, white cotton thread or with an aerosol spray, available at theater- and film-supply houses, that simulates spider webs. These supply houses also carry cobweb guns that contain a fan that blows a rubber solution into fine filaments that cling to the set. When talcum powder or Fuller's Earth is sprinkled onto any of these methods, the spidery patterns are more visible to the camera eye. Cobwebs are essential for haunted houses, deserted locations, and to indicate that an area has not been cleaned in some time.

The production can purchase photographic wallpaper that comes patterned in a variety of materials: wood, stonework, brick, and tile. Dry brushing or spraying a dark tone in areas can age the paper.

It is especially important to age newly created costumes to give the appearance the clothes have been worn, laundered, and lived-in. Many period films destroy any sense of believability by presenting costumes that look too new, like they've come out of a costume shop.

On *Blade Runner* (1982), production designer Lawrence G. Paull used warm grays and applied dust to naturally age the set. Costume designer Charles Knode designed some of the costumes and found others in used clothing stores. "Charles Knode and I talked about the costumes," Paull explains. "Deckard wore a wonderful shirt that had all these colors in it, but they were so tied into one another that it had a muted plaid effect. All the costumes were very browned over, very heavily aged, and crusted over." Knode achieved this effect by laundering the costumes in a washing machine filled with strong black coffee. (A basic method of aging costumes is to wash them repeatedly, until the desired effect is achieved.)

Costume designers shop in used clothing stores where they can purchase garments that have been naturally aged by wear and time. Costumes that are seen outdoors and have been soiled can be treated with Fuller's Earth, mud, food stains, artificial bloodstains, or whatever the situation calls for. If the character's clothes need to be torn, have missing buttons, loose threads, or some other form of disrepair, the costume designer would execute this as part of the pre-production process.

Aging sets for a period movie is a team effort from the production designer, costume designer and director of photography. Master cinematographer Gordon Willis (*The Godfather Trilogy, Pennies From Heaven, Zelig*) offers great insight into why many period films may look pretty but not all realistic.

"Period movies are a tableau form of filmmaking," Willis explains. "They are like paintings. If you're going to move, don't move with a zoom lens. It instantly lifts you right out of the movie because it's such a contemporary, mechanical item. It's not right for the turn of the century. Tracking can work. You lay it in at the right level and you're not really aware of it. On a period movie, you should put distance between you and the audience visually. They usually do this great wardrobe job on period movies, and everybody shows up with their pretty cars or horses, and the props are great. Then along comes some guy who's going to photograph this on the very latest Eastman stock and with the very sharpest lens, and when he's done, the visual is so defined, it's so immediate, it looks like it came out of the one-hour photo service. The visual is so contemporary it looks like a party with everybody dressed up walking around in period clothes; it does not put you back to where it belongs."

Contemporary life doesn't always look new. Age is character, a sign of life and experience. This must be applied to every film design with special care given to period works where the design team is using new materials to create the illusion of what life, a lived-in life, looked like in another era.

Texture does not only apply to age. Surfaces, clothes, and architectural materials, like most other elements of production design, involve texture: smooth, rough, patterned, ribbed, nappy, shiny, dull—the full range as found in life. It is texture that brings life to a design. If a set is flat in tone and texture, it will appear as artificial. Texture represents materials, status, wealth, and poverty.

### Learning About Texture

- Observe and study the texture of the surfaces around you. Identify their patterns and nuances.
- Create a texture diary of photos, clippings, and samples of materials.
- Visit lumberyards, masonry, hardware stores, and other resources that carry construction and building materials. Learn to recognize the physical properties of each variety of the major materials; wood, stone, brick, glass, tile, and metal.
- Paint several test boards an off-white color. Practice aging by spraying the surfaces with India ink. Create a range of results from new to old; control the gradations by the amount of ink and water mixture you apply.

# Chapter 9

## ARCHITECTURE

Production design in film was born out of collaboration between three separate art forms: the decorative arts, theater, and architecture. The decorative arts have a long tradition tracing back to the beginnings of many cultures. Theater stagecraft traces back to the Ancient Greeks and Romans, continuing through Shakespeare, to the beginnings of vaudeville, burlesque, and Broadway. Both these artistic disciplines influenced film art direction, but the most significant influence on production design was architecture. At the beginning of the twentieth century, as film was being born, an artistic revolution was being forged in modern architecture.

Most early filmmakers maintained a theatrical style of simple painted backdrops with little cinematic relationship between the characters and their settings. In 1897, Georges Méliès, a magician turned filmmaker, opened Star Films Studios and brought the art of theatrical illusion to the cinema. Méliès went beyond his contemporaries during the days of early cinema. He applied with cinematic technique his magical stagecraft of trap doors, chutes, revolving panels, flats and backdrops painted with architectural elements. A conjurer, Méliès used special camera effects to make scenic elements magically disappear or transform into each other. In 1899, he created an elaborate staging of *Cinderella* and one of *Jeanne d'Arc* in 1900. His most famous film, *Le Voyage dans la Lune/A Trip to the Moon*, was made in 1902. Méliès stunned viewers with an image of the human-like face of the moon struck by a flying rocket ship. Among Méliès' experiments with design and cinematic storytelling is an underwater scene accomplished by photographing a woman costumed as a mermaid, through the glass plane of a decorated aquarium, with several moving backdrops painted with sea monsters behind her. For another film he turned music hall beauties into the astral constellation of the Great Bear. Méliès created a mechanism to animate giant, moving, designed tableaux and had elaborately painted backdrops featured in his films, which often called for multiple costume changes.

Architecture was brought to the cinema in full force in the 1910 Italian production of *Cabaria*. A complete architectural approach was applied to this film, including the construction of stairways, platforms, and walls built out of wood and then surfaced with a plaster and fiber composition to bring scale and texture to the set construction in a recreation of third-century Rome. It was the first time the term "film architecture" was applied to a film production. Prior to *Cabaria*, filmmakers used painted backgrounds and hand drawn décor to illustrate the setting and had not yet discovered the application of physical three-dimensional design to cinematic storytelling.

## The Development of Shot Design and Sequential Storytelling Through Production Design

The Russian director Sergei Eisenstein is best known for his landmark work in editing structure known as montage, but Eisenstein was a trained architect who also experimented with dynamic design ideas in his films, and composed shot by shot to reveal the elements of settings through composition and editorial montage.

Eisenstein began directing theater and mounted productions of Ibsen's *Brand* and *Peer Gynt*, Shakespeare's *Twelfth Night*, *King Henry IV*, and *King Richard III*, Molière's *Tartuffe*, and Strindberg's *Erik XIV*. He created architecturally dynamic drawings of the productions in his own hand. They stressed movement, angles, and sharp curves. Eisenstein continued to incorporate design throughout his film career. In depicting the Russian Revolution, *October* (1928) made dramatic use of the Winter Palace and towering statues of a horse and a soldier.

Eisenstein came to Hollywood in the early 1930s and prepared productions that never made it before the cameras. One, *Sutter's Gold* was to be a reconstruction of the San Francisco docks. Eisenstein sketched buildings, boats, and details of elaborate fountains, supplemented by copious notes on the production design. Examination of these materials in *Eisenstein at Work*, by Jay Leyda and Zina Voynow, demonstrates Eisenstein's deep understanding of production design as an integral element of cinematic storytelling. The drawings and notes are typical of a designer's precision and dedication to scope and detail. Eisenstein's architectural training allowed him to think like a designer and to make design a part of each frame, to tell the story by relating design to narrative and character.

After designing a production of Theodore Drieser's novel *An American Tragedy* (which also remained unfilmed), Eisenstein traveled to Mexico for the unfinished *Qué Viva Mexico!* Dynamic imagery designed for this production included a foreground shot of three skulls with a procession of monks and a stark cross in the background, a woman's profile framed next to the Pyramid at Chickén, a hacienda courtyard, and the massive sky and bared landscape of the region.

For *Alexander Nevsky* (1938) Eisenstein designed all of the armor, headgear, and weapons. Cathedrals and bridges are integral elements in the environment of this epic film. *Ivan the Terrible* (1945–1947) was a medieval, expressionistic production with angular costumes, characters framed by sweeping arches, weaving procession patterns of people, and an overpowering use of space and grandeur, all of which project the power of the principal character. Elaborate makeup and hair design depicts the dramatic transformation of Ivan throughout the multipart work.

Eisenstein's films are often discussed and analyzed in reference to his innovative and elaborate experiments in editing montage. His sense and execution of production design was central to the way he contrasted and intercut movement, space, and the characters' relationship to the environment. The production design values enhanced Eisenstein's editorial creations and contributed to his film artistry.

## The Development of Applying Design Aesthetic to Cinematic Storytelling

As the cinema entered the 1920s, the aesthetic possibilities attainable through production design seemed unlimited. *The Cabinet of Dr. Caligari* (1919), directed by Robert Wiene and designed by Herman Warm, Walter Reinman, and Walter Rohrig, boldly demonstrated how a nonrealistic production design could create a nightmare world.

*The Cabinet of Dr. Caligari* was a dynamic expressionist experiment in applying design to create an environment for the demented machinations of the evil Dr. Caligari and his somnambulist Ceasare who commits murder under the influence of the doctor's madness.

The sets seem interconnected, representing the claustrophobic, distorted world of Caligari's reign of terror. The environment is created to trap all the characters in the doctor's web of deception, control, and violence, both physical and psychological. Built entirely on a sound stage, the design was created with the stagecraft of the day—constructed and painted flats. But *Caligari*'s innovation was the three dimensionality of its design. While films of the time used painted flats in a manner similar to the stage, *Caligari's* world has depth, dimension, and a carefully worked out design that creates the illusion that the many sets are part of a single large environment. This is accomplished by connective graphic elements that link through consistency of design. Separate city street sets were edited together during the post-production process so that they appear to lead from one to another in a web that traps the participants of the story.

The town is designed with distorted, contrasting angles. The set, like all those in the film, is painted, and does not pretend to be realistic but appears to be a dimensional expressionist work that comes alive off a painter's canvas. This painterly and surrealist world creates a mood we accept with the demented plot of Dr. Caligari, the master of many disguises. He is first seen with a stovepipe hat, black, imposing glasses, and long, stringy white hair. At one point his white gloves have black lines painted on them.

Alan, one of the two protagonists in the film, has a high-backed wooden chair in his room. Jagged patterns are on the walls constructed in a distorted perspective.

Streets are lined with twisting architecture. Windows are not square but angled with stark, slashing lines that indicate the bars of a prison cell. The jutting angles in the town create a contrasting, conflicting mood.

A carnival comes to the town. The tents are off-angled, and a children's ride spins in a tilted circle against a backdrop of mountains that root the town in a geographic distance from any nearby society. A black railing cuts through the composition, creating a space for people to enter that goes beyond the frame, indicating that a large expanse exists outside. Men wear pointed hats. Jagged triangular shapes are everywhere; a tent is textured with dark, dry-brushed slashes.

After a murder is committed, the windows in buildings become even more distorted and are transformed into knife-like shards.

Cesare escapes to the rooftop of canted angled poles. A narrow bridge-like road is lined with sparsely dressed trees. A prison is designed as a vaulted triangle, with the number 5 painted on the wall. An asylum building has three arches and identical gunboat windows. White painted lines in the courtyard lead to the arches. They make the pattern of an op-art sunburst. The interior of the hospital is also cave-like, and outside walls have tentacle black lines. Caligari is in the asylum office. He begins to hallucinate and sees animated, white painted words appear on the walls, ground, and sky. Art-directed trees are bare and twisted. Caligari changes disguises, which helps him succeed in capturing the hero—evil triumphs over good.

*Dr. Mabuse der Spieler* (1922) and *Metropolis* (1927), both directed by Fritz Lang used architectural interpretations of a city to express not only visual but social and political ideas, and to evoke deep emotional states in the audience. *Metropolis* is a silent science-fiction film that used production design to contrast the rich, powerful upper class that controls the futuristic city with the poor who run Metropolis with their sweat and blood.

The city aboveground is majestic with towering, glittering skyscrapers, planes flying through and around the spires and suspended highways that allow traffic to flow along the upper floors of the high-rises climbing up the angled narrow roadways. One building is constructed of stacked platforms; another is topped with a star-shaped headpiece.

The master of Metropolis presides in an office with large doors and a massive window. He sits behind a huge curved desk. An instrument panel controls the master's universe; he can close the drapes to shut out his view of the city by the push of a button. A large staircase that leads to his office represents his power and inaccessibility to all but the privileged.

Below Metropolis is the industrial power that gives it life through the work of the enslaved. Men dressed in black with black caps enter through a tunnel barred with a prison gate; they trudge toward their workstations. Two massive steel tanks spew steam. There are steep flights of stairs, clocks, panels, levers, and a huge thermometer that keeps track of the power stress level. Above, a mechanical monster's face with a tooth-lined door brings the industrial behemoth dynamo to life.

The marriage between modern twentieth-century architecture and film art served many purposes. For the daring futuristic architects, it was a way of promoting modernism. It released moviemakers from the stilted painted backdrops used extensively in the past. The dynamism of twentieth-century architecture gave filmmakers a sense of the new and the future to come.

## The Modernist School of Design Makes an Impact on the Look of Films

Modernistic design permeated the exteriors and interiors of film sets with glamour and opulence to raise the spirits of audiences suffering from the effects of World War I and the Great Depression. Architectural style dominated the tenor of film content and was a strong visual element, more than just an environment for the characters. It informed the narrative with a positive and hopeful worldview—the message the major studios were committed to promoting.

The major studios of the classical Hollywood studio system embraced modern architecture and selected it as the principal look to project a burgeoning, rising America. Paramount hired Hans Drier to define the direction of the studio's visual style. Drier had studied architecture in Munich, Germany, where he supervised projects for the government in West Africa. Drier had designed for the legendary Universum-Film AG, known as UFA from 1919 to 1923. Hans Drier made Paramount into a Bauhaus workshop, integrating European modernism into films depicting American life.

RKO featured a streamlined Art Deco, Neoclassical architectural style for its signature look, as typified in a series of Fred Astaire–Ginger Rogers musicals produced there.

The series of musicals Fred Astaire and Ginger Rogers produced at RKO were known for their modern, elegant settings that supported the sophisticated choreography of American's iconic dance couple. Production design is often influenced by circumstances presented to the filmmakers. Fred Astaire had a clause in his studio contract that required he be photographed in a full frame where he could be seen head to toe when dancing. This prevented directors from breaking up his fluid movements with close-ups, montage, or other methods that would detract from the total impact of seeing him whole, as if on stage. This turned out to pave the way for production designers to feature large scale sets that illustrated and communicated the carefree world of ballrooms, clubs, and almost any place they could design a dance floor.

The team of producer Pandro S. Berman and art director Van Nest Polglase produced the settings for many of the famous Astaire-Rogers couplings shot in classic black-and-white. White was a principal color to allow the couple to take center stage. Astaire was often costumed in dramatic black, usually a tuxedo, and Rogers in a stunning flowing or form-fitting gown in a color that stood out from the white surroundings.

Their film sets featured white pianos, music stands, tiered platforms, and tables and doors. The scale was large, expansive. The locale was often a cosmopolitan hotel in New York City or London. Nightclubs were designed with large tiered bandstands, multilevels for diners' tables, and a spectacular dance floor that changed shape from film to film and was always shiny, spotless, and inviting.

In *Top Hat* (1935), a men's clubroom has high-backed chairs, drapes, and a large stone fireplace in a space with high walls and no ceiling in sight. Elegant men wearing top hats and tailored formal clothing relax in the masculine atmosphere.

Astaire dances in a room with light colored walls, white couches, vases, and a painted sky with a puffy clouded background. A London hotel has large, white doors, a decorated floor, elegant stairway, a huge stage, and chandeliers. Diners sit by a canal while gondolas carry happy, wealthy people. A French hotel has an overpass, Deco panels, and large planters. A room has a large bath, lots of white, and a bed on a circular-stepped platform. A garden has manicured hedges. All of the architecture and décor was constructed on the RKO sound stages for this and every Astaire-Rogers picture.

The Fred Astaire/Ginger Rogers RKO films offer a glimpse into a life without care. Designers created the settings that they imagined the masses dreamed about. The films were carefully designed, coordinated in décor and tone, to service the dance and the fantasies of the moviegoers.

MGM embraced modernistic sets as far back as 1924. Mogul Louis B. Mayer hired Romain di Tirtoff, the artist known as Erté. Di Tirtoff created the high-life world of the glamorous well-coifed that went on nightclub rendezvous and lounged in luxurious boudoirs. For the MGM film *Paris* (1926), Erté designed a triangular space with geometric imagery that anticipated the Art Deco style later employed in U.S. skyscrapers.

## The Architect as Production Designer

Many production designers have come out of an education as an architect and have brought structural design concepts to cinematic storytelling. Stephen Goosson designed *Oliver Twist* in 1922, *The Hunchback of Notre Dame* in 1923, *Lost Horizon* (1937) for director Frank Capra and, for Orson Welles, *The Lady From Shanghai* (1948), which contained the memorable funhouse mirror climax.

Goosson began his career as an architect in Detroit before working as an art director for Lewis Selznick, David O. Selznick's father. Goosson's style developed over a quarter century. He designed the first futuristic city of the 1930s in *Just Imagine* (1930), set in 1980 when American society is divided by technology. Goosson built a New York City miniature in a balloon hanger four hundred feet long and two hundred feet wide. He brought elegance to *Little Lord Fauntleroy* (1936), and Art Deco to Frank Capra's *American Madness* (1932). Stephen Goosoon's astounding career includes art direction credits on 1,300 motion pictures.

Robert Boyle graduated from USC as an architecture student and went on to work with Alfred Hitchcock on *Saboteur* (1942), *Shadow of a Doubt* (1943), *North by Northwest* (1959), *The Birds* (1963), and *Marnie* (1964).

Ken Adam studied architecture in London and worked for an architectural firm, later making the transition to production design while working with William Cameron Menzies on *Around the World in 80 Days* (1956). Adam designed many films of the James Bond Series, *Dr. Strangelove or: How I Learned to Stop Worrying and Love the Bomb* (1964) and *Barry Lyndon* (1975). Lawrence G. Paull, who designed the *Back to the Future* trilogy (1985, 1989, 1990), as well as *Blade Runner* (1982), was trained as an architect and city planner, giving him an understanding of urban environments that has served him well artistically as a production designer.

The Bauhaus and German Expressionism movements influenced Ken Adam.

"One of the first films that really impressed me as a kid was *The Cabinet of Dr. Caligari*," he says. " Once I started expressing myself as a designer, I always leaned toward the choice of the theatrical. I find it dull to do a room as it is. I feel as a designer your function is to give a reality to the public that is real but departs from the dullness that is very often part of the actual place. The style is not only reflected in my modern films but even in some of my period designs. It is nearly always a heightened reality-stylization."

Lawrence G. Paull's contribution to these films traces back to his training as an architect and city planner before joining the Twentieth Century Fox art department where he apprenticed under veteran art directors Walter Tyler and John DeCuir. Both the *Back to the Future* trilogy and *Blade Runner* demanded the overview of a city planner who understood all the elements that go into constructing a functioning city: the architecture, streets, sidewalks, means of water, and electrical power, and governmental facilities. By understanding the scope, Paull was able to create cities that went beyond the camera frame and functioned as a cohesive unit.

## Construction

The design ideas for a film set are ultimately built for the production. The process from idea to completed set is parallel to the traditional architectural process with the exception of the fact that a film set is a temporary structure. The ideas for a set must address the concerns of the screenplay. They should be cinematic, visual, and communicate the vision of the director.

The concept drawings put those ideas on paper for the first time. They serve the purpose of communicating the production designer's visualization to the director. Once the director and producer agree, the art department proceeds with the process that will result in the completed set.

Detailed working drawings that address materials, scale, size, and architectural design are created. Next, a draftsman makes a plan of the set based on those working drawings. The plan looks like any architectural plan and serves the same purpose. The construction coordinator studies the plan. Materials are ordered. The set can be built in the studio or in part at a shop or warehouse and shipped to the studio where it is assembled. A crew of carpenters and other artisans as needed are put on the project by the construction coordinator, who is like a construction foreman on a traditional building project. The construction coordinator must also determine how long it will take to build the set so it can be coordinated with the shooting schedule.

## Use of Space

The characters in a film exist in the context of the space in which they appear. Space can express power, oppression, freedom, fear, joy, paranoia, and a myriad of emotions, moods, and atmospheres based on the relationship between the characters and their environment.

*Nicholas and Alexandra* (1971) expresses power by placing the royal couple in a corridor with a series of overhead arches, lavish columns, a royal carpet, and, on

Set construction on location for *Keeping the Faith* (2000), directed by Edward Norton. Courtesy production designer Wynn Thomas, Spyglass Entertainment, Touchstone Pictures, and Triple Threat.

each side, a row of male staff bowing their heads. The perspective frames the hall as an entrance to the seat of power by emphasizing its orderly perfection seen in a straight-on composition.

To recreate a place or time, the production designer must study the architecture involved. Recreation involves research to understand the design, the materials, techniques, and tools used in the original construction.

For *Little Big Man* (1970), directed by Arthur Penn, production designer Dean Tavoularis researched teepees needed for the Native American sequences. He examined teepees created for Twentieth Century Fox Studios over the decades. Tavoularis found them to be ugly, orange, with yellow zigzags designed out of suede with inch and a half stitching. Tavoularis and his art department did their own research and found an authentic Cheyenne teepee in a Pasadena, California museum. When examined it, they found it was meticulously stitched so it would be waterproof. The material was thin, translucent buffalo skin that glowed at night when there was a light inside.

Tavoularis found a tannery in downtown Los Angeles, bought the hides, sewed them together, and then ran them through a machine that shaved the skin to a fine texture. The hides were tinted a muddy cream color and cut to the authentic dimensions. This led to a standard of authenticity as the crew designed and created arrows, spears, harnesses, beadwork, and the rack for beef jerky. Traditional Indian materials were replicated. When the film was complete, *American Heritage Magazine* told Tavoularis that *Little Big Man* was the first film to show deference for the way the Native Americans really lived.

## Post-modern Film Design

Futuristic stories challenge the designer. Architectural ideas have to be projected to create an ultra-modern world that's never been seen. Often production designers rely on design concepts from the past to create the future.

This concept, called post-modernism, developed in architecture during the 1970s as a reaction against modern architecture of the time. In production design, post-modernism brings a duality of meaning to the narrative of a film. Charles Jencks, an expert in post-modern architecture, offers insight into how production designers use

post-modernism in film to echo the past and put the present and future into context: "A post-modern building is doubly coded—part modern and part something else: vernacular, revivalist, local, commercial, metaphorical, or contextual. In several important instances it is also doubly coded in the sense that it seeks to speak on two levels at once: to a concerned minority of architects, an elite who recognize the subtle distinctions of a fast-changing language, and the inhabitants, users, or passersby, who want only to understand and enjoy it."

*Dune* (1984) envisioned a medieval world. *A Clockwork Orange* (1971) was set in a near future that was both crumbling and gleaming with modernity. *Blade Runner* (1982) is set in an Asian-inspired Los Angeles, a third world nation, lit with neon lights combined with Egyptian and Mayan architectural elements.

A story taking place forward in time can be researched through the paintings and designs of futurists throughout the twentieth century and by studying science fiction films that have presented the future through design. (However, the danger in the influence of other movies is of creating a derivative design that is not responsive to your story and characters.) The production design for films that followed *2001: A Space Odyssey* (1968) influenced generations of science fiction designs. There is a genealogical link between *2001, Star Wars* (1977), *Blade Runner* (1982), and *The Matrix* (1999). *2001* created a new standard in science fiction films. The models were highly detailed, the motion of flight was realistically depicted. The environments were developed and designed in response to research and the perceptions of experts based on scientific fact, not purely imagination as the genre had relied upon in the past.

*Star Wars* benefited from this new technology, but the design of the spacecrafts was dirtier, more funky, and expressed the nature of a story that had its roots in the science fiction of old, like *Flash Gordon*. Like *2001*, George Lucas's film created a futuristic universe with its own logic and visual representation.

*Blade Runner* went further with the idea of *Star Wars*'s lived-in environments and continued *2001*'s tradition of a total future world seen through Los Angeles as a third world county. Where Kubrick used a large team of technical consultants to develop the design of his film, Ridley Scott and production designer Laurence G. Paull functioned as city planners to create the high-tech, neon, neo-noir, city.

*The Matrix* invented its own cinematic technology to depict the characters' ability to stop action while performing martial arts fight scenes. Like Kubrick, the Wachowski brothers sought new ways through technology to create images never before seen. The mythical narrative of *The Matrix* was made possible by Kubrick's landmark film that utilized myth and the act of visual experience to tell a story.

All four films expanded the genre through visualization and images that told a cinematic story in an experiential manner. They didn't solely rely on plot and dialogue, as traditional films had for decades.

### Learning More About Architecture

Production designers and filmmakers involved with the design of their film can benefit from an overview of the history of architecture. Any period in world history can be researched, but design ideas are often a synthesis or fusion of past architectural styles and concepts.

- Take a course.
- Read a book. Suggestions include:
  Arnheim, Rudolf. *The Dynamics of Architectural Form.* Berkeley, Calif.: University of California Press, 1977.
  Benevolo, Leonardo. *History of Modern Architecture.* Cambridge, Mass.: M.I.T. Press, 1971.
  Le Corbusier. *Toward a New Architecture.* Translated by Frederick Etchells. New York: Dover Publications, 1986.
  Egbert, Donald Drew. *The Beau-Arts Tradition in French Architecture, Illustrated by the Grands Prix de Rome.* Princeton, N.J.: Princeton University Press, 1980
  Gebhard, David. *Lloyd Wright, Architect.* Santa Barbara, Calif.: The Art Galleries, University of California, 1971.
  Honour, Hugh. *Neo-Classicism.* Harmondsworth, England: Penguin Books, 1968.
  Gropius, Walter. *Scope of Total Architecture.* New York: Collier Books, 1955.
  Hiller, Bevis. *Art Deco.* London: Studio Vista, 1968.
  Neumann, Dietrich, ed. with essays by Donald Albrecht, Anton Kaes, Dietrich Neumann, Anthony Vidler and Michael Webb. *Film Architecture: Set Designs from Metropolis to Blade Runner.* Munich: Prestel, 1999.
  Watkin, David. *A History of Western Architecture.* New York: Thames and Hudson, 1986.
- Study the films of Michaelangelo Antonioni, King Vidor, and Fritz Lang. Screen these films: *Artists and Models* (1937), *Batman* (1989), *The Black Cat* (1934), *The Crowd* (1928), *Dodsworth* (1936), *Female* (1933), *The Fountainhead* (1949), *Grand* Hotel (1932), *l'Inhumaine* (1924), *Lost Horizon* (1937), *Men Must Fight* (1933), *Mon Oncle* (1958), *A Nous la Liberté* (1931), *Playtime* (1967), *Sunrise* (1927), and *Things to Come* (1936).
- Take an architectural tour of the cities you visit.

# Chapter 10

## PERIOD FILMS

The term "period film" is generally applied to a story that takes place in a time before the present era. Most stories take place in specific time frames, although a writer may decide to remove all "clues" to the era, to make the story "timeless," or to set a piece generically in the Roaring Twenties, for example, instead of placing it specifically in 1923. The production designer deals with the physical reality of the screen story's time frame. Unless instructed otherwise, the designer must make decisions that address the specificity of the time period the film will visually project. Generalizing the time and place can weaken a story or disorient the nature of narrative. New York in 1961 is not the same as New York in 1968. They are both in the 1960s, but stylistic, cultural, and political factors changed dramatically during these years. If the time period in the design of a motion picture is generalized, it will not enrich the specificity of the particular story being told. A generalized design (in a realistic film) does an injustice, both to those who know the period intimately and to viewers who do not. In one case, the nonspecific design violates the trust between filmmaker and the audience member, and in the other, it cheats the viewer out of a historically accurate visual experience. The 1960s were not all tie-dye and psychedelic colors. The 1970s were not all bell-bottom slacks, disco, and bulky haircuts. History, cultural habits, and style are complex. A broad sweep of society is evidenced in every single day.

When designing a period film, determine the exact time period specifically—down to year and month, if possible. This will make all decisions easier. Time and place can be directly researched. A firm sense of place and time can provide the story with an added dimension and grounding. Establish the parameters of the time period with the director and writer. What point of view and attitude toward the era are to be presented to the audience?

For *The House on Carroll Street* (1988), directed by Peter Yates, production designer Stuart Wurtzel had to turn the clock back thirty years on New York City. Originally the title was *The House on Sullivan Street*, but the filmmakers weren't able to use it for legal reasons. Once the title was changed, Wurtzel did look at Sullivan and Bleecker Streets in downtown Manhattan as possible locations. There was an interior courtyard that was needed and a view from one house to another, but the designer determined the area was not visually interesting for the camera. The project was a low-budget production, so Wurtzel began looking at the Park Slope neighborhood in Brooklyn and found it was much less changed than the Manhattan location and would keep the budget down. Wurtzel asked Yates if the lead female character could be looking for a job in Brooklyn and the script was changed. "Residential sections have changed less, businesses always have to be upgraded with each decade, because they're reflecting what people are buying," Wurtzel explains. They shot in a Greenwich Village location that at the time was still accurate for the time period of the story. Exteriors were staged and photographed in Park Slope, Brooklyn. A chase sequence indicated in the script was to be shot in the Sheridan Square area, but when the budget was worked up it would have cost as much as $170,000. "It was an enormous headache for the cinematographer, Michael Ballhaus; he wasn't going to be able to move as fast as he wanted to," Wurtzel recalls. "So it became a chase done in the Strand Bookstore, which is very period to begin with. I was always changing book titles, and I hung overhead lights, which Michael loved because we had all this light."

Wurtzel maintained the mood and point of view of the script and the director's interpretation. The story concerns a woman blacklisted as a Communist during the McCarthy Era who uncovers an espionage plot. The mood of the times was created with a cool color palette and period perfection in the architecture.

The biggest challenge for the art department was to make Grand Central look like the 1950s for a complex chase sequence that had up to110 different camera setups. First, it took weeks of scouting trips to find each location. The storyboards were then given to Michael Ballhaus who adapted and contributed to the final compositions.

Before shooting, Wurtzel and the art department changed the lettering on the information booth and covered the electric information sign with a period billboard they prepared ahead of time. The clock over the main arch was too modern and was not there during the 1950s, so a fifty-foot American flag was hung in front of it. The electrical sign atop a modern Merrill Lynch booth was covered and strong backlight coming from Musco lights outside the window wall, placed by the camera crew, hid the aluminum base of the booth. To make the booth go black on film, Wurtzel and his crew used two-inch black masking tape to cover it. All the individual electrical track information signs were changed back to the manual type of the period.

At the outset of a production, the experienced production designer will often know more about the period than the director will. Time and place is the production designer's job, but every film requires research and decisions on how the period details relate to the narrative.

Many films take place in the "now." But again, don't generalize the design, even for a contemporary film. Always be specific about time, place, cultural, and stylistic issues. A design that blurs the exactness of time and place does little to contribute to the visual rendering of the story.

## Time

Often a screenplay states the time frame of the story to the year, month, day, and hour, but it can be less specific. Stories set in a timeless era are the hardest projects to design. With rare exceptions, the time period should be established within the production design even when the screenwriter may only hint at it. The majority of viewers will recognize décor, architecture, cultural trends, hair, and dress that will firmly plant a rootless story. Don't forfeit control by diffusing the narrative power of production design to a muddle of the time period that may look familiar but isn't quite right—it will distance the audience from the characters and deprive them of the positive impact time and environment has on them.

*Sunnyside* (1979) is about a street kid who tries to end local gang warfare. The film opens with a stock shot of Queens Boulevard, in Sunnyside, Queens, New York, where the story takes place. After that one establishing image, the entire film was shot in Los Angeles in nonspecific locations that were not true to the story or narrative locale. None of the locations were convincing for the story, which was full of movie clichés adding up to one formless failure. The film adaptation of the hit play *Grease*, directed by Randall Kleiser in 1978, was set in the 1950s, but the period is overexaggerated and mixed with 1970s elements to make the film attractive and more commercial to young audiences. Olivia Newton John's crimped hairstyle and the disco-tinged title song didn't help matters much.

## Time and Place

To visually establish a sense of place, several factors must be determined. Where does the story take place? What country, city, town, street? Is it on the water, on an island, in the air, outer space, underwater, or in another universe? Is it an imaginary land, like Oz or Pleasantville or the planet Arakis of the imagined world of Frank Herbert's *Dune*? What is the scope of the environment? Does the story take place in one room, an apartment, out of doors? Are there contrasting settings, or is the mood and style consistent and connected?

To visually create an environment there are myriad elements and details that identify and communicate the sense of time and place necessary to fully tell the story. These details are influenced by factors that govern life and society, art, behavior, economics, politics, religion, and social mores.

The great Italian film director Federico Fellini once said he would never make a film in America because he wouldn't know what shoes the actor should wear. This one piece of apparel, just one visual detail, communicates information about the characters, where they are and what time frame the story is taking place in.

How do we decide what shoes to buy? The factors include availability, color, cost, functionality, materials, peer pressure, self-image, style, and trends. This one example is a window to the innumerable choices to be made for each movie and the designer's considerations behind each selection.

What is an environment? The items that follow are components, items, and details that together make up the environmental world of a film.

## HOME OR APARTMENT

The pictorial details that comprise film characters' home and apartment environments are crucial to the production designer. These items must be carefully considered so that they honestly interpret the script and the point of view established by the director. Such details can include: air conditioners; number and layout of rooms; architectural style; bathroom supplies and appliances; bedding; bookcases; books; chairs CDs, children's room (toys, décor, artwork, stuffed animals); color and texture of walls, floor, and ceiling; construction materials; doors; fans; flowers; food; furniture; floor coverings; floor materials; home computer; home entertainment (television, VCR, DVD, stereo, radios, sound system); home office equipment; kitchen appliances (refrigerator—including magnets and pictures, stove, microwave, coffeemaker, Cuisinart); kitchen tools; liquor cabinet or bar; location (where do the rooms face? what can be seen out of the windows?); lighting fixtures; linens; magazines; mirrors; musical instruments; newspapers; pantry and refrigerator supplies; personal paperwork; pans; plants; posters, art work, and photographs; pots; radiator covers; rugs; tablecloths; tables; telephones; towels; vases; knickknacks; candlesticks; windows; window treatments; and specialty items relating to the specificity of the story and characters.

## EXTERIOR STREET

Equally important are the architecture of apartment houses or homes, cars, vehicles, garbage cans, landscaping, signage, streetlights.

## LANDSCAPE

The outdoor areas of a set design also influence the mood, atmosphere, and descriptive qualities of the production: foliage, bodies of water, dirt, indigenous animals, rocks, sand, terrain.

## RESTAURANT INTERIOR

Many film scenes take place in restaurants. Don't overlook this important venue in designing a set. Be sure to consider architecture, chairs, color of walls, condiments and bread on tables, décor, dinnerware, food served, host podium, ice buckets, napkins, reservation book, silverware, side table for desserts, staff dress, tablecloths, tables, wall coverings.

In composing a sense of time and space be aware of what raw materials are available. Go through supply company catalogues in every range of décor and functional design. Remember, as a filmmaker you must make informed decisions. Every element that is a part of the on-screen time and space environment can be chosen, altered, added, or taken away.

Films that are successful in capturing the time period of their story include:

*The Godfather* (1972)—director, Francis Ford Coppola, production designer Dean Tavoularis, director of photography Gordon Willis. The film takes place in the late 1940s. The old-world nature of Don Corleone is captured in his dark and oppressive office. Wooden blinds and a solid wood desk define his power and authority. The Kodacrome color scheme reminds viewers of home movies from parents or grand-parents, creating a sense-memory connection. Kodacrome is a film stock still manu-factured by the Kodak company. The current film stock has bright, saturated colors but within a normal range. The Kodacrome film stocks of the 1940s and 1950s pro-duced bright, saturated colors that popped out more vibrantly than those in nature. When this color scheme is used in a period feature film taking place in the 1940s, 1950s, or 1960s it creates a visual mood of the period with brighter, sharply defined saturated colors that are reminiscent of most people's perception of those time peri-ods. Perfect period cars, the Art Deco exterior of Radio City Music Hall, and a gar-den football wedding all bring the period to life with documentary detail. Hairstyles and clothes look authentic and lived-in, not just a fashion statement.

*Barry Lyndon* (1975)—director Stanley Kubrick, production designer Ken Adam, director of photography John Alcott. The eighteenth century was meticulously recre-ated through the study of paintings, architecture, and literature. Most of the film was shot on location in Europe. The majority of the costumes were real eighteenth centu-ry clothes retailored for larger modern bodies. Wigs were carefully selected for authenticity and for how they related to the individual character. The film was shot by candlelight. Décor includes a period bathtub, candle fixtures, and paintings of the period hung high on the large walls. *Barry Lyndon* is widely considered to be the most successful achievement of period filmmaking. It is the collaboration of design and photography that produces the reality of the time past and here preserved.

*Pat Garrett and Billy the Kid* (1973)—director Sam Peckinpah, production designer Ted Haworth, director of photography John Coquillion. Set in the old West of the title characters. One of the rare Westerns (Clint Eastwood's *Unforgiven*, 1992, designed by Henry Bumstead, is another) where everything—including buildings, interiors, exteriors, terrain, props, and costumes—is worn, aged, dusty, and unro-mantic, devoid of romance and myth.

*Boogie Nights* (1997)—director Paul Thomas Anderson, production designer Bob Ziembicki, director of photography Robert Elswit. Time-capsule accuracy capturing the 1970s, using the porn industry as a metaphor for family and the technological transition between film and video. The 1970s design style of disco fashion and gaudy décor is accurate and realistic, not exaggerated or satirized in the way, for instance, television's *That 70s Show* insinuates the time period. The combination of story, context, and environmental recreation in *Boogie Nights* takes the viewer back to the not-so-distant past.

Other recommended period films to screen and study include:

*The Age of Innocence* (1993)—Martin Scorsese's film captures the life of New York's aristocracy in the 1870s. Production designer Dante Ferretti transformed many New York locations back in time; the New York Art Director's club was redec-orated as a residence, and the Bronx Botanical Gardens and 23rd Street were period reconstructions built by Ferretti and his art department in the upstate town of Troy, New York. This is an example of exacting period detail, down to the pattern of the dinner plates, men's top hats, and flower arrangements. *The Age of Innocence* understands and captures the mood, atmosphere, pace, and culture of the time.

*The Conformist* (1971)—fascist Italy in the 1930s. Authentic period design is presented in an expressionistic, stylized manner. Production designer Ferdinando Scarfiotti used a distinctive Art Deco look to define the decadence of the characters and the times. The most arresting image is a room with light streaming through Venetian blinds, which was influenced by an Ernst Lubitch film that captured the attention of director Bernardo Bertolucci and of Scarfiotti. This became the signature image of *The Conformist* and inspired Paul Schrader to hire Scarfiotti and to recreate it in *American Gigolo* (1980).

*The Day of the Locust* (1975)—this film is a scathing exposé of the dark side of the Hollywood Dream Factory. Production designer Richard MacDonald recreates the Hollywood soundstage, sets, offices, and back lot of the 1930s. Based on the novella by Nathaniel West and directed by John Schlesinger, the production design captures the brutal power and excess of the studio chiefs, shattered dreams, and the idyllic community that surrounded the studios. The film's chaotic and devastating climax presents a realistic social class riot in front of a gala Hollywood premiere with the stylistic inventions of the Hollywood studio style. This expressionistic nightmare, seen through the eyes of a dissolute young man with visions of art, is a complex and emotionally wrenching sequence built on a sound stage.

*The Doors* (1991)—Oliver Stone's film about Jim Morrison becomes a study of the Los Angeles rock and Hippie scene in the 1960s. Concert venues are meticulously recreated; the Sunset Strip is brought back in time to when the burgeoning youth counterculture was transforming an America that had been dominated by the style and morality of "The Greatest Generation." One of the best examples of accurate hair, clothing, and pop culture style from the 1960s, designed by Barbara Ling.

*Glory* (1989)—the definitive pictorial creation of the Civil War. Production designer Norman Garwood did intensive research on the terrain, battlefields, and facilities. A group of men known as "recreators" were essential in achieving such authenticity. These men dress up in Civil War uniforms that are detailed with missing buttons, salt stains, and scuffed boots. They were not only consultants to the design team but also appeared on camera, on horseback as soldiers. Fort Wayne was built in exact detail; the construction took twelve weeks and the set was three hundred feet square. Dunker Church was built for the first sequence of the film in a 1930s railyard transformed into a Victorian railyard. The brickwork was so accurate to the historical original that every missing brick was actually missing.

*GoodFellas* (1990)—the Martin Scorsese film, designed by Kristi Zea, is one of the great contemporary gangster movies the covers the 1950s, 1960s, 1970s, and 1980s in the lives of mid-level mobsters. The accuracy of each era heightens the fact that the characters survive through the decades, rarely changing. The Ray Liotta character, based on the real life mob informant Henry Hill, does change; his character represents the drug culture of the 1980s and its impact on the mob.

*The Last Emperor* (1987)—China's Forbidden City, recreated in exacting detail and contrasted by the emperor's experiences in exile in Europe and in a prison camp, demonstrates how contrasting environments impact on the story and characters. The décor ranges from Ancient China to Art Deco in Europe, to the drab, gray, blue world of the Chinese political prison. Directed by Bernardo Bertolucci and designed by Ferdinando Scarfiotti.

*The Last Picture Show* (1971)—production designer Polly Platt took a town in West Texas and brought it back to the 1950s by changing façades, aging brick, and redecorating interiors. This black-and-white film directed by Peter Bogdanovich was the first contemporary film to de-romanticize the 1950s. The design strips the era of nostalgia and shows the desolation and barrenness of a town falling apart physical and morally.

*Malcolm X* (1992)—a masterful biopic directed by Spike Lee covering the scope of Malcolm X's life. Production designer Wynn Thomas had the challenge of creating a massive number of settings depicting Malcolm's childhood home, his coming-of age-years in Harlem, the headquarters of the Black Muslims, his pilgrimage to Mecca, and the climax in the Audubon Ballroom where the controversial civil rights leader was assassinated. A landmark look into a segment of African American culture and an epic recreation of American history.

*Tucker: The Man and his Dream* (1988)—a meticulous rendition of America in the 1940s. Director Francis Ford Coppola, producer George Lucas, and production designer Dean Tavoularis found a new way to represent the American dream on film by telling the true story of a maverick car inventor who defied the Detroit power-brokers. Director and producer put their own Tucker cars into the film and rounded up the remainder of existing models. The cars represent forties style, the domination of car culture in America, and a creation unseen by most Americans. The Tucker is a metaphor for American ingenuity and design as pop culture.

*The Wedding Singer* (1998)—the 1980s are a decade often presented as over-the-top in films, all big hair and outlandish colors. This sweet romantic comedy lovingly captures the style of the decade without parody. The environments are authentic and believable recreations that serve the story. Directed by Frank Coraci and designed by Perry Andelin Blake.

# Chapter 11

## GENRES

All screenwriters would like to think their original stories are just that, but over one hundred years of cinema history have demonstrated that film narratives can be codified into categories. Critics and theorists call these categories genres. The original genres created during the classic Hollywood studio era included the Western, melodrama, science fiction, the gangster film, the musical, the war film, comedy, horror, and fantasy. Over the course of the twentieth century, filmmaking subcategories and hybrids have appeared, including the screwball comedy, film noir, slasher, and biker films. Each genre has its own visual conventions that the production designer can support or subvert. The Western town has been depicted as historical, mythic, a thriving central area, or a run-down, desolate place. Study the genre of each film you screen for the visual components that comprise and interpret the genre conventions. Look for added visual elements innovated by designers to interpret and expand the story.

Essentially, the production designer is establishing period, time, and place, but establishing the genre is just as important. Audiences who are fans of a particular genre know and love the narrative and visual traditions of that genre and expect authenticity or discovery.

### Research

In addition to the specific research related to each individual project, the director, production designer, and director of photography should familiarize themselves with visual design principles of the genre and how they define the parameters of the cinematic storytelling's visual and narrative style.

What follow are some notes about the design conventions utilized in, and the type of research useful in creating, several popular genres.

## THE WESTERN

Westerns contain recurring geographical settings such as Texas, Montana, Oklahoma, and Colorado that narratively connect to the history of the era.

The physical environment of the Western is comprised of landscape, terrain, architecture of the Western town, and modes of transportation—the wagons, horses, stagecoaches, and steam-driven trains. Other aspects of the physical environment are the clothes and "props" of the inhabitants—handguns, rifles, holders, leather, felt, and spurs—and the Western bar where tough-drinking men gambled and confronted one another. The Western convention of pictorial composition features two-thirds blue sky and a lower third of brown, dusty dirt to capture the early days of America before development. The production designer works in this frame to create environments in big sky country that are vast, functional, and rarely intended to be permanent. Dirt roads and paths would later give way to blacktop.

For an understanding of the American West, read the work of James Fennimore Cooper. Read *The Ox Bow Incident* by Walter Van Tilberg Clark, and *Warlock* by Oakley Hall. Study the paintings of Frederic Remington, who visualized the old West in a prolific series of paintings that are an American archive of Western images.

Western films to study for a greater understanding of production design in this all-American genre include: *Bad Day at Black Rock* (1955), *High Noon* (1952), *My Darling Clementine* (1946), *Rio Bravo* (1959), *The Searchers* (1956) *Silverado* (1985), *Stagecoach* (1939), *3:10 to Yuma* (1957), and *The Wild Bunch* (1969).

*The Man Who Shot Liberty Valance* (1962)—this black-and-white Western was directed by John Ford, designed by Hal Pereira and Eddie Imazu. with set decoration by Sam Comer and Darrell Silvera. The story begins as the old West is becoming civilized (the vast majority of Westerns take place in an earlier time). This film makes the transition between the rugged old West and the societies of modern drama. The Shinbone wooden train station is a place where people who will settle and develop the burgeoning town arrive. Along with the train, horse-drawn carts have replaced the old stagecoach, houses now have porches and white picket fences—an image of an imminent suburban America. The town is bustling with new shops and a church. There are poles and cables that bring power to the town, a connection with the larger country around Shinbone.

There is a newspaper office and a funeral parlor, staples of most Westerns. But an old stagecoach, a relic of the past, is out of commission, covered with dirt and dust to remind the people of Shinbone how far they have come as they confront the age-old Western conflict of bad guys in black hats who want to destroy progress and tranquility.

Hank's Saloon has swinging short doors, a convention in all Westerns. There is a barbershop next door. Peter's Place is a restaurant where the townsfolk eat. It has a rough brick stone wall, the tables have checkerboard cloths. The kitchen has a wooden wall and stone walls. There is a chalkboard to keep track of free meals given to the Marshal. Half-sized swinging doors connect the dining room to the kitchen. The kitchen is more than just a functional space. While the staff prepares man-sized meals for their customers, they have conversations that develop the other characters and plot. This working space is an arena for discovery and understanding of the characters and their lives. In Westerns that take place in a less settled time, settlers eat simple meals cooked and eaten at home. Peter's Place is another connection with the modern world where public eateries are a gathering place for society to meet and develop their community.

The saloon and Peter's Place are on opposite corners to demonstrate the conflict between the old and new West. A makeshift schoolroom brings hope that education will bring civility and progress. The newspaper office becomes a space where political and social movements are made. The saloon becomes a meeting place for political change as the town's moral consciousness emerges.

John Ford uses these Western conventions for multinarrative purposes. The bar is a hard-drinking gambling establishment and a place for political change. The restaurant is a place to eat and a stage for confrontation and drama. The home of the John Wayne character is a home, a memory of the past, a symbol of power destroyed by a coward, and a remnant of the old America West—history and myth alike.

*Red River* (1948)—Howard Hawks directed this John Wayne star-vehicle. This Western begins in 1851 and covers a rancher's odyssey as he goes from St. Louis to California to settle into the cattle business and later moves the entire herd across the wilderness to Missouri for the price of twenty dollars a head. *Red River* represents a segment of the Western genre that is dedicated to the exploration of the wide-open spaces and the settlement of the old West. These films are largely shot on location in western states such as Colorado, California, and Montana. The principal challenge for the production designer is to find landscapes in a controlled area that can create the illusion of vast travel, without a lot of movement for the film company. For *Red River*, art director John Datu Arensma had to locate areas where wide camera shots could represent a progression of states as the story moved across the country. The wide shots of the troupe on horseback, covered wagons, and cattle as far as the camera eye can see must match with close-ups of individuals or small groups in dialogue scenes that are recreated under studio conditions. Nighttime campfire scenes filled with character development and plot exposition were designed and shot on the sound stage for artistic control, to avoid the natural weather elements. The settings had to be altered slightly each time because in the story every campfire was held at a different location during the long trip.

*Red River* utilized an effective narrative device created in the art department. Throughout the film, pages of a diary are shown full-screen in script written by hand in ink. These texts are a break from the constant movement of the company and the series of reflections and relationship developments revealed in the campfire sequences. This literary device is a historically correct form of documentation that reveals an inner-voice not reachable in the scenes of mass migration. The scenic artists or a member of the art department skilled in the art of handwriting would create the many pages of material provided by the screenwriter.

*The Outlaw Josey Wales* (1976)—Clint Eastwood stars in and directed this gritty, revisionist Western for his Malpaso Company. Production designer Tami Larsen, set decorator Chuck Pierce, and construction coordinator Al Littleken created Western towns that are not romantic or poetic as the ones pictured during the Hollywood studio era. The towns are still in progress, there are structures still going up, wooden studs and framing are bare. There are tents on the outskirts of town to indicate the builders are sleeping on the premises as they work. Nothing looks very permanent. The architecture is basic, utilizing unfinished wood and raw planking. Simple signs identify the business inside. A saloon is run down, in disrepair since the silver lode ran out. The wooden swinging doors are flayed and chipped. All the buildings' exteriors and interiors are dirty. Although they are new, the effects of the harsh weather have already taken its toll.

This revisionist approach is an attempt to capture the history of the real old West. The film takes place during the Civil War era and presents the dark side of everyone: Union soldiers, townspeople, Indians, and even the good guys. Eastwood is an anti-hero looking for revenge.

A great deal of the film was shot on location. The landscapes combines trees in bloom contrasted by those that are bare.

The texture of props, décor, architecture, and clothing is worn, dirty and lived-in. Eastwood portrays the West as a dangerous place constantly shifting, growing, and being destroyed by those without Christian morals. This and other Clint Eastwood Westerns set the tone for the genre in the 1980s and 1990s.

## THE GANGSTER FILM

Gangster films are urban crime dramas. They focus on the low end of a city—its back-alleys, ghettos, and desolate night streets where crime breeds. The genre depicts the underground society of criminals. The dramas take place in backrooms, the outskirts of town, private clubs, bars, houses of ill repute, after hour joints, and factories turned into the business of crime. The challenge of the production design is to reveal to the public what is in most lives off limits, the subculture of the gangster who lives a separate life from the honest working man. Criminals live and work among and around us.

Contrast is always an element in a gangster movie. Men rise out of humble beginnings to the top of the crime heap. In *Scarface* (1932) Tony Camonte, the Italian mobster portrayed by Paul Muni, comes from an immigrant background. His mother, dressed in peasant clothes, toils in the kitchen, the center of their modest family home, while her son lives the high life, obsessed with a view from a high-rise pad of an electric sign that proclaims, "The World Is Yours." After Tony is gunned down, the sign, more than a prop, becomes the final image and suggests that crime may look glamorous, but it doesn't pay.

The locations in a gangster film create anxiety. They are stripped of the safety of Main Street America. They are the fringes where criminals can operate out of the mainstream. The back alleys are not traveled by honest citizens and are largely unwatched by law enforcement. They provide an environment to stalk, to administer punishment, and to hide illegal activity.

The gangster genre uses dark alleys to communicate danger and trouble to the audience. These establish an atmosphere of fear and doom. Ghettos are locales that prove a haven for criminals and a place of business where they can take advantage of the disadvantaged. Desolate night streets represent the time and place when gangsters can run free to commit crimes. The honest citizens are home. Those out on the lonely, unwatched streets are either part of the criminal society or their prey. After-hour clubs, luxury apartments, and palatial homes are the playgrounds of the criminal element. These locations are decadent, always open and active. They are settings for the corruption of morals, drink, drugs, sex, and violence. They represent the prize enjoyed by shiftless criminals, while honest, hardworking "patsies" sleep.

Prisons are the price paid for the criminal lifestyle. In contrast to the extravagant dens of iniquity, they are large, bleak buildings with claustrophobic cells and steel bars that frame the criminal. The work areas are the scenes of a violent subculture. The bleak dining areas, with their long tables filled with tension, are a platform for communication, misery, and occasional violence. The exercise yard represents the outside, free world, but it is fenced in and surrounded by barbed wire and armed guards in high towers. It is a metaphor for the prisoner's longing to be free. Prisons are an inevitable reality in the life of a gangster, a place to survive, get educated in the way of crime life, and do penance for their criminal excesses.

The city in a gangster film can be specific—New York, Los Angeles, and Chicago are perennial settings—or a gangster film can be set in a mythic, generic urban area.

Gangster films to study include these notable examples: *The Big Heat* (1953), *Casino* (1995), *Gangs of New York* (2002), *The Godfather Part II* (1974), *Good-Fells* (1990), *Little Caesar* (1930), *The Roaring Twenties* (1939), and *Scarface* (1983).

*The Public Enemy* (1931) is a Warner Bros. gangster movie that launched James Cagney to stardom. The film starts in 1909 then travels to 1915, 1917, and 1920. The mood of the times is established first with the exterior of a brewing company; there are saloons on three corners, and people carry open buckets of beer.

The Red Oak Club has a brick exterior and in 1909 has a canopy bearing its name. When we see it again it is 1915, and there is no awning. There is a badly torn poster on the brick wall. These are hard and seedier times. Inside are saloon doors, pool tables, and a sign that reads "Don't Spit on the Floor." A petty gangster plays piano and lords over his young students in crime.

The Western Fur Trading factory is on a deserted street filled with expensive furs hanging on the walls. A speakeasy has an imposing door with a sliding panel, a convention in gangster films of the 1930s. A bar has a counter top with a wooden rail and a deep ridge close to the customer's edge. From the interior the backward word "Bar" can be seen in plain letters. There is a low rod holding a half curtain in the window.

In 1920, a family liquor store is abuzz with the public stocking up before prohibition sets in. This is a generic city: a gas truck reads GASOLINE, a warehouse is called U.S. BONDED WAREHOUSE, there are barrels of illegal beer hidden, and a florist truck is used by the bootleggers.

Cagney and his partner move up the crime ladder; they meet with others at a large, round table; he is dressed in gangster finery, a long coat and a sharp-brimmed fedora.

His family home is in stark contrast to the crime life. It is traditional, old-fashioned, with a credenza and homey furniture that represent the taste and humble status of his mother.

Cagney parties in a large, multileveled, elegant nightclub. He meets a flapper, played by Jean Harlow, who has a flat designed for her fast and superficial lifestyle. She has a white, porcelain sculpture, a divan, tall plants, and a view of the cityscape from her window that contrasts squalor with her decadent but high style.

A horse stable is upscale and represents the good life led by gangsters. A mob room has the obligatory round poker table. There is also an alley with a dirt floor that reminds us that these men live on the dark side of life.

A pawnshop, the stage for many a crooked transaction, is the scene of a holdup. Cagney is gunned down in front of the Western Chemical Company. It is night and raining hard. There is a stairway to an elevated train platform. Cagney collapses in the street and is brought to a hospital. The family is told he is coming home. In the last image the door is opened and he is dead, tied up like a mummy, and falls onto the living room floor of the loving family home. The contrast is devastating. The message inscribed at the end of the film is that the public enemy is not a man but a problem society must solve.

### THE PRISON FILM

The prison film is its own genre, unlike any other: Men and women incarcerated behind bars. Prisons are colorless blocks, uniform and confining—universes unto themselves cut off from the outside world. *Riot in Cell Block 11* (1954) and *Birdman of Alcatraz* (1962) are classics of the genre. Effective reinventions are in *The Shawshank Redemption* (1994) and *The Green Mile* (1999).

The main difference between the original prison genre film and later reinventions like *The Shawshank Redemption* and *The Green Mile* is that most older prison films were photographed in black-and-white for gritty realism, and the reinventions were shot in color to create mood and a sense of humanity. Most of the black-and-white prison films were shot on studio sets. Over the decades many prison films have been shot on location, either in shutdown facilities or in insolated areas in functioning prisons. Older hardcore prison films contain cells, cellblocks, work areas, a cafeteria, and the warden's office—grim, godless places. The reinventions and more modern prison films show the incarcerated population in television, game, and weight rooms. The reinventions use artistic license in color palette and design for dramatic objectives and to tell more complex stories than those of the stereotypes and archetypes from the original prison genre that began early in cinema history and came of age in the 1930s, 1940s, and 1950s.

### FILM NOIR

Films of the classic postwar film noir period were photographed in black-and-white. Scenes take place almost exclusively at night. The shades are down in the gangster's office, the lights are off. Ceiling fixtures are hung low. Floor lamps are less than five feet high. The visual style is related to German Expressionism. Oblique and vertical lines dominate in opposition to the horizontal line of the classic Hollywood Western. The interiors are filled with jagged light shapes: trapezoids, triangles, and vertical slits. Shadows, empty streets, rain, docks, piers, and alleyways prevail in this doom-laden genre.

Film noirs to investigate include: *The Big Combo* (1955), *Boomerang!* (1947), *Brute Force* (1947), *Call Northside 777* (1948), *The Glass Key* (1942), *The Killers* (1946), *Kiss Me Deadly* (1955), *Laura* (1944), *The Naked City* (1948), *The Set-Up* (1949), *T-Men* (1947), *They Live By Night* (1949), and *You Only Live Once* (1937).

In *Double Indemnity* (1944), an insurance agent is duped into murdering the husband of a femme fatale for her love and the payoff from a double indemnity clause he has deceptively engineered. This defining film noir was directed by Billy Wilder and designed by Hans Dreier, Hal Pereria, and set decorator Bertram Granger.

The locale is Los Angeles. The story is told in flashback and is anchored in the doomed protagonist's office. The flashback is a convention of many film noirs, platforms for how the characters have arrived at a place of dark destiny and hopelessness. There are custom file cabinets with many small drawers designed to store the many individual policy records. The agent has a desk with a banker's lamp, a customary ashtray (most everyone smokes in a film noir), and a Dictaphone that he uses to confess his crimes and supply the exposition throughout the narrative. The lighting by director of photography John Seitz is very high-key, more black and white than shades of gray.

The femme fatale lives in a spacious Spanish-style home with heavy door panels, an iron-railed staircase, and white stone arches. Venetian blinds throughout the film create long stabs of accusatory light everywhere.

A market where the couple has their clandestine meetings to plot the husband's murder has rows of shelves stacked to perfection with canned goods. The top pyramids of cans, as well as all the others, have their labels facing out. Precisely lined, the food enclosed in metal frames the doomed couple like a prison.

The interior of the insurance company is an impressive set that contributes to a subtext in the story. The floor space is huge to indicate the power and might of companies who collect money readily but dole it out very carefully. The set has two levels. The bottom level is filled with uniform desk setups where the employees do the detail work of the company. It is an open space with no privacy. The second level is a balcony that runs around the entire office. Here, the powerbrokers of the company can keep watch. The company brass is physically on top while the workers toil below. The managers have immediate access to their spacious offices and the birds-eye view of the operation.

Noir conventions in *Double Indemnity* include a revolving door, a barbershop, a cigar stand, and a forest area overlooking the lights of the City of Angels.

*Kiss of Death* (1947) is a Twentieth Century Fox film noir directed by Henry Hathaway, designed by Lyle Wheeler and Leland Fuller, proudly states in its opening that all scenes, interior and exterior were photographed in New York State at the actual locations associated with the story. This gives a firm sense of physical reality to this tale of a reformed prisoner who helps the authorities capture a psychopathic criminal, without sacrificing the artistic control production designers bring to a project. Realism is necessary for a film noir. The audience must believe this is an extension of their world; the designer and cinematographer can darken the emotional environment only once this is achieved.

The filmmakers staged scenes at the New York City Criminal Court Building and the assistant district attorney's office, inside Sing Sing prison, a church facility for children, restaurants, clubs, and New York apartments. The choice of locations, how they are presented on camera, the subtly of the set dressing to create character, and the high-key photography of Norbert Brodine give the film reality and drama. *Kiss of Death* was well ahead of its time in shooting on location (a process that wouldn't really flower until the early 1970s), while Hollywood was still building generic crime sets instead of capturing the grit of real, solid environments that contained history, character, and a sense of a life lived. The designer's role in this film was to arrange, rearrange, and add décor elements to give *Kiss of Death* its naturalistic distinction.

*The Maltese Falcon* (1931) is John Huston's directorial debut, designed by Robert Hass, is a studio creation that elevated the conventions of the private investigator mystery genre to a high art. The film takes place in San Francisco and the principal set is the office of the legendary Sam Spade, created by novelist Dashiell Hammett and portrayed by the equally legendary movie star, Humphrey Bogart.

Spade shares an office space with Archer, who is murdered at the beginning of the story. The office has a view of San Francisco. There are windows on both sides of Spade's desk. His credentials are framed on the wall. The front door is framed in heavy beaded glass so light can come through, but no one can see through the clouded surface. The name of the office is hand-lettered in black paint. This convention is consistent in all film noir's detective and gangster films from the 1930s to the 1950s.

In the corner of the office are black file cabinets and stacked up boxes of case papers. There is an overhead lamp, table clock, and curtains blowing from a partly opened window. A water cooler is standard décor, as is a door marked "Private." An outer office has a wooden rail and an art-directed view of the city. The private eye's office serves as his home as well. This location is inexorably linked to the genre and is the setting for meetings, confrontations, gunplay, romance, repartee, and the unraveling of a mystery.

## NEO-NOIR

Neo-noir is film noir in color. These films were made after the historic period and usually take place in a timeless present that echoes the forties and fifties.

See these neo-noir films: *Against All Odds* (1984), *At Close Range* (1986), *Basic Instinct* (1992), *Body Heat* (1981), *Blood Simple* (1984), *Death Wish* (1974), *Dirty Harry* (1972), *The Grifters* (1990), *Guncrazy* (1992), *The Last Seduction* (1994), *Mortal Thoughts* (1991), *Red Rock West* (1993), and *To Live and Die in L.A.* (1985).

*After Dark, My Sweet* (1990), directed by James Foley and designed by David Brisban, is a neo-noir. At first historians, theorists, and critics wouldn't accept noir in color or noir made after the initial Cold War period in which it was developed. The French named and codified film noir; it was not formulated consciously by the filmmakers. In the 1990s, filmmakers who admired and studied film noir began creating contemporary films, often timeless in narrative, then evolved the design style and adapted the use of color and texture to create the now popular subgenre known as neo-noir.

*After Dark, My Sweet* begins with a boxer in a ring. The reoccurring image is indicated with just the ropes of the ring and a black background. This may have been due to budgetary reasons, but the effect reaches back to the 1940s and 1950s of a man confronting another man in a dark, seedy arena. The image is in the mind of the protagonist who is about to meet a femme fatale and get sucked into a criminal vortex.

A bar has a blue and orange wall, the liquor bottles in a recessed wooden section, and a large stack of beer cases in the back. The window wall is green, the bar top light green.

The photographic style of the film is high key with a lot of contrast. There are dusty roads and tumbleweed everywhere. The femme fatale has diamond shaped windows on the white double doors to her home, an inviting entrance to her snare. The rooms connect to the bedroom. The walls are made of thin, slated wood; the headboard is also constructed out of wood. The protagonist lives in a run-down trailer across from her house.

The interior of the femme fatale's station wagon is orange. A young boy kidnapped as part of her plot wears an orange shirt. Color everywhere is saturated. A poolroom has a yellow wall and wood paneling. The overhead lamps have a large Budweiser Beer logo.

Orange and a contrasting deep, ultramarine blue substitute for the extreme light and dark that would be seen in a black-and-white film noir, but the color is not just stark, it's seductive, and the clash of hot and cool create an atmosphere of impending doom. The clothes, décor, architecture, and props are carefully chosen so they do not look like 1980s style. The dialogue and a few narrative clues convince us this is contemporary, but the style and the conventions of noir create the atmosphere achieved in the original genre. This is not retro style but a world that time has passed by. Neo-noir asserts that the motivations of criminals and those who seek adventure on the dark side never really change.

*The Hot Spot* (1990) is a defining neo-noir directed by Dennis Hopper and production designed by Cary White and John Frick with art director Michael Sullivan. The film appears to take place when it was released. The lead, Don Johnson, is dressed in his *Miami Vice*–style clothes. The light, textured fabrics and pastel colors did not exist in the 1940s or 1950s, although the behavior of the characters and the nature of the narrative are identical to film noirs of that time. A cocky, arrogant guy with no apparent roots comes into a desert town to take it by storm but is up against a femme fatale and constantly tempted by the moral corruption around him.

Many scenes take place in the bright of day, not in the constant night-world expected in the original noir conventions. The photography is high-key, and the color is full of depth, contrast, seduction, and doom.

It is Texas; there are telephone poles, a train station, a bar, and a strip club with no frills, featuring the obligatory dance pole. The main action takes place in a used car lot that symbolizes corruption, wheeling, and dealing. Old cars give the story the illusion of age; triangle strips of bright color plastic fly on strings. The salesman is the great American con man. The office is dark; there are a lot of fans to remind us how hot it is, physically and emotionally. Light cuts in through Venetian blinds, the classic convention that always achieves a sense of mystery, danger, and a netherworld away from the cleansing sunlight outside in its purity.

The mood is dark and seedy. The house of a repo suspect is littered with nude photographs. The town features Old West architecture. The bank exterior is brick; the interior is wooden framed partitions. There are decorated metal cages for the tellers.

A painted "Drink Coke" ad from decades past is a mural on a brick wall badly faded and chipped. The femme fatale is blond, dressed in a white, sleeveless blouse, red skirt, and white-framed sunglasses and rides in an open white convertible with a 1950s pink steering wheel.

The color palette of the film is pastel, beige, and clay colors. Johnson's room is sparse, bathed in a blue light from the street at night. The femme fatale's house has pink gathered drapes in the bedroom, a stained-glass wood framed door, wood paneled walls, light blue upper walls. The windows are topped by red-scalloped trim. An arch leads to the outside where colorful Chinese lanterns hang on trees. Inside, is a wooden slatted bar, lots of arches and stone walls. The pink drapes connect the woman's femininity to her steering wheel. There is a large, life-size, formerly ferocious stuffed bear linked to her husband, and a line of cuddly stuffed animals against balcony posts that represent the little girl in the woman.

The other woman in the story is a brunette. Her house has an ornate white fence and gate. She is seen in natural light, the other woman in blue or lavender gelled light.

*The Hot Spot* takes place in a small town, not the big city, but the web of doom in a noir comes from the desires of the characters, not just the environment. The locale becomes a den of sin. The morals of the characters designate their fate and physical space. The common shared areas are manipulated to illustrate and indicate that all is not all-American and apple pie here.

### HORROR

Classic horror films produced by Universal Studios featuring Frankenstein, Dracula, the Wolf Man, and the Mummy were set in environments influenced by the ravaged land of twentieth-century war-torn Europe and featured destroyed Gothic structures, castles, marshes, mad scientist's laboratories, haunted houses, and German Expressionist–influenced architecture and décor.

While horror films of the past are often set in a decrepit house or seedy part of town, contemporary horror films can take place in suburbia, the city—almost anywhere, and during any time of day. A "normal" environment can be the perfect place for a contemporary horror narrative, allowing the design to act in contrast to the horrific action and events.

Horror films, old and new, to study include: *The Amityville Horror* (1979), *Carrie* (1976), *Dracula* (1931), *The Exorcist* (1973), *The Fog* (1980), *Halloween* (1978), *The Hills Have Eyes* (1977), *The Last House on the Left* (1972), *Night of the Living Dead* (1968), *The Mummy* (1932), *The Omen* (1976), *Poltergeist* (1982), *The Texas Chainsaw Massacre* (1974), *Wolfen* (1981), and *The Wolf Man* (1941).

*Frankenstein* (1931) is one of the Universal horror films that set the standard for the horror genre and were the aesthetic template for hundreds of films throughout the decades. For *Frankenstein*, director James Whale and art director Charles D. Hall created an expressionistic environment that reflected and became a metaphor for the ravages of war. Twisted trees, rocky roads, and a graveyard with a tilted cross and a skeleton—a symbol of death—set the tone.

The film's Goldstadt Medical College has an amphitheater ringed with lights, charts of human anatomy, and large jars housing human brains. This genre often relates science with man's tampering with nature that results in a living horror.

Castle Frankenstein is high up on a hill. The interior is a towering space with thick, wooden beams, a large wooden table, stone walls, electrodes, an instrument panel, rough hewn stone steps, irregular sized stones, columns, chains, and a slatted wood floor. In the mad scientist laboratory, the lifeless body of the Frankenstein monster lies on a table, awaiting the life-giving jolt of electricity from the heavens.

In contrast, Baron Frankenstein, the father of the man who created human life run amok, lives in an elegant home with high narrow windows, large framed paintings on the walls, ribbed columns, paneled wooden walls, and recessed shelves.

The surrounding area has a courtyard with large scale Tudor houses. The film ends with images of mountains, a dark art-directed studio sky, a tall wooden windmill that is burned to the ground by angry townspeople who think they've killed the monster (don't think the device of leaving a plot open for the sequel began in the 1990s).

*A Nightmare on Elm Street* (1984) was directed by Wes Craven and designed by Greg Fonseca. This modern era horror film contrasts the everyday life and environments of the young characters with the nightmares they share, which enter an apparently real world.

A house is idyllic with a front yard. The interior has a Tiffany lamp, off-white drapes, flowers; it's very homey, with a patterned couch and a large overhanging porch.

The color palette is cool, without red, so that the bloody, gory scenes will provide a full shock treatment when the color is introduced. A teenage girl's bedroom becomes a house of horrors when she begins to climb the walls and deep open scratches appear on her body. Blood is everywhere.

The local high school is a generic suburban environment, but the basement is an underground nest of malice, with its old boiler and corroded pipes. The heroine's house has a basement with a similar visual theme, and it is there that the confrontation with the notorious Freddy Krueger occurs.

Wes Craven, a master of contemporary horror, understands that true terror can strike in bright daylight in a comfortable, seemingly secure space. The contrasting horror scenes have their roots in traditional genre elements that in the past were shown in a contrived total environment. Craven orchestrates the design to surprise and shock. After each scare the viewer is returned for just long enough to life as we know it—but not for too long.

## MUSICALS

The American musical is a celebration of the stage. The concept of characters breaking into song and dance frees the designer from realism and inspires expressionistic, artistic spectacles that are infused with fun, entertainment, and drama. The classic American film musical was a popular genre during the 1930s, 1940s, and 1950s. Backgrounds and settings were implied, impressionistic, and painted with a broad, lavish, and, at times, lurid brush. The design of a musical creates an environment that visually expresses and supports the story while functioning as a space for elaborate performances. Imaginative, decorative, and filled with exuberance, the musical can take place in a faux New York, or Los Angeles, a stage filled with ascending platforms, rows of white pianos, an elegant ballroom, or a period setting more grand and illusionary than its realistic counterpart in a dramatic film.

All films that have extensive music numbers or use music and lyrics as a narrative device are classified as the musical genre. There is a qualitative difference between the classic Busby Berkeley musicals that were light on character and plot and filled with imaginative large-scale production numbers that reveled in artifice, and later musicals such as *Fame* that take place in naturalistic environments. The style of having musical numbers bursting into the narrative occurs in all musicals, but as far as production design is concerned, whether the treatment is realistic or fantastic demands a different visual approach. Designers who have worked on Broadway stage musicals have a good understanding of the nonrealistic musical. Those without this design experience will need to research and study the style on stage and in film. Realistic musicals are similar in approach to nonmusical films, but often they are visually stylized to support the narrative and musical concepts.

Since the 1960s we have seen the death and rebirth of the genre. Musicals can take place anywhere—the stylized Berlin of *Cabaret* (1972), the realistic rock and sand formations of *Jesus Christ Superstar* (1973), the New York streets from the original *Hair* (1979), the bare stage of *A Chorus Line* (1985) shot in a real location, slightly augmented for the camera, or the glitzy, sleazy nightlife of *Showgirls* (1995) and *Coyote Ugly* (2000), two films that take place in real places that are exaggerated and romanticized for commercial consumption.

The musical is a genre that has often been reinvented. *Brigadoon* (1954) is a classical American stage musical that was adapted to the screen. When Hollywood filmed a stage musical, they would attempt to open it up, expand the locations and the limitations of the stage, but the production design style often retained the theatrical artifice of the stage. *42nd Street* (1933) was originally a movie musical, which was later successfully adapted to the Broadway stage—twice. Lloyd Bacon and Busby Berkely combined realism for the backstage story with elaborate, stagy song and dance numbers that are the musical within the film. The Hollywood musical reigned from the 1930s into the early 1960s. In the 1970s, a new musical form arrived. *Saturday Night Fever* (1977) celebrated the beginning of the disco era. The film does not have any dramatic scenes expressed by the characters in song, as in classic movie musicals such as *Showboat* (1951), *Oklahoma!* (1955), or *My Fair Lady* (1964). A painted sky on a cyclorama in the dance numbers for *Oklahoma!* sets the perfect balance between artificiality and realism, bringing the classic stage musical to the screen without losing its theatrical heart and soul. The dance numbers in *Saturday Night Fever* are used to show the nightlife and desires of the characters and are scored with songs by the Bee Gees and contemporary disco musical artists. *Fame* (1980) is about a high school for the performing arts. Here the production numbers express the talents and emotions of the characters. Songs performed by two cast members are presented as song performances rather than people breaking into song in the classic musical convention, but the purpose is the same. These songs express narrative and character elements and allow the performers to directly express themselves to the audience in musical form rather than in dramatic dialogue in a scene structure. *The Wiz* (1978), a contemporary musical take on *The Wizard of Oz*, was taken from the stage to the New York City Streets with theatrical license. *All That Jazz* (1979), Bob Fosse's autobiographical film, is presented in combination of Broadway glitzy, gritty realism, and Fellini-esque fantasy. There are production numbers interwoven in the dramatic narrative structure that express the life, work, and fantasies of the main character Joe Gideon. *Showgirls* and *Coyote Ugly* use music and dance as entertainment and erotic titillation, not for narrative purpose. *Moulin Rouge* (2001) is an original period musical that uses the classic convention of having the characters expresses themselves and the narrative in song. The music consists of love songs that were written long after the film's time frame, creating an alternate universe where the past and future come together.

## SCIENCE FICTION

Futuristic worlds, planetary exploration, other solar systems, and space vehicles are some of the conventions expected in this genre. Science meets fantasy, humans encounter extraterrestrials, giant ants, blobs, and pods inhabit. High or low-tech science fiction films defy reality; imagine the future; and free the imaginations of designers, special visual effect teams, and makeup artists to take us to a planet of apes, a galaxy far away, long ago, or to the depths of the ocean. Screenings should include: *Blade Runner* (1982), *The Matrix* (1999), *Star Wars* (1977), *Things to Come* (1936), and *2001: A Space Odyssey* (1968).

*Invasion of the Body Snatchers* (1956) is a classic low-budget black-and-white film, directed by Don Siegel and designed by Ted Haworth, is deceptively simple and powerful in impact. An alien society plans to take over the world by making identical copies of human bodies in pods that take over when the victim falls asleep. The pod person looks just like the real thing, but has no emotions and plots with the others to turn society into beings without human feelings. The metaphor of a less humane population growing as the Cold War progressed during the 1950s succeeds here, because the film's design of the average U.S. town looks so normal and typical of the era. It makes the narrative and the various transformations even more terrifying than if the design were deliberately spooky. This had a great influence on the resurgence of horror films in the 1970s, 1980s, and 1990s that relied on horror coming to everyday life. The challenge of *Invasion of the Body Snatchers* was designing the pods and executing the chilling special effects. Production designer Ted Haworth conceived the idea at a companion's home. Haworth was taken by a pair of drapes with an autumn motif illustrated by a skeleton of leaves. "I went home that night, and I made the first pod," Haworth remembers. "My wife had just had a baby, and I wanted to give the whole impression of a baby being born, so this slithering image came out, and the foam kept pouring out. It was a combination of looking at that curtain, a bubble bath, and the idea of doing it without special effects." Haworth sculpted the pod shapes using hairpins shaped as webs and then applied a texturing compound to form the pod and colored it like an autumn leaf. Haworth designed and built a greenhouse on the sound stage. The roof was slatted so moonlight could create a creepy atmosphere. All the actors were cast in a dental plaster so a perfect head-to-toe representation of each actor was available. On cue, the pods would foam and create the illusion of life being replicated

*Alien* (1979)—this Twentieth Century Fox film, directed by Ridley Scott, launched a successful franchise and brought a microdetailed industrial look to the interior of space vehicles. The design was conceived through the influence of graphic artist H. R. Giger who is credited with "Alien Design." Production designer Michael Seymour, and art directors Les Dilley and Roger Christian, worked with Giger's sketches and elaborated his concepts throughout the complex, crowded, and detailed environment. Director of photography Derek Vanlint supplied the atmospheric smoky light and an effective use of colored gels to transform the color of the design materials. The ship's interior is designed with contrasting and connecting textures and architectural elements. A multisectioned unit with clear covers that flip up hold the crew in hibernation. When the chambers open, the flaps create a butterfly metaphor that visually supports the story as the crew wakes up after a long sleep during the long space voyage.

Snake-like, coiled pipes line a wall. Mayan relief patterns of oblong and square shapes texture other walls. There are computers with many graphic patterns on the screens. The main computer communicates with the crew by a series of text messages that help drive the narrative. The interior of the ship looks funky, functioning, and lived-in. There are long passageways. Every shot is busy with design and operative elements. A reptilian nature to the design links with the Alien and its many forms, which slowly kills off every member of the crew but for one survivor. The Alien has a long snake-like head, large pointed teeth, tentacles, and cold marble-like eyes, and it slobbers with goo, saliva, and remnants of the victims it's ingested. The ship is a labyrinth of rooms, pipes, toggle switches, monitors, and images that recall factories of the industrial revolution. A metal camera iris consisting of connecting sections that fan open and closed controls a tunnel. The juxtaposition of high-tech and low-tech environment creates a spooky, flying factory of terror where the ever-evolving Alien relentlessly stalks human life.

### THE WAR FILM

Battlefields, ravaged cities, jungles, beaches, air, sea and land combat, tanks, helicopters, airplanes, and a cache of weapons are the settings of the war film. Also military bases, barracks, trenches, rubble, ruin and destruction of property and human life etch the imagery of war upon the screen. The conflicts may change from the Civil War to World Wars I and II, then Korea or Vietnam, but the grim reality of the antiwar film or the patriotic fervor of a John Wayne glory brigade rely on historical research and recreation of a time and place where freedoms are won and lost, and blood is spilled. War films are a genre that requires the assistance of the military for arms, equipment, and scholarship.

The principal difference in the production design of the antiwar and patriotic war film is the creation of the battlefield. Antiwar films tend to emphasize the enormous destruction war brings to cities and the landscape. The battlefields are strewn with debris, rubble, and a massive loss of life. The patriotic war films tend to make the battlefields more generic, less specific, and less futile. A sense of period and geographical place can take a backseat to the heroics of the good guys. Some are detailed and historically accurate but don't emphasize loss, hardship, and the confusion of war.

War films from past and present to study include: *All Quiet on the Western Front* (1930), *Apocalypse Now* (1979), *The Bridge on the River Kwai* (1957), *The Dirty Dozen* (1967), *Full Metal Jacket* (1987), *Hell Is for Heroes* (1962), *The Longest Day* (1962), *Paths of Glory* (1957), *Platoon* (1986), *Pork Chop Hill* (1959), *The Red Badge of Courage* (1951), *Sands of Iwo Jima* (1949), and *Saving Private Ryan* (1998).

With *Bataan* (1943), art director Cedric Gibbons, his associate Lyle Wheeler, and set decorator Edwin B. Willis created a believable World War II Philippine battlefield in the studio with documentary detail. There are village homes, roads, military vehicles, and a barrage of explosions and debris. The Americans blow up a bridge in stages until they render it impassible. The foliage is dense and accurate for the region. The uniforms are authentic and aged with dirt and bloodstains in this black-and-white film. The audience sees the soldiers hack through indigenous plant life. Weapons are period accurate, rifles and machine guns on turrets—part of the arsenal. There is a downed plane, shovels, and camouflage nets on helmets. There is always the indication of a sky above, and in several scenes, a low, white, milky fog covers the ground. The production design of *Bataan* provides an environment for a story that recreates the brutal experience of war.

*Tora! Tora! Tora!* (1970)—this epic war film, which required cooperation from the governments of the United States and Japan, recreates Pearl Harbor on December 7, 1941, in documentary detail and narrative tone, unlike the Jerry Bruckheimer–produced *Pearl Harbor* (2001), in which the attack serves as a backdrop for a love triangle and ends with a patriotic action scene so that the film could have a "happy" ending.

*Tora! Tora! Tora!* is a huge production that employed three Japanese cinematographers and four art directors, including Richard Day and Jack Martin Smith, and two set decorators. The sets include many military and governmental offices on both sides. Actual U.S. and Japanese naval ships were used and mock-ups were created of selected sections. The production also had a fleet of planes to bring realism to the attack recreation. Explosions were created the old-fashioned way—without computer wizardry. The Hollywood aesthetic convention here is that all of the offices look like sets. They are not aged, don't look lived-in, and are sparsely decorated. We see just enough to identify the purpose of the room. The Japanese offices are done in old-world wood trim and have a miniature pagoda or a piece of Japanese ceramic. A German office has a huge Nazi flag and leather chairs. The American offices have light blue walls and a no-nonsense sense of style—they are all work, with no extras. The exterior design includes hangars, barracks, piles of sandbags, and heavy artillery. The design suits the documentary approach but has not aged well since its release in

1970. There is little sense of connection between interiors and exteriors as the story constantly shifts back and forth. *Tora! Tora! Tora!*—whose Japan-set sequences were originally to have been directed by the great Akira Kurosawa—was directed by Richard Fleischer, a Hollywood professional who maintained an art direction tradition that was about to be radically changed over the remainder of the decade.

## SUBVERTING GENRES

During the studio era, Hollywood produced genre films that largely stuck to the rules and conventions. Since the 1960s, filmmakers have created variations on the standard genres, subgenres, and even some new ones evolved from others.

A production designer creates out of narrative, character, and the director's intent. There are parameters the designer must accept and deal with—time, place, and the like—but these are all filtered by artistic intent and artistic license. It is essential for the production designer to understand the pictorial elements that make up each genre. These visual elements identify and define the nature and genre of the story. Many contemporary films are made up of two or more genres.

Stanley Kubrick and Robert Altman are both filmmakers who took artistic pleasure in subverting genres. Kubrick's *Full Metal Jacket* (1987) takes place in two historically correct locations rarely seen in Vietnam War film. The first section of the film is an exact recreation of a Marine training facility. The pristine set by Anton Furst, which includes sterile, uniformed barracks and meticulously manicured grounds, contrasts with the outrageous behavior of the characters, as boys transform into men and then into killing machines. Vietnam films historically take place in the jungle, but the second section of *Full Metal Jacket* takes place in the city of Hue, built on location in England to specification of the actual battle area. The destroyed city is filled with rubble and destruction and is the site of a female sniper whose very presence and death symbolized the immorality of the Vietnam War. The city location goes against audience perception of Vietnam while showing another dimension of America's inability to understand its perceived enemy. When Kubrick took on the horror genre with *The Shining* (1980), he turned the haunted house convention into an exploration of familial drama and writer's block turned into psychosis.

Robert Altman directed *McCabe and Mrs. Miller* (1971), a Western set in a mining town where a gambler and prostitute join in a business enterprise, only to be stopped by the corporate power of the time. The monochromatic palette, the dusky cinematography, and the distressed wooden environment present an unromantic view of the old West.

Both Altman and Kubrick reinvented film noir: Kubrick with the existential *The Killing* (1956) that uses space to put the characters into a universe that dwarfs them, and Altman in *The Long Goodbye* (1973). Altman transposed Raymond Chandler's private eye Marlowe from the 1940s and 1950s to 1970s L.A. for a culture shock.

### Genre Is Storytelling

Although some designers are known for mastery in a particular genre—for example, Henry Bumstead has designed many superior Westerns—production designers should ideally obtain the skills to design any project. Genre is the framework of narrative. Be aware of conventions, but remember that production design is a physical representation of a particular story, and it must be convincing to serve *that* story and those particular characters.

## Genre Exercises

- Design a genre film in sketches and notes. First try to work in the classical form of the genre, then deconstruct your ideas to expand the original conventions.
- Keep a genre diary. Make notes about each film you see. What's the genre? What are the conventions? What are the exceptions? Many current films are constructed of a combination of genres. How do the conventions work together? What mood and atmosphere do the combinations create?
- See a Broadway stage musical. Read a Western novel. Watch a true-crime film. Screen a war documentary.

# Chapter 12

## BUDGET AND SCHEDULING

Having an idea is the first stage in making a film. Then the concept is shaped into a narrative and written up as a screenplay, the working plan for the cinematic story. After revisions and many drafts, a shooting script is prepared. This is the version used as a blueprint for the development of the physical production. Then the planning of the production takes place. This phase, pre-production, is crucial in visualizing the film and preparing the production design.

During pre-production, the production designer must move through several distinct phases and tasks, including storyboarding, budgeting, design, and construction of the sets. The triumvirate—director, director of photography, and production designer—are occupied with the creation of the look of the film.

### Budgeting

The key to financial control of the project is the establishment of a line budget that covers all aspects of the production design. A detailed budget is drawn up so each department will be fully supported and the producer can monitor where and how the money is being spent. The following line budget items for the art department can be applied to all films. On a low-budget production these jobs can be combined into the responsibilities of a few, which will cut back on salary expenses. Research, negotiate, and budget each of the following items applicable to your movie.

The production designer is responsible to the producer for the budget allocated to the art department. Producers often don't understand what's necessary to create and build the design in terms of crew, materials, and construction costs. Production designers have different approaches in dealing with producers.

Production designer Kristi Zea likes to take an aggressive approach: "Most of the time I'll say, 'Don't tell me what you have in the budget. I'll tell you what I think it's going to cost, and then we'll go from there.'" Zea's philosophy is this: If a firm number for the production design budget is given to her at the outset, the producer will assume the design can be done for that price. Zea's approach is to first find all of the locations and determine, based on the demands of the script, what is involved. She then submits a budget. If she is told the number is way above what is available she will work with them, cutting back until the production design budget is within the means of the company. Working up front in this manner, Zea feels, puts less pressure on the designer and the art department. The production can follow her expenses as she stays on budget without worrying. This allows Zea to do what she does best and is hired for—to design movies. Production designer Bruno Rubeo feels that producers and production managers do not understand the budget needed for the art department to function properly, "Art direction is an area that is not clearly understood by money people," he says. "The politics are half the battle." Rubeo sees the role of the production designer as administrator and artist. He finds the money people in the film business are only concerned with the bottom line, always willing to cut the production design budget regardless of whether it damages the project artistically. The director trusts the designer, but the keepers of the budget may not. Rubeo believes trust is significant. The producer must have confidence that the designer will do what is artistically best for the film within the budget considerations. Fiscal matters are also the concern and responsibility of the production design. The designer consults with the art director, the construction coordination, and the set decorator to understand what each scene will cost. If aspects of the design are impossible to accomplish given the budget, the designer is responsible for reporting the situation to the director.

### Projecting the Production Design Budget

The following must be computed to determine the art department budget:

- Production designer—salary, per diem expenses, transportation, meals, housing.
- Art department operating costs.
- Art director—salary, per diem, etc.
- Assistants to production designer and/or art director—determine whether assistants are necessary and what their deals will be. If you are a filmmaker, producer, production manager, or if you are a production designer working on a low budget film with a small crew and you have fiscal responsibility over the art department, remember that any and all deals can be negotiated as deferred payments. This means the production doesn't have to pay out until the film is completed. If you can negotiate points of the film, rather than a cash payment, money only goes out when the film is sold and has broken even from its initial cost.
- Set designers: how many are needed? What are their salaries and expenses?
- Illustrators: how many? Will they work freelance per drawing or on staff?
- Production assistants: How many are needed for the art department? PA's are paid at the standard daily rate the production pays out.
- Purchases: A detailed accounting of all items purchased for the art department.
- Rentals: A detailed accounting of all equipment, supplies, materials, and facilities.
- Miscellaneous Expenses: Always build in a contingency for Murphy's Law.

## SET CONSTRUCTION
- Construction coordinator: salary, expenses.
- Labor costs, salaries for carpenters and construction crew. Will the crew be getting union or nonunion wages?
- Loss and damage: in every construction project there are unexpected and unwanted mistakes and accidents that must be absorbed by the budget.
- Set striking: salaries, fees, and carting costs paid out for the set to be taken down after the filming is complete.
- Set restoration: materials and equipment fees to restore a location or set.
- Fees to store sets if necessary.
- Purchase of materials: the cost of lumber, nails, etc.
- Greens purchase: cost of plants, sod, and other landscaping materials.
- Platforms: cost of building, buying, or renting platforms for building sets.
- Miscellaneous.

## SET DRESSING
- Salaries for the set decorator, lead man, and/or buyer
- Labor and material costs to install carpet and drapery
- Labor and material costs to create and manufacture décor items
- Fixtures: cost for practical lighting, lamps
- Rentals: cost for rental of décor items
- Miscellaneous

## PROPS
- Property master and assistant salaries
- Loss and damage expenses
- Labor and materials cost, for manufacturing props
- Miscellaneous

## WARDROBE
- Costume designer and dresser salaries
- Cleaning and fabric dying costs
- Loss and damage
- Manufacturing: labor, materials costs
- Purchase of costumes/clothes
- Rental of costumes/clothes
- Miscellaneous

## MAKEUP AND HAIRDRESSING
- Makeup and hairstylists salaries
- Makeup and hairdressing supplies
- Wig purchases/rentals
- Prosthetic makeup appliances
- Miscellaneous

## LOCATIONS

- Location fees and rentals
- Police/firemen/security
- Travel fares
- Hotel costs
- Living expenses
- Mileage and parking
- Location restoration
- Purchases
- Rentals
- Phone/postage/delivery services
- Miscellaneous

## FACILITIES EXPENSES

- Stage rentals
- Back lot rentals
- Parking
- Telephone
- Postage/messengers/delivery services
- Miscellaneous

## Scheduling

The production designer works closely with the production manager who is in charge of planning and supervising the shooting schedule. All planning and scheduling in the art department is predicated on the shooting schedule. Create a scheduling board that details all art department deadlines. Back-time all dates to determine when to begin each step. Maintain daily communication with the production manager.

## Budgeting Tips

- Plan a realistic budget. Err on the high rather than the low end to avoid surprises and disasters that would delay, halt, or (heaven forbid) shut down the production.
- Keep a file on prices for vendors and services.
- Practice budgeting by drawing one up based on a feature film you have seen. Study the tape or DVD and make a line budget of what you determine were the resources necessary for the production design.
- During production, keep checking and revising production design budget as necessary.
- Be creative. Tap all of your natural and personal resources for what is needed to mount the production design. Call in all of your chips. Get friends involved. Go over all the skills, objects, materials, equipment, and locations they have access to.
- Network—bring in who you know to shrink the budget and enrich the production design.

"analyze that" Calender

S.H. = Sobel House set
U.S.A.O. = U.S. Attorney Office
I.D.E. = International Diamond Exchange
SS–Sing Sing Prison

## April

### Shoot 1

| | Monday | Tuesday | Wedensday | Thursday | Friday |
|---|---|---|---|---|---|
| Shoot: | | | START SHOOT / I/E Car Dealership / Int'l. Diamond Exchange (D) | Int. Morretti's Steak Hse (N) | Int. U.S.Atty.Office (D) / I/E F.B.I. Car, T.S., W.W.F. |
| Rig-Grips | S.H., U.S.A.O. | S.H., U.S.A.O. | S.H. | S.H. | |
| Set Dec. | | | | | |
| Paint | | | | | |
| Const. | Shop | I.D.E., install display cases | I.D.E., install safe | Shop | Shop |

### Shoot 2

| | Monday | Tuesday | Wedensday | Thursday | Friday |
|---|---|---|---|---|---|
| Shoot: | I/E Ben's Car (D) / Ext. Sing Sing Prison (D) | Int. Memorial Chapel (D) | Int. Sobel House (D) | Int. Sobel House (D/N) / Foyer, Master Bedroom | Int. Sobel House (N): / Hallway, Michael's Room |
| Rig-Grips | | | | Sing Sing Prison Mess Hall | Sing Sing Prison Mess Hall |
| Set Dec. | | | | | |
| Paint | | | | SS Mess Hall | SS Mess Hall |
| Const. | Shop | | Shop | | |

### Shoot 3

| | Monday | Tuesday | Wedensday | Thursday | Friday |
|---|---|---|---|---|---|
| Shoot: | I/E Sobel House (D): / Guest Room | Int. Sobel House (N): / Kitchen, Family Room | Int. Sobel House (N): / Hallway, Guestroom / Living Room | Ext. Sobel House (D): | I/E Sobel House (N): / Sobel's Office Dream (part) / F.B.I. Car |
| Rig-Grips | Sing Sing Prison Mess Hall | Sing Sing Prison Mess Hall | Sing Sing | SS | SS |
| Set Dec. | Sing Sing Prison Mess Hall | SS Mess Hall | Sing Sing Padded Cell | Sing Sing Padded Cell | SS Vitti's Cell |
| Paint | Sing Sing Prison Mess Hall | SS Mess Hall | SS Mess Hall | Sing Sing | Sing Sing |
| Const. | | | Shop | Shop | Shop |

### Shoot 4

| | Monday | Tuesday | Wedensday | Thursday | Friday |
|---|---|---|---|---|---|
| Shoot: | Ext. Sobel House (D): | Int. Sobel House (D): / Dining Room | Int. Rigazzi (D) / Ext. NoGo (N) | Int. NoGo (N) | Int. NoGo (N) |
| Rig-Grips | SS Detail | NoGo Restaurant/Sing Sing / NoGo/Sing Sing | NoGo/Sing Sing | SS Detail | SS Detail |
| Set Dec. | | NoGo/Sing Sing | NoGo/Sing Sing | SS Detail | |
| Paint | | NoGo/Sing Sing | NoGo/Sing Sing | SS Detail | |
| Const. | Shop | | | | Shop |

### Shoot 5

| | Monday | Tuesday | Wedensday | Thursday | Friday |
|---|---|---|---|---|---|
| Shoot: | Int. Sing Sing (N) / Rec. Room, Cell Block / Vitti's Cell | Int. Sing Sing (D) / Mess Hall, Pay Phone | | | |
| Rig-Grips | | | | | |
| Set Dec. | | | | | |
| Paint | | | | | |
| Const. | Shop | Shop | | | |

Production design calendar for *Analyze That*, courtesy Wynn Thomas, Warner Bros., Baltimore Spring Creek Productions, and Tribeca Productions.

# Chapter 13

## WORKING IN THE STUDIO

Shooting under studio conditions gives filmmakers optimum control over the production of their projects. Sets can be constructed and shooting can take place without weather interruptions, crowds, and other distractions.

During the classic Hollywood studio era, each company—MGM, Columbia, Paramount, Universal, and Warner Bros.—maintained fully equipped art departments containing carpentry shops, prop rooms, and costume rooms that could support any genre and any size production.

For the contemporary filmmaker, there are fully equipped studios in Hollywood and New York City that independent filmmakers can rent for their productions, but not all low-budget filmmakers have the finances to shoot in a studio. Fortunately, studio shooting has become redefined over the last twenty years. Any large commercial interior space can be turned into a studio. Filmmakers have shot in unused factories, empty schoolrooms, community centers, garages, and barns and have converted almost any open interior space into a movie studio. Electricity and water are essential. Additional expenses could be air conditioning or heating. If the power is not sufficient, a generator must be rented. The filmmakers rent, lease, buy, or borrow the space and transform it into a working movie studio. At a minimum, you will have to set up the space with the following:

- An area to construct **standing sets**
- Overhead rigging for lights
- Junction boxes with plenty of cable
- An area to prepare and serve food
- A substantial support crew to maintain the facility
- Security
- Transportation to and from the set
- An art department area set up with supplies to create drawings
- Shipping and receiving access to get supplies in and out

When a film company is working in a studio, the production designer is responsible for setting up the art department and getting the sets ready for the first day of shooting. The pre-production process for studio production is the same as location work. The schedule must be planned day by day and back-timed so that the art department will be ready for the first day of shooting and can proceed with other sets to be ready, as needed, according to the schedule. While location work requires alteration, possibly some construction, and mostly set decoration and painting, designing and building a set from scratch on the studio floor is a major construction undertaking, so building hours must be determined accurately by consulting and working carefully with the construction coordinator.

The advantage in studio work is the crew will not be interrupted by inclement weather or the many conditions that come from working in a space where you don't have total control. When you rent a studio for a particular period of time, it is yours to work in.

A well-planned design and construction period should stay on schedule with some supervision. More crew can be put on if work falls behind or the schedule of what sets are shot when can be changed in consultation with the production manager.

If you are working in a space that has been converted into a studio, you can build the set and shoot it in the same place. If the production is renting studio space to shoot the film, it may be necessary to construct the set at a workshop and transport it to the studio when it is ready.

Remember this:

- A fully equipped workshop space must be available
- The construction schedule must be structured to coordinate with availability to the stage
- Stable sets must be built, so that components can be transported easily and later stored if the production chooses
- The set must be constructed so it is completely safe for the actors and production crew

The art department must get the exact dimensions of the studio and report to the director whether the facility space is adequate for the production designer's plans and for the manner in which the film will be photographed and produced. When selecting a studio space, check to make sure there is enough distance from the floor to the underside of the photographic lights hanging from the grid. The top of the set should be at least two feet or more away from the lighting equipment to avoid fire hazards. The dimensions of the studio will dictate how the space should be used and how the sets should be built.

## Advantages of Shooting in the Studio

Control is the principal advantage of shooting a film in the studio. What can be accomplished in the production design is limited only by the budget and skills of the art department. A fair-sized studio allows the filmmaker to work continuously. There are no company moves to make as there are in working on location. It is always day or night in the studio. Power is readily available, as is space for the art department to set up shop. Over the decades, studio construction and decorating techniques have made great strides. Many studio sets in contemporary films look as authentic as location work. In the 1970s, filmmakers left the studio for the real world on location. They are still doing just that in the new millennium but with the art and craft of studio production design they can now have it all inside and on the sound stage.

## Safety Procedures

- All exits and lanes must always be kept clear to avoid accidents, maintain easy mobility, and as an escape route in the event of fire
- Walkover boards should be put over all cables so the cast and crew won't trip over them
- Secure and brace all flats and scenery
- Keep all structures and materials away from the lighting instruments to avoid a fire
- Spray all sets and materials with flame retardant
- Build security handrails onto all offstage platforms and steps
- Check all materials carefully and avoid those considered to be hazardous

## The Grid

The grid is a honeycombed framework at the top of a studio, also known as the **flies,** that overlooks the staging area. Catwalks are walkways that allow the crew to move about the grid, which contains the hoisting, **rigging,** and lighting equipment.

Scenery and sets can be raised from the grid utilizing several different methods:

- Wheeled carriages from overhead beams
- Chain tackle
- A pulley system
- Rope
- Motor-driven hoists

The walls in a commercial studio are marked with footage indicated at regular horizontal intervals from one end of a wall to the other. If you are working in a makeshift studio, the walls should be marked for footage counts so that design elements can be identified by number.

The studio plans, elevations, and working drawings are assessed by the construction crew before the set is built, and all measurements and materials are checked before proceeding. Any problems or questions are put to the production designer and resolved before construction begins.

## Workshops and Tools of the Art Department

Often, the conditions under which low-budget film sets are built are far from ideal. Understanding what is required is helpful in innovating and improvising production design methods, based on the budget and the availability of materials to the production company.

The construction shop is made up of areas for storage of materials and tools, woodworking, framing of flats, assembly, and painting. Paint bins and cabinets for hardware and brushes should be stored near the painting area, which also requires an operational industrial sink. Lumber racks and tools should be stored near the woodworking shop. Space is needed for power tools, drill presses, table saws, and workbenches for carpentry.

The property shop is an area where all props to be constructed are designed, built, finished, and stored. An area away from the woodworking and painting shops should be designated for props. If the prop shop is too close to where the crew is painting and engaging in carpentry, specks of paint and chips of wood can impede and damage prop work.

All work areas should be well lit for aesthetic and safety reasons. The crew must see the colors and textures under optimum lighting conditions. Working with construction tools requires a clean, bright working space to avoid accidents. Power outlets should be plentiful and conveniently available. A large assembly staging area is needed to frame flats and to put the set together.

The majority of tools and equipment needed to build a set concern woodworking. They include measuring and marking tools, a selection of saws, and pairing tools. Power tools such as power saws, a sander, and a router are necessary, as are boring tools and a large selection of drill bits. Sets are constructed of wood and metal, so wood-joining tools such as hammers, wrenches, staple guns, and screwdrivers should be on hand. A vise, pipe cutter, and threader is needed for metal work. A welding setup is recommended should consist of oxygen and acetylene tanks, and welding attachments and nozzles. Construction materials include lumber, metal, and conduit pipe. Duck canvas and muslin are used to cover wooden-framed flats. A large selection of nails, screws, bolts, and washers are essential.

### Flats

Flats are framed units used to form walls, rooms, and other design structures. Framed and cross-braced out of wood, flats can be covered with canvas or burlap and treated with sizing so they can be painted, or they can be covered with prepared board or plywood that has been sized. Flats covered with fabric are easy to work with but are not as effective as hard surface flats in their ability to look like real walls or to support wall hangings. Soft flats are effective for painted or photo backings positioned outside of windows. If the set will have a ceiling, it is recommended that it be built out of flats covered with soft materials like canvas or fabric. Flats can be connected together, called a run, to create walls or stand-alone elements of a set. All flats should be treated with fire retardant for safety.

If the production design budget can't afford to build flats and is working in a rented studio, the facility may use flats that can be repainted and utilized for the set. Network with other filmmakers or theater groups who may have flats that can be borrowed or rented.

The painting crew paints the flats to the color specifications of the production designer. Sawdust, sand, and dirt can be mixed into the paint to texturize the surface so that it takes on the character of a plaster wall on camera.

Flats can be built out of 3" × 1" or 4" × 2" lumber and braced vertically and at the four corners. Most large commercial studios can accommodate flats that are from ten to fifteen feet high. Most smaller studios have eight to ten foot ceilings. Flats should be four to six feet wide for easy handling. For a run of flats, lash line and lash eye hardware is used to connect the flats together.

Wild walls can be moved during shooting to accommodate the camera and the director's staging plan.

## Materials and Use

To create ornamental and architecture contours for the set, the art department uses various materials—most commonly, papier-mâché, timber frames, plastic foam, wood, stone, fiberglass, molded glass, and Styrofoam.

Papier-mâché is useful to create forms; fine details can be indicated with plaster. It is created by dipping tissue, paper towels, or newsprint torn into strips in a mixture of wheat paste and glue. It is squeezed into a mass, applied to a surface, and modeled into shape. Wire screening can be shaped into the desired form onto which the Papier-mâché is then applied.

A timber frame covered with wire mesh and canvas can be shaped to create the illusion of rocks. It is also a good foundation for turf, peat, and sawdust. Plastic foam can be sprayed, hardened, and shaped into forms. **Corbels**, projected stone or wood that support a horizontal structure like a beam or an arch, can be carved out of wood. Fiberglass is effective for creating any detailing moldings. Fiberglass cloth can be produced in a similar method to papier-mâché, put into a mold shaped to the design, and then released. Sheets of manufactured fiberglass can also be cut into forms and shapes, and molded glass is a durable surface that holds detail well.

Shell moldings are made of plastic sheets, laid over rocks, wood, or any material whose texture you want to copy, and then put into a device that, via a vacuum, molds the plastic to an exact replica of the material.

Styrofoam is available in block or board form. It is a lightweight, inexpensive, and versatile material for sculpting and shaping into decorative forms. Styrofoam can be cut with a hot wire tool, blade, or a jigsaw. The surface of Styrofoam can be aged with a blowtorch or a flame gun or dissolved with acetone, paint thinner, or carbon tetrachloride applied by brush or spray. When painted with oil-based or aerosol paint, the surface will begin to dissolve, resulting in both color and the illusion of aging. Pieces and sections of Styrofoam can be secured with dowels or adhesive glue. Styrofoam is effective to create rock and stonework. Because it is so light, Styrofoam can be used for falling-rock effects. It is safe and no one will be injured.

It can be sculpted into columns and statues. A hard glaze can be created on Styrofoam by lightly applying a flame to the surface. Styrofoam board can be cut and shaped into scenic signs that can be placed over location signs and easily secured with a light guide line.

Be very careful when working with Styrofoam. It is fragile and can easily crack or damage. If not secured properly, it can fall or blow over.

A WARNING: When Styrofoam burns, it gives off noxious fumes. So be sure all flame work is done in a well-ventilated area.

## Painting

The set must be painted once built. In the most basic manner, set painting is similar to painting an apartment or house; the painter covers the surface with paint. The difference is that the designer is not just selecting a fashionable or pleasing color but one that suits character and story, as well as mood and atmosphere. Painters who work in an art department have different skills than professional house painters. Often, they have to age their work; every wall cannot look as if it were just freshly painted. Scenic painters have to have a wide knowledge of paint pigments and texturing techniques.

The paint crew uses many application techniques to create specific scenic effects. They use spray paint for shading and aging effects. Sand or sawdust can be added to the paint to create specific areas of rough texture. Paint can be applied with a sponge, paper, or rags to create areas of dense color. Dry brushing one color over another is an application technique that suggests metal, stone, or wood. Allowing several wet colors to flow together on a flat surface creates aging, plaster, and earthen effects. Applying a transparent dark color over a light opaque coat creates a shadowy texture. Brushing a dark tone onto a light background simulates a natural wood grain. Applying light varnish gives surfaces a sheen, and additional coats will give the appearance the area is wet. A dark matte surface appears without detail. A dark glossy surface takes on the nature of polished wood. Dry-brushing a lighter tone onto the painted surface of a flat creates highlights. Splattering and splashing paint of another color onto a painted surface can also create aging effects.

Vertical painting doesn't take up a lot of floor space. For vertical painting the set or scenic elements are mounted on a frame braced against a wall and painted from a **scenic loft** that allows the painter to reach the upper areas and the horizontal expanse. If available, a scaffold that meets safety standards can be used to paint a large set. The most convenient and accessible method is to paint horizontally with the set elements lying flat on the shop floor.

NOTE: Dulling spray is another essential art department tool that constantly comes in handy during production. It reduces glare and unwanted reflected light on the set.

## Three-Dimensional Weight-Bearing Construction

These structures include steps, ramps, and raised platforms or levels.

The parallel, a platform used to create various heights in staging areas, is the most common construction architecture. It is a hinged trestle structure that opens, supporting a top and can be folded flat to be stored. The parallel is lightweight, easy to put together and transport. It is sturdy and can adapt to triangular shapes as well as a standard rectangle.

Platforms can be made out of steel, which interlock and are secured with bolts. Platforms are made of three structural members—the top, rail, and post. The top, which bears weight, is supported by rails running parallel. Irregular and freeform platforms are constructed by individual methods that best support the structure. **Ramps** can be constructed to facilitate access to the platforms.

Structures that don't have to bear weight can be supported with lightweight framing just so they can hold their shape. These would include columns, trees, and rocks that are art-directed.

Walls containing a window, fireplace, recessed bookcase, or doors are difficult to handle if built in one piece. Build the flat with a cutout for the addition and then just plug in the desired unit, also built separately, making the flat easier to handle.

A door flat is built with a framed-out doorway with a metal saddle at the bottom. Scenic doors do not need to have working locks. The door is held secure by ball-catch inserts. Design and build the appropriate style door with accompanying hardware and doorknob.

Window flats contain a stable window-frame built into them. Transparent plastic is used instead of glass. If the window is to be broken as part of the action, special plastic sheets or very thin glass is used. Remember that safety is paramount if the action takes place anywhere near the actors or crew.

There are design situations where the camera will be shooting on both sides of a wall as when rooms are connected. To achieve this, either place flats back to back or cover a single flat with material or board on both sides. Back to back flats must be well secured. In either case, both sides of the flats are decorated.

If a window, door, staircase, or fireplace does not have to be operational or will not be physically used by the actors, a dummy can be substituted to save time, materials, and money.

Arches can be built in three pieces: a top piece, containing the arch curve and two columns that attach to the right and left of the top piece.

## Bracing the Set

If the set or scenic pieces are not self-supported or solid, they must be braced or weighted so they will be safe for the actors and crew to work with.

Techniques to secure the set include:

* Bottom weighting—by placing heavy metal weights or bricks at the bottom of the set or scenic piece

- Suspending wire or rope from the top of the set to the ceiling grid or supports
- Bracing struts made of inexpensive timber can secure the corners or verticals of a set or piece of constructed scenery
- **Grummets** are fittings secured at the top of a flat to hold a stabilizing wire, cable, or rope in place
- A **flying iron** is a hinged metal ring plate that allows scenery to be suspended safely
- **Sandbags** placed behind the set on the floor piece will help to secure it

Flats can be joined together by lashing, the use of securing bolts, L plates, U plates, pin hinges, or C clamps, and floor braces are weighed down by sandbags.

## Methods for Anchoring Objects to Flats

Members of the art department use many methods to secure design elements to flats. These include:

- Staples applied with a staple hammer or staple gun
- Mirrors and framed pictures can be supported by Z-Hooks
- Plastic putty
- Magnets
- Velcro
- Masking tape

Practical lamps on set should be secured with metal back-plates. The wiring is taped to the back of the flat secured and grounded for safety.

A roll of gaffer's tape is a handy and essential staple for the art department. Keep a good stock of it, for it can be used to secure objects to the set, to tape down cables, wires, and ropes. Gaffer's tape can also hold back drapes, mark the floor for furniture and décor positions, and identify ropes and cables used to lift scenic pieces.

## Openings

If the camera can see out of a window in an interior studio set, a backing must be created to give the illusion there is something outside. Backings can be on a flat stretched with canvas or other material. A hard backing is made of wood, board, or other solid materials. A backing can be painted or be a photographic blow-up. A translight is a **transparency**, a photographic backing that allows light to pass through it. A backing can depict a cityscape, landscape, or whatever the screenplay and design plan calls for.

If you are not using a scenic backing outside a window, put up blinds and close them so that the exterior view can't be seen. Lighting from behind the blinds can create the illusion of sunlight. Trees, bushes, a brick wall, a sky cloth, or a cyclorama can be positioned behind the opening to create a view outside a window. The view can be made to look realistic by using real materials or given a poetic quality by creating an art-directed look achieved by painting or using designed objects behind the opening.

A partial hallway can be built just outside a doorway opening in a set. A stairway can be indicated with just a few steps visible to the camera. Building a partial set that appears to be an adjoining room can create the illusion of another room existing beyond an open doorway. These techniques are useful to give the appearance of connecting space. An isolated room set has a tendency to look like a set. When signs of the existence of a larger space are visible, the set will appear more realistic and expansive. An actor can make an entrance or exit using the partial set area. To save space, the area indicated could be built as a separate set by building it side by side or, if studio space is limited, by constructing it later after the first set is struck.

A scenic backing is the most cost-effective way of creating a view out of an opening. The degree of realism can be controlled by the photo-realist quality of the painting on the backing. A photographic backing may be even more suitable. The distance of the camera to the backing also determines how believable the view will appear. The further away the backing is from the opening or the camera, the more realistic it will look. The lighting of the backing is critical in creating the atmosphere of daylight or an outdoor night scene.

A painted flat decorated with a mirror, framed paintings, or photographs can imply another room existing outside of a door opening. The addition of a table, chair, or piece of furniture will bring an even greater sense of realism to the impression that an adjoining room exists.

Another method of handling a door or window opening in a set is to block the view with swaged drapes, Venetian blinds, or a partially pulled up shade. These techniques will also give the impression there is life beyond the opening with little effort by the art department.

Backings must be designed and positioned properly to achieve their desired effect. They must cover the distance of the opening so the background images do not appear too small or too far away. If the backing is incorrectly angled, the camera will overshoot the upstage end of the set. If the backing is too close to the opening, the director of photography won't be able to light it evenly. Make sure that the lighting in the room doesn't cast shadows onto the scenic backgrounds. Objects placed too close to the backing will also cast unwanted shadows on the backing.

If the windows in a set opening are glazed or made of frosted plastic, no backing is necessary. A branch shadow, artificial snow, or lighting can indicate season; light outside the opening can help indicate the weather or the time of year the scene is taking place.

### Cycloramas

A cyclorama is a background suspended on curved piping, a wooden **batten**, or curtain track from the top of the studio. Gently curving around the sides of a set, a cyclorama runs along two or more studio walls and creates the panoramic illusion of a landscape, sky, cityscape, infinity, or void. The cyclorama can be made out of many diverse materials, from canvas to linen, scrim to velour. The cyclorama, known as a cyc, can be stretched taut by being wrapped around a pipe or batten on the floor, or folded and held down on the studio floor by weights. The design on the cyclorama is created by the production designer and painted directly on the material by the scenic artists.

During the Hollywood studio era, a cyclorama was often used for musicals and fantasy films, to indicate realistic background through painting; earlier audiences accepted it as a cinematic convention. For contemporary films, a cyc works best when used to create expressionistic, theatrical, unrealistic effects or to place a scene in a space that transcends time and place.

A cyclorama was the answer for the challenge of making the art-directed train, in *Murder on the Orient Express* (1974), directed by Sidney Lumet, appear to be really moving as it sat in a studio. "It was very hard to look out of the window and see any distance without being aware that you were looking at the studio floor and that the carriage was at an inappropriate height," production designer Tony Walton explains. " So that in addition to fogging up the windows somewhat, we made huge wraparound cycloramas very close to the train. They were made of rear projection screen material and painted with acrylic paint." The outdoor illustrations gave the impression the train was passing through various landscapes.

In *Heaven Can Wait* (1978), directed by Warren Beatty and Buck Henry, production designer Paul Sylbert also employed a cyclorama to create the illusion that there really is a waiting area in the beyond where the departed are assigned their final destinations. "I started out with the idea of Maxfield Parish for heaven. I wanted a real heavenly heaven," Paul Sylbert explains. " I did experiments with cloud material. I wanted to create a rainbow on the stage using a fine mist and lights at 28 degrees like it is with the sun when you hose your garden and you see the rainbow. It is just the sun striking particles of water forming a prism, but the angle and the intensity has to be right. The sun is almost horizontal when that happens. I was never able to get the spray fine enough without soaking things and I was never able to get the light intense enough from one direction. I did something else." Paul Sylbert's solution was to create a place between heaven and earth. His assistant was a former Navy man who found a grid of steel strips that are the structure used for a ship's decking. It allowed 85 percent of light to pass through. The decking was covered with wet muslin. The structure was lit from underneath and there was a white cyclorama behind it so there would be no horizon line. Buckets of dry ice were placed in the four corners of the stage. "We tilted them and the froth began to rise. It was a world without shadows."

To save money, seamless paper can be hung as a cyclorama. The upside is the paper is inexpensive, comes in rolls in a variety of colors, can be stapled or suspended from the top of the studio and taped to the floor, and provides a good painting and decorating surface. The downside is seamless paper easily tears and can be damaged by handling. Light too easily bounces off the paper's surface, which interferes with the rendering of dark tones. Wide areas of a cyc require several sheets that must be taped, resulting in joints that can readily rip apart.

Cycs can be constructed out of plywood or any prepared board. This approach avoids the wrinkles caused when working with paper or fabric and can support lightweight décor pieces. A hard surface can be painted and textured with sawdust. Note that hard surfaces may cause acoustic problems for sound recording.

When using a cyc, the floor can be painted the same, a related, or contrasting color. Cyc joins can be hidden with cover units painted the same color and by pieces of furniture, décor, or platforms.

Sky effects can be created with a cyclorama in many ways. A pale blue gelled light will give the illusion of a sky. Photographic slides of sky scenes can be projected on the cyc by way of a scenic projector. Stars for a night scene can be achieved by attaching small, white Christmas lights to the cyc or by placing a foil gobo pierced with pinholes in front of a white light. A gobo is an opaque or black sheet on a wooden or masonite frame that is put in front of a light on an adjustable stand. Gobos can be cut into shapes and patterns to form shadows on a set.

A cove unit is used to hide the join between the floor and the bottom of the cyc. It is a six or twelve foot structure with a 45-degree, sloping surface of plywood or fiberglass on a hollow wooden frame. The curve is necessary to allow the light on the floor and cyc bottom to be graded or blended by the director of photography.

Scenic planes—two-foot-high, vertical, self-supported plywood boards—can also hide the join between the bottom of the cyc and the floor. The planes can be shaped with a saw to indicate hills, roof, trees, or any number of forms appropriate to the scene. Many colors can be used for a cyclorama, including off-white, shades of gray, light blue, or black. If matte effects are going to be used, the cyc can be painted cobalt blue or green for that special effect work.

## Ceilings

*Citizen Kane* was not the first film to feature sets with ceilings, but most films made prior to, and many after, the 1941 American classic were shot on sets without ceilings. It still is a decision to be made by the filmmaker. No ceiling on a set makes it easy for the crew to light and record sound, but camera angles are restricted (no extreme, low-angle, Orson Welles shots) and realism is challenged. Ceilings add dimension, verisimilitude, and a clear definition of space. Lighting and sound recording are compromised, but with proper design and planing, a partial ceiling can afford the look that is needed, along with the freedom of movement for the cast and crew.

## Floors and Ground Areas

Floor and ground areas are critical elements of a production design. The floor of an apartment or home can be constructed out of myriad materials from wood to tile to stone. The age and condition of the surface is important to the period and the economic status of the characters. Outdoor ground areas, whether they be dirt, grass, rock, or a smooth or rough terrain can be a wide palette of color and texture depending on the region, time period, and the intended mood of the design. Floor and ground areas can be real, constructed, or duplicated with other materials. Considerations for these vital areas, the base of your design where the characters plant their feet and move through the narrative, must involve and answer all of the questions discussed for every other aspect of architecture and décor of the production design.

A designer may manipulate the height or angle of a floor for dramatic effect. For the production design of *The Freshman* (1990), Ken Adam wanted to give the social club—where the mob figure played by Marlon Brando in this comedy held court—a sense of power and the aura of his character in *The Godfather* without imitating that classic film. Adam forced the perspective by lowering the ceiling and raising the floor of the set, to make Brando appear even bigger than he was.

When Terrence Marsh designed the submarine for *The Hunt for Red October* (1990), he had to enhance the practical lights for aesthetic and practical cinematographic reasons. The actual subs have fluorescent lights overhead. Marsh increased those and added units under the floor to create an upward glow. The actual submarine did not have lights under the floor. This addition to the design contributed to the dramatic tension of the film, based on the Tom Clancy bestseller.

For the film adaptation of the Broadway hit musical *The Wiz* (1978), a reinterpretation of *The Wizard of Oz* featuring African-American performers, production designer Tony Walton had to come up with a solution in creating the famed yellow brick road for this Sidney Lumet film shot on location in New York City. Painting it on was out of the question, because the company was moving fast and they were shooting in the winter, so conditions wouldn't allow the paint to dry in time. The solution was yellow Congoleum linoleum that was rolled out on the floor of the former World's Fair New York State Pavilion (which was cracked and had to be smoothed out with concrete first). To cover the surface of a city bridge, space heaters were employed to soften the material, which hardened in the icy weather. The result was as memorable as the studio-created original back in the 1939 film starring Judy Garland.

Molded rubber mats can be painted to simulate cobblestones, bricks, or tiles. Fiberglass can be treated to look like pavement. Artificial grass or real sod can be used for landscaping exterior scenes on a studio floor. A floor can be laid with secured plants. Area carpeting can be secured to the floor with gaffer's tape.

### Procedures for Building and Erecting Sets in a Studio

- Stage plans and evaluations are studied.
- Key location points for where the set will be positioned are marked on the floor using the studio wall footage markings and overhead lighting grid.
- Access routes and fire lanes are created and maintained.
- Scaffold work and large platforms are done first.
- Any scenic structures that will need to be suspended are hung early and lifted out of the way of construction.
- Start construction in the back of the stage and work forward to maintain the optimum floor space for the construction crew to work in.
- Carefully brace each scenic element as it is built.
- Section off and logistically organize each working area to avoid accidents and to create a production work environment.
- Learn and follow all studio safety and fire rules. If you are setting up your own studio space, create written work, safety, and fire rules, and post them where all the construction and production crew can see them.

- Handle and lift all flats carefully, using two handlers for each flat.
- Carefully hide all flat joins with tape or fabric.
- All positions of flats, furniture, and décor should be carefully marked on the studio floor with chalk or gaffer's or masking tape.

In addition to safety lanes and fire exits, make sure the set and the staging area doesn't block access to workshop areas, entrances, and exits.

When construction is completed the production designer checks the set and any modifications necessary are made by the construction crew before shooting begins. In addition to door and window trim, decorative trim, either painted on or practical is used for baseboards, chair rails, wainscoting, cornices (a lightly framed three-dimensional trim) and mantles. Framing must support the trim.

## Camera Blocking in the Studio

When planning the shot list, creating the storyboard, and during camera block be aware that overshooting the set can be caused by several situations:

- When the camera is shooting at a 45-degree angle at a shallow depth set
- If the flats are too low for the camera composition
- Extreme low-angle shots and not enough height in the set to support them
- When the camera is shooting at a steep, downstage angle
- When the camera is shooting into a window or a door without a backing
- When reflective surfaces reveal off-set areas

During camera rehearsals, or as the director of photography is framing and designing the angle, movement, and composition of each shot, the production designer or art director checks the set as seen through the camera, making aesthetic, logistical, or technical changes as necessary. The floor manager and the art department check to see that the set is secure and that nothing will impede the work or safety of the actors or crew.

During shooting, the proper continuity of the set must be maintained. This is done by the script supervisor, but the art department staff must assist in the physical process of dressing the set and keeping a close eye on the continuity of the production design, which they know better than anyone on set.

## Rehearsals

Actors rarely get to rehearse extensively on the completed set. While the director is rehearsing during pre-production, the set is being constructed, so rehearsals are conducted in a rehearsal studio or, in the case of a low-budget film, wherever the filmmakers can work. During rehearsal the director wants the actors to get a sense of what it will be like to work in the logistics of the actual setting. The blocking also must be worked out and then transferred and refined on the set. It is essential that the art department prepare the rehearsal space by taping off the dimensions of the set on the rehearsal area floor and by using available tables and chairs to represent architecture, furniture, and décor. Once the set is built, the director should continue rehearsals to get the actors comfortable with their cinematic environment. If there isn't time for on-set rehearsals before shooting, they should continue during production while the crew is working, during setups and between takes.

## Striking the Set

Never **strike** a set until the producer and director give clearance to do so. There is always the possibility of retakes due to camera or performance problems or script changes. The routine for taking down or striking a set must carefully follow procedures. The film or tape shot of each set should be checked by the director, production designer, and editor to make sure the production is ready to strike a particular set. Detailed Polaroids or photographs should be taken of each aspect and view of the set for reference, in case it has to be erected again. The production designer or art director should carefully supervise the process of striking the set to ensure that nothing is damaged and that it can be properly stored or sold to another production. The following is a list of steps required for the proper striking of a set:

- Move all technical equipment out of the way first.
- Remove all props, furniture, practical lamps, drapes, and rugs.
- Take down or roll up the cyclorama.
- Take down all studio lighting.
- Remove all plants and landscaping elements.
- Remove everything but the architectural elements of the set; the flats, doors, and windows.
- Remove all moldings, arches, and attachments (doorknobs, handles, etc.).
- Secure all windows and doors with gaffer's tape or rope.
- Stack up all sandbags and weights away from the set.
- Carefully release all lashing wire and ropes, a wall at a time. Make sure there is enough crew on hand to guarantee that nothing will fall when all the secure lines are taken down.
- Remove all nails, hooks, braces, and hardware from the flats.

## Storage

Store any scenic pieces and flats, for use on the next production or for possible future rental or sale. If storage is not available, make every attempt to arrange a sale of flats to a theater group, school, or other filmmakers to recoup some of the production design costs. If you are going into production on another project within the next several months, a storage fee may be a good investment. Don't just destroy or trash the materials. If other options are not available, you may be able to carefully dismantle the set and sell the raw materials as scrap.

## Transportation of the Set

A truck or van is necessary to transport the sets and scenic pieces. A scenic trolley used to cart the flats from the studio to the transportation vehicle is not essential but easier than carrying everything by hand.

If you can store the sets and props, here's another set of procedures to follow:

- Photograph everything separately for reference. Catalogue every item in detail. Cross-reference the text with the photos.
- Store the flats vertically, with dividers, so they can be easily pulled out without incurring damage.
- Stack all platforms.
- Roll up all cloth **scenic paintings** and fabric around thin wooden poles to avoid wrinkles and creases.
- Don't roll up scrims; this causes creases that won't smooth out. Fold all scrims fan style for a better result.
- Fold all cycloramas as you would a drape and bag them for storage.
- Put all props on shelves clearly labeled and coded to match the catalogue book.

## Getting Familiar with Working in a Studio

- Take a studio tour; ask permission to be an observer during a working session.
- Visit area studios. Get specs of the facilities and any literature with information concerning the operation of the studio and their rules.
- Scout unoccupied factories and other large spaces with potential to be transformed into a motion picture studio. Measure the dimensions and draw up a studio plan. Does this suit your production needs?

Screen behind-the-scenes documentaries on films shot in a studio. Watching the cast and crew working under studio conditions can be helpful. Many DVDs have segments that contain these documentaries and interviews with production designers investigating the process.

# Chapter 14

## WORKING ON LOCATION

Working in the studio offers control for filmmakers. Working on location presents conditions of controlled chaos, especially when shooting in exterior locations of populated urban areas. In the studio a set can be built to the exact specifications of the design and shooting can proceed without unexpected delays. On location the filmmakers will encounter the natural weather elements, the wondrous unpredictability of the sun, and a spectrum of interference in the form of onlookers, noise pollution, house rules restrictions, laws, and science.

### Scouting Locations

You will encounter two possible situations when on a search for a location to film a scene. The location you consider a candidate for selection will either be perfect for your film as it stands before you or will need modification to be transformed to fit into your production design plan for the film. Be skeptical if you arrive at the notion of perfection too easily. Don't settle. Does the location fit the aesthetic, practical, and technical attributes the film requires? If modification is necessary, how much needs to be done? What will the transformation cost? If those questions are answered to your satisfaction another phalanx of inquiries to make include the following:

- Is the location available?
- Is the space large enough for a production crew to work in?
- Is there adequate parking?
- Is the location accessible by public transportation and by car?
- Can you get permission to modify or transform the location?
- How long will you need the location for pre-production work?
- How long will you need the space for shooting?

## Transforming a Location

Design and plan what alterations need to be made and meet with the owner of the property. The work must be done in pre-production and maintained during production.

Production designer Kristi Zea did several transformations of actual locations for the 1989 film *Miss Firecracker*. The house in the film was supposed to have belonged to the main character's grandmother. The concept was that artifacts passed down from generations were still in the house. The actual location was an empty house that had begun to deteriorate. The roof was in poor condition, so the art department put up plastic to prevent leaking. The house had been empty, so it was dressed by Zea and her staff. They put in two televisions, one on top of the other. One worked and the other did not. They researched people's homes in the area where older women or widows were living. They saw family pictures all over the walls, and everything was dark and dusty. Zea decided that the Holly Hunter character left the house pretty much the way it was when she took it over. Her character lived in two or three areas of the house where she added her personal belongings. The rest of the house was left decorated just as the grandmother had left it.

The Southern town of Yazoo City had the right look for the film. A local pool hall that needed very little work had a counter with jars of pickled eggs, a southern delicacy that Zea highlighted in arranging the location.

An amusement park where the Miss Firecracker contest took place was created on location by the art department. The chosen location was close to the town and was a plot of land inhabited by squatters living in a trailer. They relocated them and leveled the area. Trees and undergrowth were cleaned out. A stage for the contest and houses were built. Then an actual carnival company was hired that had the appropriate style required by the script and were set up to Zea's instructions.

As soon as shooting is completed the location must be restored to its original condition. Check the dailies first to make sure the scene is complete. Repair any damage and remove all signs that a film company was ever there. Leave the location as you originally found it.

## Shooting at One Location for Another

Decades ago, producers realized that the high cost of shooting in Los Angeles or New York City made it enticing to shoot in Canada. The incentives were impressive; lower costs, good facilities and support, a range of locations that they were convinced would successfully play for the East and West coasts of the United States. For many producers the bottom line dictates creative decisions imposed on the director. Production designers continue to do their best to use locations in Canada, but those are rarely the best artistic choices. New York locations are often filmed in Los Angeles, where the architecture, colors, and the light are not the same.

If your story is set in one place, but it is financially necessary to shoot in Canada or another lower-cost area, be as specific as you can:

- Utilize confined areas—the wider the shot, the more that is revealed. Control your design illusion by limiting the scope of each shot. The wider the shot, the harder it is to create the intended illusion of time and place transformation.
- Interiors are easier to manage and to match with architectural style.
- Limit exteriors or plan to shoot exteriors in the area where the film takes place.
- When working on location the production designer must modify what exists there to create the intended look for the film. Often the designer must cover up something that would betray the period in the transformation of the location. Television antennas can be removed or blocked from the camera's view by trees. Overhead power and telephone lines can be avoided by the composition or covered by billboards. Signs created by the scenic artists can effectively disguise the existing area. Roads can be created with gravel, tanbark, and peat.

Martin Scorsese's *Mean Streets* (1973) art directed by William Sardell remains one of the most surprising examples of a New York film shot mainly on locations in Los Angeles. After a long struggle to get *Mean Streets* made, Scorsese was compelled to build the set for Tony's Bar in Hollywood. The apartment Charlie (played by Harvey Keitel) lived in was shot in an office building on Hollywood Boulevard. And yet, the film has been acclaimed for its realism and specificity to New York City's Little Italy neighborhood. The churchyard of the old St. Patrick's Cathedral was shot on location in the Big Apple, and the exterior of the bar was found off Broome Street, but the climax of the film set on New York roadways and the ending on the streets of Little Italy were shot in Los Angeles. As different as those thoroughfares may be, especially the back streets where the protagonist's car crashes, careful location selection and camera placement succeeds in convincing the audience the entire film was shot on location in New York. There are many such neighborhoods across the country, and although there are similarities—restaurants, specialty food shops, and social clubs—none are as distinctive or well known as the home of the feast of San Gennaro. The feast was shot at the real event but the careful matching and selection of the Bronx locations stand up to the specific geography of the original.

## Matching a Location and Studio Work

If you are using the exterior of one location to represent the interior of another, the architectural structures must match. If trees, buildings, or any architectural elements are established in the exterior view of a location that would be visible in the interior, they must be recreated either on a backing in a **miniature**, or setting outside the window of the studio set, or the interior location to be used.

If the exterior of a building doesn't match the interior, the shot should be positioned carefully during post-production either from the best angle to link them architecturally or by cutting to another shot before making reference to their relationship to each other. A direct cut of a badly matched exterior and interior may destroy the reality you are trying so hard to achieve.

Often a scene will require a combination of location and studio work to create a consistent production design. A spectacular and impressive example is the classic scene in Alfred Hitchcock's *North by Northwest* (1959), production designed by Robert Boyle, when a crop-dusting airplane menaces Cary Grant. The sequence required a totally flat landscape so Grant would have no place to hide. After scouting South Dakota and Kansas, Boyle remembered the Tulare Lake Basin in the San Joaquin Valley where he was raised. There were no cornfields there, but one was needed as a place where Grant could hide from his overhead attacker. The art department planted corn there in time for the location shoot. The shots depicting the explosion of a tanker truck and Grant being peppered with bullets from the plane were special effect scenes that needed to be photographed in the studio using rear-screen projection. Boyle had to recreate specific sections of the exterior location on sets in the studio that perfectly matched the location. Availability of the location or the nature of the action may demand studio and location work be combined. Recreating and matching design elements are an essential skill of the art department.

## Putting It All Together

Finding all of the locations that fit together to form the design world of the film is a major challenge for the production designer. Contemporary filmmakers often don't have the luxury of building everything in the studio, so they must search for each individual element that, when seen in the continuity of the film, totally creates a consistent environment for the characters and story, while serving the director's vision of the project.

How have production designers accomplished this feat on the movies we see and believe in, as the world in which the film exists and evolves before our eyes? Here is a range of examples:

*After Hours* (1985)—director Martin Scorsese, production designer Jeffrey Townsend. Contemporary New York at night, a Kafkaesque comedy. This film was shot on the quick and on the cheap, on location in New York. In addition to shooting at the Moondance Diner on Sixth Avenue, the production used the Emerald Pub on Spring Street for the bar tended by John Heard. The large and threatening iron gate in front of Griffin Dunne's workplace was found at the Metropolitan Tower on Madison Avenue.

*The Age of Innocence* (1993)—director Martin Scorsese, production designer Dante Ferretti. A series of locations were utilized to recreate upper class New York in the 1870s. The opera house that opens the film is the Philadelphia Academy of Music. The Beauforts' luxurious home was shot at the National Arts Club in the Gramercy Park section of New York. Long Island's Old Westbury Gardens were selected as well as numerous locations in Troy, New York. River Street in an upstate town on the Hudson River was the setting for turn of the century Wall Street. Mrs. Mingott's salon, which in the film is not far from Central Park, was shot at the Phi Kappa Phi fraternity house at Troy's Rensselaer Polytechnic Institute, and the home of Newland Archer's parents was the Federal Gale House, a residence hall of Russell Sage

College. The scene where Archer and May Welland walk through a white aviary was photographed at the Enid A. Haupt Conservatory of the Bronx Botanical Garden.

*Annie Hall* (1977)—director Woody Allen, production designer Mel Bourne. Throughout his long career Woody Allen's films have explored his beloved isle of Manhattan. Three movie theaters that represent the City's intellectual film community are used as locations: the Beekman, the New Yorker, and the legendary repertory house, the Thalia. Brooklyn's famed Coney Island amusement park is featured in a flashback. Annie's apartment was on the Upper East Side. Other locations include the Hamptons, the Wall Street Tennis Club, and Central Park.

*As Good As It Gets* (1997)—director James L. Brooks, production designer Bill Brzeski. The apartments of the Jack Nicholson and Greg Kinear characters were scouted on 12th Street in New York's West Village, Helen Hunt's place near Prospect Park in Brooklyn. The New York City restaurant where she worked was constructed on the ground floor of the Barclay Hotel in downtown Los Angeles.

*Basic Instinct* (1991)—director Paul Verhoeven, production designer Terence Marsh. Shot on location in San Francisco, this sexy thriller goes to Montgomery Street for Michael Douglas' apartment and to the Tosca Café on Columbus Avenue. Sharon Stone's notorious leg-crossing interrogation scene was shot on a set at Warner Bros. studio in Hollywood. The Stentson Bar is a lesbian country-and-western bar south of Market Street in 'Frisco. The chase sequence was shot on hilly Kearney Street and Stone's sex-trap digs were located south of San Francisco at a beachfront estate in Carmel Highlands. The conclusion of the film, when the Jean Tripplehorn character is shot, was photographed on Broadway in Oakland, California.

*Blood Simple* (1984)—director Joel Coen, production designer Jane Musky. This audacious first film by the Coen Brothers was shot on location in Texas. The quirky neo-noir took place at Mount Bonnell Park above Lake Austin where M. Emmet Walsh gets his instructions to murder John Getz. The illicit affair takes place at the Heart of Texas Motel. The body is buried on Farm Road, South of Hutto, which is northeast of Austin. Walsh burns the X-rated photos of the lovers at the Old Grove Drug Building on Sixth Street in Austin and the gory climax was shot in an apartment building above a restaurant on the same block, with the location serving as the place Frances McDormand moves into.

*Blow Out* (1981)—director Brian De Palma, production designer Paul Sylbert. The company went to Philadelphia to shoot this audio takeoff of Michaelangelo Antonioni's *Blow-Up* that had also been the inspiration for Coppola's *The Conversation*, a film that first translated the photos to sound. Here, John Travolta is a soundman for a "cheapo" exploitation film when he actually records a murder in progress. The director's hometown of Philadelphia was the base of operations, with the car accident sequence taking place on the Wissahickon Bridge. Travolta meets Nancy Allen (Mrs. De Palma at the time) at the 30th Street Station. Travolta jeeps through the central plaza of the Philadelphia City Hall in Penn Square and crashes into the window at the famed Wanamaker's Department Store on Market and 13th.

*Clerks* (1994)—director Kevin Smith. This black-and-white first feature film was made for only $27,000 in Kevin Smith's home state of New Jersey. When working on a no-budget film (after lab costs and purchasing stock, how much could be left for production design?) filmmakers must use creative thinking to get the film done. Smith shot at Quick Stop Groceries in Leonardo, New Jersey. RST Video was next door, just as the video store is in the film. The scene at the undertakers was shot at Postens Funeral Home in Atlantic Highlands.

*Dazed and Confused* (1993)—director Richard Linklater, production designer John Frick. Linklater shot in his hometown of Austin, Texas. The majority of the film was shot at the Bedickek Middle School. The burger joint was the Top Notch Restaurant, and the alfresco party was done at West Enfield Park.

*Desperately Seeking Susan* (1985)—director Susan Seidelman, production designer Santo LoQuasto. This post-modern classic was shot in New York and New Jersey. When the Madonna character arrives in New York she is in the Big Apple's Port Authority Bus Terminal. Rosanna Arquette gets her hair done at the Nubest & Co Salon on Northern Boulevard in Manhasset. The East Village was the location for a shopping sequence featuring St. Marks Place and a second-hand store, Love Saves The Day, on Second Avenue at East 7th Street. The Aidan Quinn character works as a projectionist at the Bleecker Street Cinema. The production shot at New Jersey locations in Tenafly, Edgewater, and Lakehurst, as well in Roslyn Heights in Nassau County, Long Island.

*Dirty Dancing* (1987)—director Emile Ardolino, production designer David Chapman. This popular low-budget film is set in New York's Catskill Mountains in the early 1960s. The look does capture the spirit of the 1960s, but the music and the moves are from the 1980s. *Dirty Dancing* was shot in "the mountains" but they were the Appalachian mountains rather than the Catskills. The resort was neither Grossinger's nor Browns but Mountain Lake Hotel in Mountain Lake, Roanoke, Virginia. The relocation fooled even those who spent their youth in the upstate New York playground where all comedians worth their salt cut their eyeteeth before anyone ever heard of a comedy club.

*The French Connection* (1971)—director William Friedkin, art director Ben Kazakow. As a study in contrasts, this gritty New York movie starts on the streets of Marseilles, France then cuts to Popeye Doyle getting drunk at the foot of the Manhattan Bridge on the Lower East Side. A suspect is tailed on the Triborough Bridge and staked out at Ratner's Restaurant on Delancey Street. Frog One is found at the Roosevelt Hotel on Madison Avenue, shops at Ronaldo Maia Flowers, and looses his tracker at the Grand Central subway stop. The bad guys meet in front of the Capitol Building in Washington, D.C. Popeye lives at the Marlboro Housing Project on Stillwell Avenue in Brooklyn. The landmark chase sequence begins at the Bay 50th Street station and, during the five week shoot under the Bensonhurst elevated railway, goes down the Stillwell line to 86th Street to New Ulrecht Avenue, violently concluding at the 62nd Street station. The Doral Park Avenue Hotel on Park Avenue is where Devereaux the French celeb stays and the drug deal and shootout goes down on Wards Island.

## Tips for Working on Location

- Scout and research each location carefully. Make sure the requirements and support needed for the productions are available and can be either supplied or brought in.
- Familiarize yourself with as many regions as you can for their potential as locales. The well-informed traveler has a good understanding of the vistas that can be captured by the camera and put to narrative use to filmmakers.
- Plan to make the cast and crew as comfortable and focused as possible when working on location.
- Do community outreach before, during and after location work.
- Be prepared for weather conditions a location may present.
- When in Rome. . . . Don't behave as an outsider when on location. Show appreciation for your welcome.

# Chapter 15

## LOW-BUDGET PRODUCTIONS

On a big-budget studio production, monies are available to support the art department. The production designer has the staff, facilities, equipment, and budget necessary to carry out their plans. Money can always help greatly to solve problems. Low-budget films have limited financial resources. Some low-low-budget independent films proceed without a production design, or members of the art department convince themselves that the film can be shot on real locations without a production designer to the oversee the realization of the vision of the film.

However, in order for a filmmaker to fully realize the vision and objectives for a project, the design of a film must be addressed. Even a low-budget film can have an effective production design by understanding the purpose and responsibilities of the craft. Cost-cutting approaches are necessary. Consider the following:

Consolidate jobs. On a large scale, well-financed production filmmakers can afford a large art department where each member has a specific job. This is not always realistic on low-budget films where the filmmaker may not have access to all the crew specialists, so plan B has to go into effect. The art department can be scaled back. Each person working with the production designer can wear several hats. It is the process of production design that's important, not how many people work on the crew. The set decorator can also do props. The property master could paint the sets during pre-production. Regardless how small the crew is, use the most capable person for each task.

On a low-budget film, the production designer can be responsible for the work of many, doing the labor of the key art department positions. Production assistants with limited experience and on-the-job training can support the designer. On a big production, the designer designs and then supervises, but on a low-budget he will also have to physically do as many of the tasks himself—help to construct the set, do some scenic painting, whatever is necessary. Production designers should also have persuasive personalities, to draw others in. Teaching skills are helpful to train production assistants and others to work in the art department.

Get local art students involved in the production design of your film. Many of the skills needed for the art department are similar to those possessed by illustrators, graphic artists, fine artists, sculptors, architects, and by those from other artistic endeavors and training. With a little training and supervision from the production designer or art director these other artists can be very effective.

Get local art professionals involved. Many architects, graphic designers, artists, commercial painters, fine artists, carpenters, and others in related fields have a passion for filmmaking. With leadership and some training they can be effective on a low-budget film.

Get as many services, locations, and supplies as you can for free or at a discount. Assign a producer or team member to network, negotiate, and involve companies, individuals, and community groups in the production design of your film. This will support a small-staffed art department and keep the line budget items down.

Budget for the production design. The areas that often get neglected by independent and student filmmakers are production design, post-production, and especially sound design—which is the aural counterpart of art direction. The budget should reflect the needs of each department within realistic expectations. The budget should be created in consultation with the production designer. Each item should be listed and its cost estimated, with miscellaneous backup funds figured in if estimates are under-funded.

Keep the production design realistic as to what money and resources are available for the art department. The production designer must be fiscally responsible to the budget. Find the best deals in paint, hardware, lumber, tools, and art supplies. Research vendors, explore the conglomerate chains such as Home Depot and Staples, as well as independent vendors.

## Keeping the Production Design Budget Down

When working with a low budget to produce a film, there are ways of keeping the production design budget down, in addition to those previously discussed, without limiting the artistic and creative choices that will visually enhance and interpret the story.

Put all of the money spent on the production design on the screen. Avoid excess and waste. Building a set and then scraping it for another idea, or shooting at a location and then not using the footage because of coverage or editing or coverage problems, are just some of the mistakes filmmakers make that are wasteful of the budget. Building more then you need or spending time and money on décor details that won't been seen on camera are all traps that can be avoided by careful planning and wise allocation of the production design budget.

Make full use of studio space. Select the venue carefully—don't pay for space you are not going to use. Camera-test all materials to be used for the design. Don't employ expensive materials in areas where the camera won't directly see them.

Don't design and build what the camera won't see or is outside of the director's visualization of the film. Put the majority of the budget into the major sets. Don't squander money and effort on minor sets. Design sets to scale when possible, to reduce costs.

If available, use a stock or standby set from another production or studio that can be altered inexpensively to create the design plan for your film. Borrow, rent, or lease pre-built, used flats.

On a low-budget movie the filmmaker is always looking to cut costs. The art department is under constant scrutiny to keep spending at a bare minimum. Construction materials are expensive, but there are ways to save money. Recycled materials cost less and are just as effective in many cases. Corrugated cardboard and packaging materials can be utilized for covering or siding flats, when painted and treated appropriately. On a low-budget movie the designer can take full advantage of a cyclorama and minimize the building of scenic pieces. Put all of the design elements to good use. Create multipurpose units that can function in more than one scene or set. Use the same basic architecture, walls, doors, and windows for more than one set by repositioning walls, adding, or removing furniture and décor, and utilizing reversible window treatments.

The most effective way to keep the art department budget to a minimum is to concentrate on only what is within the camera frame.

- Be selective—imply, don't overstate, the settings
- A creative use of perspective and scale can give the illusion of size and space

Forced perspective is a useful technique to imply more with less. Hallways and room extensions can be painted or photographed and put on a backing placed strategically to give the illusion the set is more architecturally complex than it really is.

Veteran Hollywood art directors often used the forced perspective in their work. Robert Boyle gives two examples of the technique in use: "You're achieving a large space in a limited space. You bring the background up, and you force everything smaller. For the circus caravan scene in *Saboteur* (Alfred Hitchcock, 1942), we not only used midgets in the background, we went beyond that. We had cutout figures where the arms move, and we had little lights on the arms. They were supposed to be policemen with flashlights way in the background. It was at night, and you could do things like that. Those were standard ways of working in those days. The long hotel corridor for the Plaza Hotel in New York for *North By Northwest* (Alfred Hitchcock, 1959), was a painted backing of the extension of the corridor we built, and the actors came around in front of the painted backing and over to the room. That's forced perspective in a scenic painting. Then we took the same backing and used that for the reverse angle shot."

Remember, low-budget filmmaking does not have to signify amateur and shoddily mounted productions. For decades, many Hollywood films overspent and lavished resources that were not necessary. Money squandered does not enhance or support the look of a film. Money spent for amenities not directly translated to the screen are wasted. Low-budget independent filmmaking is a philosophy and can be more effective, practically and artistically, than mega-budget, bloated productions, which don't serve visual storytelling in relation to the project. Plan and think before you spend. Question all decisions and search for alternate methods and materials that will bring the same results for less output of cash resources.

John Cassavetes, the patron saint of low-budget, independent filmmaking, had a radical attitude toward all Hollywood production conventions, including those in production design. The home he shared with his wife, actress Gena Rowlands, and their family was often used as a location to make their movies. No storyboards or illustrations were drawn. The art department on a John Cassavetes film worked with what they had, and it always fit the search for the truth of the moment in the soul of his characters that the directors obsessed over. The locations were real. The art department arranged, took away, and added, but Cassavetes had a gut for detecting artifice and overmanipulation.

"Money has nothing to do with film. In the end it kills you from being creative and from inventing, finding a way to do it," Cassavetes philosophized in the documentary *I'm Almost Not Crazy*. "It makes you think, it makes the crew think. You say, 'We're in this room, how do we make this a palace?' So some fool like me says, 'We either make the picture or we don't. If we are going to make it, let's make this room a palace or let's not make it a palace. Look how easy this changes, it's a room.' And you make that adjustment but the emotions stay the same. So the emotions guide you, the sense of humor guides you, saying 'The hell with life' guides you."

Low-budget filmmakers must be inventive and use art direction ideas, principles and techniques from every kind of movie from Hollywood blockbusters to no-budget indies. Production design is adjustable to the needs and resources at hand to the filmmaker. Keep your mind open, the integrity of the film forefront, and be bold.

# Chapter 16

## GUERRILLA FILMMAKING

The purest definition of guerrilla filmmaking is making a movie on the fly, no budget, barely a script, shooting on location with a barebones crew, sometimes just a cinematographer and sound recordist, without permits or permissions, and adhering to very few cinematic, political, and social principles, laws, and rules.

Guerrilla filmmaking was born out of a spirited rebellion against Hollywood and commercial philosophic methods of filmmaking. The guerrilla filmmakers of the 1960s, 1970s, and 1980s perceived production design as a Hollywood necessity that could be done without. By shooting on a location as they found it or anywhere that was available, guerilla filmmakers kept the budget down but also relinquished a lot of artistic control over the visualization of a film and the ability for design to communicate narrative, content, and character. *The Brothers McMullen* (1995) embraces a wonderful human story and presents sincere performances, but creator Edward Burns paid little to no attention to the production design and cinematic craft of his film. As a result, the characters have no dynamic relationship to their environment. The settings tell little about the narrative or the expression of mood or atmosphere.

Many guerrilla filmmakers create stories that take place in one location. The power of choice in a one-set film is critical. The single set must serve the story. Make that choice carefully. If the film takes place in an apartment, don't settle for one apartment. For the Lower East Side Apartment in *Married to the Mob* (1988), production designer Kristi Zea used five different locations for the various rooms and views, including the outer hall doorway, kitchen, and living room. Each room was selected for its specificity to the character and situation and to create a unique living space that resonated with the bohemian transition of a woman fleeing from the Long Island mob lifestyle. This approach is available to the low-budget filmmaker who need not feel compelled to shoot at a location where one room is right and the others are artistically wrong. It may be convenient, but settling for less than the design desires is a disservice to your story.

In the 1990s, independent guerilla filmmakers began embracing production design as part of their nontraditional, low-budget production approach. Education and exposure to the little understood film craft of production design helped, and the ever-growing numbers of designers entering the field were responsible for this movement. Thomas Vinterberg and Lars Von Trier created the Dogme95 manifesto that announced that films should be shot in real locations without bringing in any outside artistic tools or altering the space in any way. This edict comes from filmmakers who are acutely aware of the impact cinematic environments have on a film, and selection of location in *The Celebration* (1998), *Breaking the Waves* (1996), and other Dogme95 films is not haphazard. A film doesn't have to be overdesigned; awareness of locale and the right artistic decisions can be made, without embracing the excess of overmanipulated visualization that Dogme95 and guerilla filmmakers consider intrusive and artificial.

Remember, creative control is paramount on all films. All economic and cinematic decisions should be made for the good of the film, not for artistic ego-gratification or by conforming to a self-imposed "manifesto." Each screen story is different and requires the filmmaker to employ good judgement, courage, and integrity toward the intent of the narrative and the conviction of the characters. Good filmmakers understand that they must forge content with aesthetic and technical issues each time out. A film with a good script, fine acting, and poor craft is just that. A movie with all craft, flash, and no substance fails to engage the hearts and minds of the viewer.

*Content + Craft = Cinema* is the mantra of the total filmmaker.

# Chapter 17

## DIGITAL PRODUCTION DESIGN

Production designers sketched all drawings by hand with pencil, pen, or marker, until computer assisted design, **CAD,** was introduced in the 1980s. This digital software allows designers to see their creations from any and all angles and views. First and second generation production designers were trained to see and understand the set from any perspective by looking at a flat drawing. In their artistic mind's eye, they were perpetually seeing their design in three dimensions. Directors often did not have this skill and don't always have this skill today; producers rarely do, and studio suits and financiers even less so.

CAD was the next step in film design, just waiting until technology caught up with it to happen. It doesn't make hand drawing obsolete; not everyone has access to technology, and some that do feel the intellect and imagination can not be improved on. Seeing may be believing, but so is trust in the collaborative artists who create a motion picture. Others are best in the modality of eye and hand coordination with their own fully loaded computer consisting of a drawing implement between fingers touching gracefully on paper, still others can make a mouse and cursor dance a graceful dance. Tools are a choice—pick the one you use best. Take the time to learn the others.

Although CAD may not accessible to all filmmakers, it is invaluable at demonstrating what a set will look like from any angle. This ability can be helpful if those involved—especially investors—have difficulty in "seeing" what the set will look like in all its dimensions and from every conceivable angle.

### Pre-CAD Effects

Prior to computer generated imaging (CGI) there were limited cinematic techniques available to the art department.

## MATTE SHOTS

Matte shots are paintings on glass that allow the filmmaker to employ backgrounds previously unattainable to them. The matte painting of a foreign locale or fantasy world is optically combined with the actors and the physical location design. Mattes are time-consuming to create and only specialized craftspeople can produce effective results—people such as artist Albert Whitlock, who worked extensively with Alfred Hitchcock. Whitlock's most celebrated work with Hitchcock is on *North by Northwest* and *Vertigo*. Whitlock was able to provide "impossible shots" for the director—like a "god's point of view" looking down on the United Nations. The chariot race in *Ben Hur* (1959) used a matte painting to create the Roman landscape expanse around the full shot of the arena.

## REAR SCREEN PROJECTION

This photographic technique was also readily used to create backgrounds during the Hollywood Studio Era and is rarely used today. A second unit filmed the scene or a still image known as a **background plate** that was later rear-projected in the studio as the actors performed in front of the screen. When combined with physical design elements it was effective, but the increase of film grain and optical distortion from the lens selection or camera position often gave it away. Perspective and movement were greatly compromised. The most common use of rear screen projection was in driving scenes, which would be filmed in a dummy car inside a studio while the rear screen material of what would be seen out of the moving car was projected and shot by the production camera along with the characters in the car. The result did not look realistic. The increased grain, mismatched color, or poorly timed movement of the background often gives rear screen away. Ironically, Hitchcock overused this technique mainly because of his reluctance to shoot on location. The artificial look of driving sequences in his films most always looked contrived and eventually came to be expected and accepted as the aesthetic of his cinematic style.

## MINIATURES

The studio system developed the idea and methods for creating shots of cars and trucks driving on a road, helicopter views of towns and cities, and other architectural expanses that would be too costly to shoot in reality. Miniatures are scale creations of such scenes in the studio. Departments were set up at each studio where craftspeople built the scenes. After meticulous construction of the miniatures out of wood and other materials, they were painted, lit, and photographed, often with a moving camera. When properly executed, the shots cut into the film looked like the real thing. Steven Spielberg made extensive use of miniatures in the *Indiana Jones* series and his epic comedy *1941*.

The carnival carousel that runs amok in the climax of *Strangers on a Train* (1951), was built full-sized by Ted Haworth's art department in the studio so Hitchcock could stage actors getting on and off of the ride. For the shots of the carousel running out of control and finally collapsing, a miniature was built and photographed.

## WATER TANKS

These are large sized vessels filled with water similar to a deep swimming pool, used to shoot scenes that take place in an outdoor body of water but actually are shot in the studio. Tanks are used to avoid the difficulty, expense, and danger of shooting on location. The scene is then staged, lit, and photographed in the tank under studio conditions. The downside of this technique, which was extensively utilized in Hollywood films during the studio era, is scale. If the scene is supposed to take place in rough, ocean waters, the waves, even when whipped up with fans and propellers, are rarely large enough to be truly believable.

## BACKINGS AND TRANSLIGHTS

A hard backing is a framed board put behind a door or window opening on a set or location to create the illusion of a background designed for the film. A hard backing can be a photographic blow-up or a painting created on a treated hard surface. Backings can also be painted on wood-framed canvas or other materials. A hard backing can only be lit from the front. A translight is a full-sized photographic transparency that can be lit from the front or the rear. The visual subject of a backing or translight can be the view out of a window or an image created to depict a scenic image in another room.

## CAD Production Design

There are now expansive options in the digital domain. Computer Graphic Imaging has changed the look of filmmaking and presents endless design possibilities. With CGI, impossible shots are now possible. CGI is having a major impact on the visualization of a movie and has become integrated into the design of a film. With CGI, filmmakers can shoot in one location and digitally transform it into another. Visual elements can be added, subtracted, altered, and enhanced.

## Virtual Production Design

CGI has the potential to make an enormous impact on production design in filmmaking. The most revolutionary aspect is the ability to create design elements, including virtual sets that a camera can pan, move through, and around. Backgrounds and views out of windows and doors can be added. Architectural elements can be added to a set or location. Telephone poles, television antennas, and other modern aspects of design can be erased or replaced for a period film. The color palette can be altered, enhanced, and reimagined by digitally painting the film frame by frame. New sets can be digitally aged and textured. Signs and text on windows and buildings can be altered. Special effects like exploding, burning down, or shooting up a set can be achieved without rebuilding or having replacements on hand during shooting.

## CGI in Contemporary Film Production

*Titanic,* which won eleven Oscars, including Best Picture, Best Art Direction and Best Visual Effects in 1998, made effective use of CGI, including computer-generated people who slid down the tilted deck of the sinking ship, falling to their deaths. Many films, including another Oscar winner, *Gladiator* (2000), have used CGI to create total or partial environments that would be too costly to built traditionally. CGI is affordable and is now used extensively for everything from explosions to flying manhole covers as in the Sylvester Stallone star-vehicle *Driven* (2001), but some production designers are concerned that these visual effects may not serve the medium as well as traditional methods.

## Successfully Merging CGI Technology with Production Design

Much of *Titanic* and *Gladiator* was convincing, but many films that make extensive use of digital technology to create images are not. The aesthetics of the CGI look and the nature of the action can give it away. The shot that closely follows a Japanese air bomb as it fell to destroy the U.S. Navy fleet in *Pearl Harbor* (2001) is an impossible shot and the audience knows it. However, viewers may become more willing to suspend disbelief as digital filmmaking becomes accepted in the ever-changing medium of motion picture making. Few realized the *Gladiator* coliseum was digitally created, but the perspective and physical relationship of the characters to their environment to real elements lacks depth. The digital illusion of space is not the same as the physical and optical reality of defining spatial relationships. CGI is often part of the special effects department rendered by **computer graphic** artists and technicians who do not have a film production design background. Many production designers lack an understanding and technical knowledge of digital creation and compositing. Only a merging of the two disciplines will produce the most effective results. Eventually this merging of skills will happen as professionals in both fields collaborate and cross train. The latest generation of moving image creators is bringing knowledge of the new technical tools to production design.

CGI, like all cinematic techniques, should be used specifically and with purpose. Soon after cinematographer Garrett Brown invented the Steadicam, it was over- and misused by auteur directors who devised long shots where the composition in motion wasn't always interested in serving the story and was along more for the lens-ride. But the Steadicam is now a vital item in the filmmaker's toolbox that can be used effectively to write cinematic language.

## Computer Animation

Digital technology can be a creative tool in itself. The results have produced all-digital films like *Toy Story* (1995), *Toy Story 2* (1999), *Shrek* (2001) and *Final Fantasy* (2001), which have pioneered and advanced the new medium.

Digital filmmaking offers unprecedented visual and narrative possibilities. It is a medium that embodies the physical properties of both live action and animation. The realism of live action and the creative invention of animation are combined with imagery that has unique aesthetic qualities of its own. Creatively, there are few limits to the possibilities offered to the design in digital filmmaking, only time and money, the historic adversaries of motion picture making. The year 2001 was a landmark for digital filmmaking, with the first Oscar for a feature length animated film awarded at the 2002 ceremony to *Shrek*. Many films that employ the medium, like *Dinosaur* (2000) and *Waking Life* (2001) and cutting edge Anime films from Japan, are gaining attention.

Digital filmmaking allows moviemakers to defy the visual limitations of both live action and animation and puts the artistic control in the hands of the designers. Locations and sets do not have to be found or built—at least not with physical materials.

Production design in animation is an exciting new frontier. Animation always had the ability to create detailed backgrounds, but CGI and the influence of live action films have brought dimension and an environmental quality. What was once largely a two-dimensional medium is now a three-dimensional one.

A new generation of animators well-versed in live action films and cinematic grammar are approaching animation design no differently than their colleagues in live action. Animation films are now bringing production designers on their projects, and this will lead to even more exciting possibilities for the animated movie.

Animation has always had its own form of production design. Disney's *Beauty and the Beast* (1991) made a crossover leap to the concept, purpose, and impact of film production design on the animated motion picture. This was achieved by designing environments that were detailed in architecture and décor and had a direct narrative and atmospheric relationship to the characters. The execution of the sets in *Beauty and the Beast* was highly detailed and sharp in focus. The filmmakers employed camera technique like sweeping crane moves, once the exclusive domain of feature films, which give dimension to all of the locales. George Lucas is an innovator spearheading the all-digital direction in live action films with his *Star Wars* franchise.

## The Future of Digital Moviemaking

Movies will always need a story, traditional or nontraditional, characters, and settings; they will always be directed, photographed, and designed. The process and aesthetics of motion pictures will always evolve and innovate. Writers and filmmakers will imagine new vistas; new tools will offer new solutions and visions.

The digital revolution is having an impact on the entire process of making a motion picture. More moviemakers are now shooting their projects on digital or Beta video rather than 16mm or 35mm film stock, for budgetary concerns. The once wide differences between film and video are now narrowing dramatically due to constant improvements in camera technology and to experienced cinematographers applying their lighting, composition, and camera operation expertise to the medium of video.

The production designer must be familiar with new cameras and digital formats.

Video does read and interpret color and light differently, and only testing and experience with the particular equipment being used will reveal the parameters of space, color, depth, sharpness, and texture available. Good design principles do not change, but new tools have their own visual properties, advancements, and limitations. The gap is closing between film and video. New digital software programs can now replicate specific film stocks, and computer chips that can come closer to reproducing the visual tonal range of film are being developed for video cameras.

# Chapter 18

## HOW TO FIND A PRODUCTION DESIGNER

One of the reasons that many independent, low-budget, and student filmmakers historically did not have a production designer as part of their project was the simple reality that they didn't know how or where to find one. Most filmmakers can locate a director of photography or editor to collaborate on their projects but come up empty when even considering the notion of having a production designer as part of their creative team. Here are a number of approaches to finding a production designer for your next project.

- Hire a professional production designer. Credits and contact information are available through The Internet Movie Database, at *www.imdb.com*; the Art Directors Guild, at *www.artdirectors.org*; and the Society of Motion Picture and Television Art Directors, at 11365 Ventura, Studio City, California 91604, (818) 762-9995. If your budget can't support a designer's fee, ask if they can recommend a student or member of their art department who is looking for a first-film design experience.
- Theater schools are a good source for beginning designers; many are interested in designing for theater and film.
- Art schools are an excellent resource to enlist members of the art department and possibly locate production designers.
- Film schools don't regularly produce production designers as part of their curriculum, but with each passing year, more film students are making the transition or becoming interested in the field. Post your request on as many film school bulletin boards and Web sites as possible.
- When all else fails put a sign reading "production designer" on the back of a crewmember. It is an interesting phenomenon, but when someone is given a specific job on a film set, they are able to focus on the task. With sufficient support from the producer, director, and director of photography the results may not

be optimum but far richer than just shooting anywhere randomly. This is a first step. Filmmakers build their own crews, collaborators, and department heads. When this works out well, the company can stay together from film to film.

# Appendix A

## 100 SIGNIFICANT FILMS FOR FURTHER STUDY OF PRODUCTION DESIGN

*The Adventures of Baron Munchausen* (1989)
*The Age of Innocence* (1993)
*All That Jazz* (1979)
*Amadeus* (1984)
*Barry Lyndon* (1975)
*Barton Fink* (1991)
*Batman* (1989)
*The Beguiled* (1971)
*Being John Malkovich* (1999)
*The Best Years of Our Lives* (1946)
*Blade Runner* (1982)
*Blood Simple* (1984)
*Blue Velvet* (1986)
*Boogie Nights* (1997)
*Bonnie and Clyde* (1967)
*Born on the Fourth of July* (1989)
*Brazil* (1985)
*The Bride of Frankenstein* (1939)
*The Cabinet of Dr. Caligari* (1919)
*Cabiria* (1914)
*Chinatown* (1974)
*Citizen Kane* (1941)
*The City of Lost Children* (1995)
*A Clockwork Orange* (1971)
*The Conformist* (1971)
*The Cook, the Thief, His Wife and Her Lover* (1989)

*The Crowd* (1928)
*Day of the Locust* (1975)
*Dick Tracy* (1990)
*Do the Right Thing* (1989)
*Dracula* (1931)
*Dr. Strangelove or: How I Learned to Stop Worrying and Love the Bomb* (1964)
*Dr. Zhivago* (1965)
*Edward Scissorhands* (1990)
*Empire of the Sun* (1987)
*Enemies, A Love Story* (1989)
*Eraserhead* (1978)
*The Exorcist* (1973
*Fanny and Alexander* (1983)
*The Fisher King* (1991)
*The Fountainhead* (1949)
*42nd Street* (1933)
*Ghost* (1990)
*Glory* (1989)
*The Godfather* (1972)
*The Godfather Part II* (1974)
*Gold Diggers of 1935* (1935)
*Goldfinger* (1964)
*GoodFellas* (1990)
*Gone with the Wind* (1939)
*The Heiress* (1949)
*How Green Was My Valley* (1941)

*The Hudsucker Proxy* (1994)
*Interiors* (1978)
*Intolerance* (1916)
*The Killing of a Chinese Bookie* (1976)
*King Kong* (1933)
*Kramer vs. Kramer* (1979)
*The Last Emperor* (1987)
*The Last Picture Show* (1971)
*Lost Horizon* (1937)
*The Magnificent Ambersons* (1942)
*Malcolm X* (1992)
*Mary Poppins* (1964)
*Matewan* (1987)
*Meet Me in St. Louis* (1944)
*Metropolis* (1925)
*Mishima* (1985)
*Nashville* (1975)
*North by Northwest* (1959)
*On the Waterfront* (1954)
*Orlando* (1993)
*Pat Garrett and Billy the Kid* (1973)
*Patty Hearst* (1988)
*The Pirate* (1948)
*The Purple Rose of Cairo* (1985)
*Ragtime* (1981)

*Rear Window* (1954)
*Rebecca* (1940)
*The Red Shoes* (1948)
*Rosemary's Baby* (1968)
*Saturday Night Fever* (1977)
*The Scarlet Empress* (1934)
*The Servant* (1964)
*Se7en* (1995)
*The Shining* (1980)
*Silkwood* (1983)
*Shock Corridor* (1963)
*Singin' in the Rain* (1952)
*Sleepy Hollow* (1999)
*Star Wars* (1977)
*The Ten Commandments* (1956)
*The Thief of Bagdad* (1924)
*The Thin Blue Line* (1988)
*Tucker: The Man and His Dream* (1988)
*2001: A Space Odyssey* (1968)
*Unforgiven* (1992)
*Velvet Goldmine* (1998)
*The Wedding March* (1928)
*The Wiz* (1978)

# Appendix B

## GLOSSARY

**abutment:** stone or brick constructed against an arch or vault to secure its thrust.

**achromatic:** an absence of color. Neutral tones such as gray, white or black.

**aging:** process of making new materials look older, worn, and lived-in.

**architecture:** the style and design of a building.

**art department:** team of artisans and craftspeople who work under the production designer.

**art director:** person who runs the art department and directly supervises the design team and answers to the production designer. If there is no production designer on a production, the art director is responsible for both the look of the film and supervision of the art department team. Art director is the original title of this position prior to William Cameron Menzies' work on *Gone with the Wind* in 1939.

**asphaltum:** tar-like substance used to age new materials.

**backing:** a mounted photograph or painting which depicts a background vista or design component.

**background plate:** a shot used as a background for rear or front screen projection.

**back lot:** exterior area adjacent to an interior sound stage used to build sets for outdoor scenes.

**bag line:** used to lift a sandbag.

**balustrade:** short posts that support a rail.

**batten:** a narrow piece of lumber used to secure a scenic drop.

**blue screen:** process in which a scene is photographed in front of a blue or green screen so that later a composite shot can be created with a digital or painted matte.

**break:** to fold or unfold scenic materials.

**breakaway:** scenic element or prop manufactured or rigged to break apart on cue.

**breakdown:** interpreting a screenplay in a series of shots to tell the story visually. Process involves creating a storyboard and shot list.

**bull line:** four strand, heavy hemp rope on a winch used to lift scenery that is not counterweighted.

**butt joint:** an edge to edge join.

**buttress:** a support that provides a wall with additional support.

**buyer:** person who purchases props, décor, costumes, furniture, and other items for the art department.

**CAD:** Computer Assisted Design. Software that allows the designer to create three-dimensional views of a set.

**camera angle projection:** a perspective drawing created from an architectural plan that presents how the completed set will look through a specific camera lens.

**canted angle:** an unusual composition that expresses a unique point of view and personal interpretation. Also known as a Dutch angle.

**cantilever:** a projecting beam that supports a balcony.

**carpenter:** wood-worker who constructs flats and sets, and works under the supervision of the construction coordinator.

**catwalk:** walkways above the set in the flies and grid.

**ceiling plate:** a metal plate utilized to suspend light scenic pieces and ceilings.

**cheek-walls:** low walls that protect the lateral edge of a flight of stairs.

**chrominance:** in video the difference between a color and a reference color of the same luminosity.

**cladding:** prepared board or plywood attached to a structure that furnishes a smooth decorative surface.

**cleat:** a wooden or metal fitting with projecting horns so a line can be secured to it.

**cleat line:** cord used to lash two scenic units together.

**clew:** a metal clamp that holds a series of ropes together that allows them to be lifted as one.

**cloth clip:** used to secure a partly rolled up backdrop on its support batten.

**color correction:** the final alteration of the color of a film or video to the instructions of the director of photography done at a film laboratory, video, or digital suite.

**color palette:** the range and scope of the colors to be used in the production design

**composite shot:** when more than one visual element is combined to create an image at the laboratory stage or through manipulation by digital software.

**computer graphics:** pictorial elements generated by digital software.

**construction coordinator:** person in charge of the construction crew and the building of sets.

**construction crew:** carpenters and other building personnel who work under the supervision of the construction coordinator to build the sets for a film.

**corbel:** stone or wood block that supports a horizontal structure such as an arch head or ceiling.

**cornice:** decorative molding just below the ceiling of a room.

**costume designer:** person who creates, selects, and coordinates all of the clothing and apparel worn by the actors in a film.

**costumer:** person who dresses and assists the actors with their costumes during the production process.

**cover set:** an interior set that can be used as a contingency in the event of inclement weather when an exterior shoot is planned.

**CTB:** color temperature blue. Blue filter that increases the color temperature of a light source in variable amounts.

**CTO:** color temperature orange. Orange or amber filter used to decrease the color temperature of a light source in variable amounts

**cut cloth:** a suspended scenic cloth cut to provide effects. An uneven edge cloth can present the illusion of foliage. A cutout can be used for a window opening or to present a view of another drop behind it.

**cyclorama:** a curved screen made out of material on which a background or color field is painted.

**diorama:** a miniature rendition of a set.

**dipping:** dyeing white or light-colored fabrics to reduce their reflective qualities on camera.

**director of photography:** Person responsible for the cinematography on a film. Also known as the DP.

**donkey:** an electric winch.

**drafting:** architectural drawings used to plan the construction of a set.

**dress:** putting furniture, décor, and props on a set.

**drop:** a large painted canvas utilized for a scenic background.

**dulling spray:** when applied to a surface, a dulling spray deflects hot spots and glare due to lighting.

**elevation:** a specific and particular view of a set.

**exterior:** an outdoor location.

**façade:** a set design element that appears to be the front or outside of a building. An architectural term indicating the front of a structure.

**flat:** a wooden frame covered with material or a board used to create the walls and other aspects of a set.

**flies:** the space above a stage where scenic backgrounds and other scenery are raised and suspended.

**fly:** scenery on ropes or wires above the set.

**flying iron:** a hinged metal ring plate that is used to hang scenery.

**forced perspective:** technique used to create depth by foreshortening the background.

**free perspective:** the exaggeration of normal perspective to enhance the illusion of depth in a design.

**french flat:** a group of flats tied together and flown over a set as one unit.

**gantries:** bridgework over a set used to hang lights and suspended scenic elements.

**gel:** gelatin or plastic material that comes in a variety of colors. When placed over lamps, they produce colored light.

**gimbal:** a device that cradles an object allowing it to be steady even though what is below it is unsteady.

**gray scale:** A gradation of tones ranging from black to white.

**greensman:** person responsible for landscaping exteriors of a film set or location.

**grummet:** a fitting at the top of a flat that secures flying cables.

**guardrail:** safety handrails built onto offstage elevated platforms.

**hard backing:** a set backing on a hard surface.

**header:** a horizontal surface at the top of a set that depicts a lintel or a beam.

**hoist:** motorized mechanism that pulls a wire cable to suspend or support scenery.

**interior:** an indoor set or location.

**irons:** hanging, flying, and flat irons support flats that are suspended by wire.

**jack:** a framed brace that holds scenery upright.

**Kelvin scale:** a system that measures the color temperature of a light. Low color temperatures have warm properties. High Kelvin light sources are cold and blue in nature.

**kill:** to remove unwanted scenic elements.

**latitude:** range of exposure in which a film stock can produce an acceptable image; the scope of contrast the emulsion can record.

**lead man:** assistant set decorator. Person responsible for located objects to decorate a set.

**leg up:** raising the height of a scenic element with supports from the floor.

**lintel:** a beam over a door or a window.

**line-set:** three to five lines on the same head block used to lift a batten or an element of scenery.

**lip:** a beveled strip that overhangs the edge of a framed scenery unit to conceal the joint crack with an adjoining component.

**local:** a crewmember hired from the region where a film company is shooting.

**location:** an actual place used to film a scene.

**location manager:** person responsible for finding and supervising locations utilized by the production company.

**mask:** to hide a portion of the background area or equipment from the camera view with scenic pieces.

**matte shot:** a composite image that uses a painting created in conjunction with the blue screen or green screen process or a digital image combined with live action resulting in a shot unobtainable by the filmmakers in the conventional manner.

**metaphor:** an image that makes a reference or analogy to an idea or theme.

**miniature:** a small-scale version of a setting, filmed to represent its full-size counterpart.

**mise-en-scène:** French term referring to staging of a film or play.

**model:** a miniature representation of a set built to scale out of cardboard, balsa wood, or other lightweight material to present a dimensional view of the set. Used to plan set decoration, camera angles, and blocking.

**move:** a preplanned rearrangement of props or scenery at a given moment during the shooting.

**muling block:** a pulley used to change the horizontal direction of a moving line.

**pedestal:** the base of a column or supporting structure.

**per diem:** a set amount of money paid daily to crew members when they are working outside of their home area; principally meant for meals, can also include other living expenses.

**peripteral:** a building surrounded by a singular row of columns.

**perspective:** the illusion of depth on a two-dimensional surface.

**photo boards:** a storyboard comprised of stock or custom made photographs, most often used in advertising agency presentations.

**plan:** a technical drawing used to construct a set.

**plot plan:** overhead view or a blueprint of a location or studio set.

**polychrome:** many-colored.

**practical:** anything on a set that actually works.

**practical location:** an existing location.

**process screen:** technique used to project film from behind a screen to create a background for the foreground action. Also known as rear screen or front screen projection.

**production designer:** person responsible for the visual look of a film.

**production illustrator:** person who renders illustrations, in drawings or paintings, of the production designer's idea for a set or moment in a film.

**property master:** person responsible for props and objects used and handled by the actors.

**pylon:** a tapered rectangular tower.

**rake:** to set at an angle; often refers to the slope of a floor.

**ramp:** a slanted surface that joins two different levels.

**rear screen projection:** projecting a still or moving image on a screen behind the action as it is being photographed.

**re-entrant corners:** corners that have angles pointing inwards.

**retrofit:** technical addition to an existing structure.

**reveal:** the side of a door or window between the outer edge and the frame that creates wall thickness.

**rig:** a piece of equipment used for a specific task.

**ring plate:** hardware that allows light scenic units to be suspended.

**safety bond:** a wire stop than ensures the stability of a scenic piece.

**sandbag:** a canvas bag filled with sand used to weight down and secure scenic structures and elements.

**scene dock:** a scenic storage area close to the studio floor.

**scenic artist:** person who paints scenic background, lettering, signs, portraits, and other things needed to be painted on a set.

**scenic loft:** a piece of equipment that allows the scenic painter to paint standing upright as the painting is raised and lowered.

**scenic painting:** a painting done on canvas or a hard surface, used to create a background for a set.

**scrim:** a translucent screen used to diffuse light.

**set:** a structure built in a studio used to create an environment for a film.

**set decorator:** person who plans, and places furniture and décor on a set after it is constructed.

**set designer:** person who conceives and draws up plans for a set.

**set dressing:** furnishings used to decorate a set.

**setting line:** drawn on the studio floor to indicate exactly where a set is to be built.

Also used to define the boundary limits to stage a scene.

**skid:** a movable trolley with pulley and rope used to raise scenery.

**snatch block:** a pulley block with removable sides that allows it to be inserted into a tackle system without rethreading lines.

**stage:** area in a studio used to build sets and to photograph a scene.

**stage cloth:** canvas or plastic sheet used to protect the floor during the painting and decoration process.

**standing set:** a permanent indoor or outdoor set.

**strike:** to take down and apart a set and scenery.

**storyboard:** a series of drawings that tell the story of a film frame by frame; used as a guide to design the film.

**studio:** production facility where sets are built and scenes for the film are photographed.

**supervising art director:** position held during the Hollywood studio system. Person who headed the art department, assigned the art director to each project.

**surround:** also called a shroud. A carry-off platform that surrounds a turntable.

**swing gang:** the set dressing crew. People who work under the supervision of the lead man to obtain necessary objects for set decoration.

**track:** an overhead rail that enables suspended curtains to be moved on runners.

**translight:** a transparent photographic blow-up used as a background for a set.

**transparency:** a still image printed on glass or celluloid and projected.

**transportation captain:** person responsible for vehicles used in a film.

**traveling matte:** a mask on sections of composite shot elements that move and change from frame to frame.

**trick line:** small line used to trigger a breakaway or trick device.

**tripping:** raising a piece of soft scenery from the bottom and the top.

**trompe l'oeil:** an illusionistic painting.

**tumbler:** pole attached to bottom edge of a scenic drop, attached by a pulley system.

**turntable:** circular table slowly rotated.

**value:** the relative lightness and darkness of a color.

**valance:** short curtain or drape that hangs from the edge of a table or shelf to the floor.

**vault:** arched ceiling.

**wagon:** a low platform on casters.

**wall brace:** attached to hardware in the studio wall, it is used to support scenery.

**wild:** any part of a set that is movable.

**winch:** a cylinder where rope or cable is wound. Used to raise scenery.

**windows:** a casement window opens on side hinges; French windows are long, reach to floor level, and open on side hinges; sash windows slide vertically within a frame and are balanced by counterweights.

**window bay:** a three-sided window that juts out from the wall-line and forms an alcove.

# Appendix C

## BIBLIOGRAPHY

Abbott, L. B. *Special Effects: Wire, Tape, and Rubber Band Style*. Hollywood: ASC Press, 1984.

Affron, Charles, and Mirella Jona Affron. *Sets in Motion: Art Direction and Film Narrative*. New Brunswick, N.J.: Rutgers University Press, 1995.

Albrecht, Donald. *Designing Dreams*. New York: Harper & Row, in collaboration with the Museum of Modern Art, 1986.

*The Art of Hollywood: Fifty Years of Art Direction*. London: Thames Television, 1979.

Arnheim, Rudolf. *Art and Visual Perception: A Psychology of the Creative Eye, the New Version*. Berkeley, Calif.: University of California Press, 1974.

Aronson, Joseph. *The Encyclopedia of Furniture*. New York: Crown Publishers, 1968.

Barsacq, Leon. *Caligari's Cabinet and Other Grand Illusions*. Boston: New York Graphic Society, 1976.

———. *A History of Film Design*. New York: New Amsterdam Library, 1978.

Begleiter, Marcie. *From Word to Image: Storyboarding and the Filmmaking Process*. Studio City, Calif.: Michael Wiese Productions, 2001.

Black, J. Anderson, and Madge Garland. *A History of Fashion*. London: Macmillan, 1990.

Boucher, Francois. *20,000 Years of Fashion: The History of Costume and Personal Adornment*. New York: Harry N. Abrams, n.d.

Brunhammer, Yvonne. *The Nineteen Twenties Style*. London: Paul Hamlyn, 1966.

Carrick, Edward, *Designing for Moving Pictures*. London and New York: The Studio Publication, 1941.

———, comp. *Art and Design in the British Film: A Pictorial Director of British Art Directors and Their Work*. London: Dennis Dobson Ltd., 1948.

Chiericetti, David. *Hollywood Costume Design*. New York: Harmony Books, 1976.

Corliss, Mary, and Carlos Clarens. "Designed for Film: The Hollywood Art Director." *Film Comment*, May–June 1978.

Dalle, Vacche, Angela. *Cinema and Painting: How Art is Used in Film*. Austin, Tex.: University of Texas Press, 1996.

Eisner, Lotte H. *The Haunted Screen: Expressionism in the German Cinema and the Influence of Max Reinhardt*. Berkeley: University of California Press, 1969.

Elam, Kimberly. *Geometry of Design: Studies in Proportion and Composition*. New York: Princeton Architectural Press, 2001.

Ettedgui, Peter. *Production Design and Art Direction: Screencraft*. Woburn, Mass.: Focal Press, 1999.

Fiell, Charlotte & Peter. *Design of the 20th Century*. Köln: Taschen, 2001.

Finch, Christopher. *Special Effect: Creating Movie Magic*. New York: Abbeville Press/Cross River Press Ltd, 1984.

Giesecke, Frederick E., Alva Mitchell, Henry Cecil Spencer, Ivan Leroy Hill, John Thomas Dygdon and James E. Novak. *Technical Drawing*. New York: Macmillan Publishing Company, 1991, ninth edition.

Gottshall, Franklin H. *How to Design Period Furniture*. Milwaukee, Wis.: Bruce Publishing Co., 1951.

Hart, John. *The Art of the Storyboard: Storyboarding for Film, TV, and Animation*. Boston: Focal Press, 1999.

Heisner, Beverly. *Hollywood Art*. Jefferson, NC and London: McFarland & Company, 1990.

———. *Production Design in the Contemporary American Film: A Critical Study of 23 Movies and Their Designers*. Jefferson, N.C. and London: McFarland & Company, 1997.

*Hollywood and History: Costume Design in Film*. London: Thames and Hudson, 1987.

Katz, Steven D. *Film Directing Shot by Shot*. Studio City, Calif.: Michael Wiese Productions in Conjunction with Focal Press, 1991.

Kybalová, Ludmila, Olga Herbenová, and Milena Lamarová. *The Pictorial Encyclopedia of Fashion*. Translated by Claudia Rosoux. New York: Crown Publishers, 1968.

LoBrutto, Vincent. *By Design: Interview with Film Production Designers*. Westport, Conn.: Praeger Publishers, 1992.

Lourie, Eugene. *My Work in Films*. San Diego, New York, London: Harcourt Brace Jovanovich, 1985.

Mandelbaum, Howard, and Eric Myers. *Forties Screen Style: A Celebration of High Pastiche in Hollywood*. New York: St. Martins Press, 1989.

Marner, Terrence St. John, ed. *Film Design*. New York: A. S. Barnes and Co., 1974.

Millerson, Gerald. *TV Scenic Design*. Woburn, Mass.: Focal Press, 1998.

Mordden, Ethan. *The Hollywood Studios: House Style in the Golden Age of the Movies*. New York: Alfred A. Knopf, 1988.

Parker, W. Oren and Harvey K. Smith. *Scene Design and Stage Lighting*. New York: Holt, Rinehart and Winston, Inc., 1968.

Preston, Ward. *What an Art Director Does: An Introduction to Motion Picture Production Design.* Los Angeles, Silman-James Press, 1994.

Reeves, Tony. *The Worldwide Guide to Movie Locations.* Chicago: Acappella, 2001.

Rogers, Pauline B. *Art of Visual Effects: Interviews on the Tools of the Trade.* Woburn, Mass.: Focal Press, 1999.

Rose, Rich. *Drafting Scenery for Theater, Film, and Television.* White Hall, Va.: Betterway Publications, 1990.

———. *Drawing Scenery for Theater, Film and Television.* Cincinnati, Ohio: Betterway Books, an imprint of F& W Publications, 1994.

Schatz, Thomas. *The Genius of the System: Hollywood Filmmaking in the Studio Era.* New York: Pantheon, Books, 1988.

Sennett, Robert S. *Setting the Scene*: *The Great Hollywood Art Directors.* New York: Harry N. Abrams, Inc., 1994.

Simon, Mark. *Storyboards: Motion in Art.* Woburn, Mass.: Focal Press, 2000.

Simonson, Lee. *The Art of Scenic Design.* New York: Harper & Row, Publishers, 1950.

Spencer, Charles. *Cecil Beaton: Stage and Film Design.* New York: St. Martin's Press, 1975.

Tashiro, C. S. *Pretty Picture: Production Design and the History Film.* Austin, Tex.: University of Texas Press, 1998.

# Appendix D

## TOOLS FOR FURTHER RESEARCH

Before the advent of the home videotape market, filmmakers had to study films in theaters, museums, and archives. Since the arrival of DVD in the 1990s, filmmakers have unprecedented access to films, to study and understand the role of production design in the cinematic process. The technical quality is superb, and films can be seen in the proper aspect ratio they were designed for. Instant access to any and all parts of a film focuses the attention of analysis. Many commentary tracks reveal important information and insight into the design of a film. Many DVDs include special features that include storyboard-to-film comparisons that facilitate study of the original storyboards and the completed shot. This single feature is a resource for demonstrating the evolutionary process from idea to physical design. DVD titles that include storyboard to film comparisons or in-depth examinations of the production design of a project include *The Abyss* (special edition), *The Birds*, *Brazil*, *Do The Right Thing*, *Men in Black* (collector's series), *The Red Shoes*, *Rushmore* (collector's edition), *The Silence of the Lambs*, *The 39 Steps*, and *Vertigo*.

Production designers still employ the pencil, paint, and ink, but digital software has revolutionized the process. Here are some suggestions for digital tools:

- Bryce 4: a 3-D application with which you design interior sets and exterior locations, it allows a camera to record a QuickTime Movie.
- Photoshop: allows digital manipulation of photographs. Drawing tools facilitate the addition of figures or other design sketches to enhance location photos for storyboard presentations.
- Storyboard Artist: contains clip file imagery to create storyboards.
- Storyboard Quick: another software package to generate storyboards.
- ScriptWerk: When used in conjunction with Microsoft Word this formatting software combines storyboard frames with screenplay pages.

# A FINAL WORD

I hope this has been informative and inspirational. Constant study and commitment to craft will allow you to grow as a visual storyteller. Apply what you have learned here and from the examples of others to your personal work as a filmmaker—that is most important. Along with a respect for the achievements of the past, ideas, communication, a point of view, and the expansion of the language of movies are sacred tenets to the motion picture creator—even now, especially now in the second century of what is called filmmaking. Good luck and forever remain a student of motion picture art. Long let it be.

# INDEX

## Books from Allworth Press

**Documentary Filmmakers Speak**
*by Liz Stubbs* (paperback, 6 × 9, 240 pages, $19.95)

**The Directors: Take One**
*by Robert J. Emery* (paperback, 6 × 9, 416 pages, $19.95)

**The Directors: Take Two**
*by Robert J. Emery* (paperback, 6 × 9, 384 pages, $19.95)

**The Directors: Take Three**
*by Robert J. Emery* (paperback, 6 × 9, 256 pages, $19.95)

**Hollywood Dealmaking: Negotiating Talent Agreements**
*by Dina Appleton and Daniel Yankelevits* (paperback, 6 × 9, 256 pages, $19.95)

**Making Independent Films: Advice from the Film Makers**
*by Liz Stubbs and Richard Rodriguez* (paperback, 6 × 9, 224 pages, $16.95)

**Making Your Film for Less Outside the U.S.**
*by Mark DeWayne* (paperback, 6 × 9, 272 pages, $19.95)

**Technical Film and TV for Nontechnical People**
*by Drew Campbell* (paperback, 6 × 9, 256 pages, $19.95)

**Producing for Hollywood: A Guide for Independent Producers**
*by Paul Mason and Don Gold* (paperback, 6 × 9, 272 pages, $19.95)

**Directing for Film and Television, Revised Edition**
*by Christopher Lukas* (paperback, 6 × 9, 256 pages, $19.95)

**The Health & Safety Guide for Film, TV & Theater**
*by Monona Rossol* (paperback, 6 × 9, 256 pages, $19.95)

**Get the Picture? The Movie Lover's Guide to Watching Films**
*by Jim Piper* (paperback, 6 × 9, 240 pages, $18.95)

**Career Solutions for Creative People**
*by Dr. Rhonda Ormont* (paperback, 6 × 9, 320 pages, $19.95)

**An Actor's Guide—Your First Year in Hollywood, Revised Edition**
*by Michael Saint Nicholas* (paperback, 6 × 9, 272 pages, $18.95)

**The Screenwriter's Legal Guide**
*by Stephen F. Breimer* (paperback, 6 × 9, 320 pages, $19.95)

Please write to request our free catalog. To order by credit card, call 1-800-491-2808 or send a check or money order to Allworth Press, 10 East 23rd Street, Suite 510, New York, NY 10010. Include $5 for shipping and handling for the first book ordered and $1 for each additional book. Ten dollars plus $1 for each additional book if ordering from Canada. New York State residents must add sales tax.

To see our complete catalog on the World Wide Web, or to order online, you can find us at *www.allworth.com.*